TIMELINE
OF
Britain

TIMELINE
OF
Britain

GORDON KERR

canary
press

This edition printed in 2008.
© 2008 Omnipress Limited
www.omnipress.co.uk

This 2008 edition published by Canary Press,
an imprint of Omnipress Limited, UK

ISBN – 13: 978-0-9537976-6-0

Printed and Bound in China

10 9 8 7 6 5 4 3 2

Cover design: Andrew McColm
Internal design: Anthony Prudente on behalf of Omnipress Limited
Images: courtsey of Corbis, Getty and iStockphoto

Contents

INTRODUCTION   *8*

PREHISTORY AND THE ROMANS   *10*
BC 8000 – AD 1065

THE NORMAN INVASION   *25*
1066 – 1299

THE LATE MIDDLE AGES   *33*
1301 – 1499

REFORMATION & RESTORATION   *45*
1500 – 1759

INDUSTRIAL REVOLUTION   *73*
1760 – 1899

THE 20TH CENTURY – PRESENT DAY   *111*
1900 – 2008

Introduction

Historically the British are an island-race, cut off from Europe and the rest of the world by the sea. This simple fact has long meant that the British tend to see themselves, not only as great mariners, but also as geographically, socially and philosophically 'separate' from the rest of the world.

According to a popular viral email, life in today's Britain is about 'driving a German car to an Irish pub for a Belgian beer. Then travelling home, grabbing an Indian curry or a Turkish kebab on the way to sit on Swedish furniture and watch American shows on a Japanese TV.'

There is certainly some truth to this statement. Clear-cut cultural identity is becoming more and more a thing of the past, the former prime minister Tony Blair famously said that 'blood alone' no longer defines national identity, and that modern Britain has been shaped by a rich mix of different ethnic and religious origins. Statements such as this have led many to conclude that national identity is no longer relevant in the lives of ordinary people, though perhaps it is actually just as important as it ever was, and it is merely what comprises 'Britishness' that has changed with time.

It has become quite normal for the British, especially the English, to feel quietly ashamed of their national heritage, and to attempt to escape it, sometimes going as far as to invent an exotic bloodline based in Europe or further afield rather than admit to being 100 per cent Brit. They do so with at least some good reason, it is generally perceived that the British have been responsible for some disasterous events in world history, such as the establishment and maintainance of the transatlantic slave trade, but it is worth remembering that they have also done some good. The British are responsible for the invention of penicillin, the telephone, the Worldwide Web and the clockwork radio – all of which might sound small and insignificant to someone who has come to take such things for granted, but have had a wide-reaching positive impact on the wider world.

In today's ever-changing political climate the notion of 'Britishness' has become a matter for passionate debate. Kipling wrote that '*the Saxon never means anything seriously until he talks about justice and rights*'. As the British government progresses with plans to issue identity cards to record and track the movements of all official British citizens, and new fears concerning the threat of home-grown terrorists seem to appear in the media on a daily basis, a book concerning the history of Britain, its many triumphs and failures, becomes ever more relevant. *Timeline of Britain* explores the chronology of this green and pleasant land, from its birth in prehistory to the present day.

PREHISTORY AND THE ROMANS

BC 8000 – AD 1065

*c.*8000

The Mesolithic Period begins. The ice sheets melt; the North Sea begins to rise. The bow and cutting tools are being used. Stonehenge is a ritual site. The population of Britain is about 30,000.

*c.*6500

The marsh connecting England and Europe is submerged, separating Britain from mainland Europe.

*c.*5000

The Neolithic Period. People engage in agriculture. Stone axes, antler combs and simple pottery are being used.

*c.*4000

The earliest-known camps or communities appear. Communal burial is practised.

*c.*3500–3000

The first ceremonial centres begin to appear. Long barrows and chambered tombs are common. Corpse exposure is practised; bodies are left to decompose or be consumed by animals and birds.

*c.*3200

Stone houses are constructed at Skara Brae in Orkney.

*c.*2500

The Bronze Age; metalworking improves; the development of bronze axes leads to improved woodworking. Multi-chambered tombs are built. Henge monuments appear. 'Beaker Folk' are building single burial sites.

*c.*2300

Construction of Britain's largest stone circle begins at Avebury.

*c.*2000

Metal objects are manufactured. Woven cloth appears in Britain. Construction begins of Stonehenge's inner ring of bluestones.

*c.*1800 – 1200

Power and influence in society passes from priests to those who control the means to manufacture metal objects.

*c.*1500

Stone circles fall out of use as religious practices change. Burials are made near stone circles or in flat cemeteries. Metal weapons and ornamentation are becoming more sophisticated.

*c.*1200 – 1000

A warrior class begins to wield power in society. The roundhouse is the most common form of dwelling; in Ireland, the 'crannóg', an artificial island constructed in the middle of a lake, is common.

*c.*1000

The earliest hill forts begin to appear. Fortified farmsteads are built.

*c.*800   The Celts start arriving from central Europe.

*c.*700   Small farming settlements with networks of fields begin to appear.

*c.*600   The Iron Age; ironworking technology becomes widespread.

*c.*500   Celtic customs and artefacts spread across Britain. Druids, the intellectual class of the Celts, begin a thousand-year dominance. Large hill forts dominate the British landscape. The chariot is introduced in Britain. In Scotland, people begin to build 'brochs' or hollow stone towers.

325   The earliest documented reference to Britain is made by Greek explorer Pytheas of Massilia; he describes its inhabitants as skilled wheat farmers who are normally peaceful, but make formidable enemies in war, especially when using horse-drawn chariots.

*c.*150	East Anglia, Kent and the Thames Basin begin to be settled by Belgic people from northern France.
*c.*100	Hill forts in southern England are fortified against the threat posed by the Belgic tribes to the east. The Gaels begin to arrive in Ireland.
*c.*90	The earliest known coins are in use.
55	Julius Caesar invades Britain for the first time; more of a reconnaissance expedition than an invasion.
54	Caesar's second invasion of Britain overcomes Cassivellaunus, King of the Catuvellauni, commanding a huge Celtic army.
52	Commius, ruler of the Gaulish Atrebates tribe, arrives in Britain and establishes his capital at Silchester (near Reading).
50	Large settlements known as 'oppida' begin to appear in England.
44	Julius Caesar is assassinated in Rome.
27	Octavian becomes emperor.

AD	
9	Rome acknowledges Cymbeline (Cunobelinus) as King of the Catuvellauni, and he becomes a tributary ally of Rome; he rules much of south-east England.
40	Cymbeline dies; his sons, Togodumnus and Caratacus, succeed him.
43	Aulus Plautius, lands at Richborough in Kent leading a full-scale Roman invasion of Britain; Togodumnus and Caratacus halt tribute payments to Rome; Caratacus leads British resistance.
44	The Romans, under the command of Vespasian, capture hillforts all over southern England.
47	The Romans occupy Britain as far west as the Severn and as far north as the Trent.
49	Caratatus wages guerrilla warfare against the Romans in Wales. The Romans found the town of Colchester.
50	Caratatus is defeated and flees to the Celtic tribe, the Brigantes, in north-east England. The Romans found London around this time.
51	Caratacus is handed over to the Romans by Cartimandua, Queen of the Brigantes, and is taken to Rome. Roman politician, Quintus Veranius, arrives in Britain to conquer the whole island.

Queen Boudicca
AD 61

Boudicca was the queen of the Iceni people of Eastern England. She was married to Prasutagus, who was endorsed by the Romans as ruler of the Iceni. Following his death, the Romans decided to assume direct rule over the region. Boudicca and her daughters led a frenzied rebellion against their Roman occupiers. Her warriors successfully defeated the ninth legion of the Roman army and destroyed Colchester – the Roman capital, as well as London. According to legend, Boudicca committed suicide by drinking poison when the Roman army, under the command of Paulinus, finally defeated the Iceni rebels.

61	Boudicca, Queen of the Iceni, leads an uprising against the Roman occupiers; she sacks Colchester, St Albans and London, killing around 80,000. The Romans begin the suppression of the Druids.

62	Boudicca is defeated at the Battle of Watling Street; she escapes from the battlefield and commits suicide.
63	Joseph of Arimathea visits Glastonbury; the first Christian mission to Britain.
70	The British Governor, Petillius Cerialis, defeats the Brigantes at Stanwick in Yorkshire.
c.77	The Roman conquest of Britain is complete; Wales is subdued; Scotland is conquered as far north as the Forth and the Clyde; Gnaeus Julius Agricola is Imperial Governor.
84	The British, under Caledonian war leader, Calgacus, lose the decisive Battle of Mons Graupius on the Moray Firth; Agricola's campaign against the Scottish tribes is complete.
87	The Romans withdraw from the far north of Britain around this time; troops are needed elsewhere in the Empire.
100	A new Roman border, the 'Stanegate Line', is established between the Tyne and the Solway.
117	Hadrian becomes emperor.
121	Hadrian visits Britain and orders the construction of a wall across northern Britain to prevent raids by Picts.
142	Roman governor, Quintus Lollius Urbicus, begins building the Antonine Wall in central Scotland, between the Forth and the Clyde.

163
The Roman army abandons southern Scotland and retreats south to Hadrian's Wall.

193	Septimius Severus becomes emperor; Clodius Albinus is proclaimed governor of Britain.
196	Clodius Albinus, attempting to become emperor, withdraws troops from Britain; the northern frontier is overrun.
197	Clodius Albinus is killed by Severus at the Battle of Lyon.
208	Emperor Septimius Severus arrives to personally oversee the reconquest of Scotland; the Caledonians wage a guerrilla war that mires the Romans in a protracted struggle.
c.209	St Alban becomes the first Christian martyr.
211	Britain is divided into two distinct Roman provinces, Britannia Superior in the south with its capital at Londinium (London) and Inferior in the north, with its capital at Eboracum (York). Septimius Severus dies at Eboracum.
c.250	The Scots, thought to have migrated from Iberia, raid Ulster and western Scotland. Angles, Saxons and Jutes from Germany attack the east of Britain.
274	Britain is under direct rule from Rome.

287	Carausius, commander of the Roman British fleet, revolts and rules Britain as emperor.
293	Carausius is deposed and assassinated by fellow rebel, Allectus.
296	Constantius Chlorus resumes the Roman conquest of Britain. The 'Empire of Britain' is brought to an end with the defeat of Allectus.
306	Constantine the Great is proclaimed emperor, at Eboracum, by his troops; he leaves Britain to fight for the throne.
311	The Edict of Toleration is proclaimed; Christianity is made legal throughout the Empire.
312	Constantine defeats and kills Maxentius; he embraces Christianity.
314	The Council of Arles is attended by three British bishops; the first British presence at a continental church gathering.
337	Emperor Constantine receives 'Christian' baptism on his deathbed; his three sons, Constantine II, Constans and Constantius rule jointly.
343	Emperor Constans arrives in Britain to quell unrest in the north.
350	Irish raiders make permanent settlements in south-west Wales.
367	An action known as the Great Conspiracy, undertaken by the Picts, the Scots and the Saxons combined with a revolt of the garrison at Hadrian's Wall, devastates Roman Britain.
369	Theodosius drives the Picts and Scots out.
383	The Roman army in Britain proclaims Magnus Maximus emperor; he conquers Gaul, Spain and Italy with an army made up of British volunteers.
388	Maximus occupies Rome but is beaten by eastern emperor Theodosius, and executed.
395	The death of Theodosius, the last emperor to rule an undivided empire; one of his sons, Arcadius, becomes emperor in the East while his other son, Honorius, becomes emperor in the West.
396	Stilicho, reorganizes Roman British defences; military authority is transferred from Roman commanders to British chieftains.
397	Stilicho repels an attack by Picts, Irish and Saxons. St Ninian is the first bishop to visit Scotland; he builds the first Christian church in Scotland at Whithorn.
402	Stilicho recalls one of the two legions in Britain to assist against the Visigoths. Local defence forces are created.
406	A barbarian force sweeps into central Gaul, severing contact between Rome and Britain; the Roman army in Britain mutinies; Marcus is proclaimed emperor in Britain, but is assassinated.
407	Gratian becomes emperor in Britain but lasts only four months. Constantine III is hailed as the new emperor by the Roman garrison. He withdraws the remaining Roman legion and crosses into Gaul to rally support. Constantine's departure represents the end of the Roman Empire in Britain.
408	Without the Romans, Britain is attacked by the Picts, the Scots and the Saxons.
410	Emperor Honorius, faced with a Goth invasion, says that Britain must organize its own defences.
411	Constantine, the last emperor of Britain, is captured and executed.
420	The death of Coel Hen, who commanded the Roman army in northern Britain. The Pelagian heresy, a controversial theological theory, is outlawed in Rome, but, in Britain, it enjoys support from a 'pro-Celtic' faction; traditionalists who are pro-Roman, support the Roman church.

423
St Patrick is born in Banna
Venta Burniae, believed to be
near Birdoswald in Cumbria.

429   Pope Celestine I dispatches bishops Germanus and Lupus to Britain to combat the growth of Pelagianism. Germanus leads Britons to the 'Hallelujah' victory in North Wales against an army of Picts and Saxons.

_c._432   The traditional date for the beginning of St Patrick's mission to Ireland.

_c._440 – 50

A period of civil war and famine in Britain, caused by the ruling council's weakness and inability to deal with Pictish invasions; the situation is aggravated by tensions between Pelagian and Roman factions; the country begins to be divided, geographically and along factional lines.

_c._445   Vortigern, a leading warlord amongst the Britons, comes to power.

_c._446   Vortigern authorizes the use of Saxon mercenaries for the defence of the north against barbarian attack.

_c._447   In the Battle of Aylesford, in Kent, Vortigern's sons, Vortimer and Cadeyrn, defeat the Jute leader, Hengest. Germanus expells the Irish from Powys and restores Cadeyrn's son, Cadell Ddernllwg, to the throne.

_c._448   Britain is ravaged by civil war and plague.

_c._450   Vortigern invites Hengest and Horsa to fight as mercenaries against the Picts.

_c._452   The Saxon settlement of Britain increases. Hengest invites his son, Octha, from Germany, to occupy the northern lands and to form a defence against the Picts.

_c._456   St Patrick returns to Ireland to carry on his mission.

458   Hengest conquers Kent.

_c._459   Vortigern burned to death while being besieged by Romano-British leader Ambrosius Aurelianus, in Herefordshire.

_c._460 – 70

Ambrosius Aurelianus takes full control of the pro-Roman faction and the British resistance effort; he leads Britons in years of fighting with the Saxons.

_c._465   Arthur is believed to have been born around this time.

_c._466   In the Battle of Wippedesfleot the Britons defeat the Saxons; the battle is so costly to both sides that there is no fighting for years afterwards.

c.470	Ambrosius assumes the high-kingship of Britain.
473	Hengest advances westward.
c.476	Invasions by Jutes, Saxons and Angles force many Celts to migrate from England to Brittany in France.
477	The Saxon chieftain, Aelle, lands on the Sussex coast.
486	Aelle fights the Britons at the Battle of Mercredesburne (possibly Seaford); the battle is indecisive.
c.487	The birth of St David.
c.490	Hengest dies; his son, Aesc, rules for 34 years.
c.493	The death of St Patrick.
c.495	Cerdic lands on the south coast and establishes what is to become the Kingdom of Wessex (the 'West Saxons'); he is the ancestor of all subsequent Wessex kings.
c.496	A Romano-British and Celtic force, under the overall command of Ambrosius and battlefield command of the legendary Arthur, defeats the Saxons at the Siege of Mount Badon; the Saxon advance is halted. However, Romano-British culture is eroded over the next 50 years; the Saxons become dominant.
c.500 – 50	Celtic monasticism spreads throughout Europe.
500	King Cadwallon Lawhir begins the expulsion of the Irish from Anglesey.
c.501	The Gaelic-speaking Scots – Christians – arrive from Ireland and establish the Kingdom of Dál Riata in Argyll, on Scotland's west coast.
508	Cerdic of Wessex defeats the British king, Natanleod, at the Battle of Netley, near present-day Southampton.
c.515	Aelle of Sussex is succeeded by his son, Cissa; Sussex becomes less important.
517	In Wales, King Cadwallon Lawhir of Gwynedd dies and is succeeded by his son, Maelgwn, who reunites Gwynedd and Rhos.
521	St Columba is born at Gartan in Tyreconnell.
530	The British of the Isle of Wight are defeated by King Cerdic of Wessex at the Battle of Carisbrooke.
c.530 – 40	There is a mass migration of Celtic monks to Brittany.
534	Cerdic is succeeded by Cynric as King of Wessex.
c.537	According to the *Annales Cambriae*, King Arthur dies fighting Mordred at the Battle of Camlann.
c.540	Gildas writes about the arrival of the Anglo-Saxons in England in *De Excidio Britanniae*.
547	Ida becomes King of Bernicia (in Northumbria).
549	Many die of Yellow Fever in Britain and Ireland.
550	St David introduces Christianity to Wales. St Ninian dies.
552	Cynric of Wessex defeats the British at Old Sarum.
556	Cynric of Wessex defeats the British at Barbury Castle.
560	Ceawlin succeeds Cynric as King of Wessex; he organizes a confederation to drive the Britons out of Wessex, and he becomes the second overlord of the southern English. Ethelbert becomes King of Kent.
563	Christianity is gaining popularity in Saxon England.
565	St Columba founds a monastery on Iona and begins the conversion of the Picts to Christianity.
568	Ceawlin of Wessex drives Ethelbert into Kent.
569	At the Synod of Victoria, St David denounces the Pelagian heresy.

*c.*570 The Northern British Alliance is formed by the kingdoms of North Rheged, Strathclyde, Bryneich and Elmet; over the next five years they wage war on the Northumbrians.

571 Cuthwulf of Wessex defeats the British in the Battle of Bedford.

574 St Columba inaugurates and anoints Aidan as King of Dál Riata.

*c.*575 Irish kings meet at the Convention of Druim Cett to settle the relationship between the King of Dál Riata and the Irish kings of northern Ireland.

577 In the Battle of Deorham, Cuthwine and Ceawlin's troops kill three British kings, Coinmail, Condidan and Farinmail. The west Saxon advance is resumed; they capture Gloucester, Bath and Cirencester.

585 The foundation of the Anglo-Saxon kingdom of Mercia in England; Creoda is the earliest-known king.

590 Irish monk Columbanus embarks on missionary work abroad; he founds several influential monasteries in the Frankish and Italian kingdoms.

591 Ceawlin is deposed; Ceol becomes King of Wessex.

597 Augustine is sent by Pope Gregory to bring the Roman version of Christianity to the Saxons; he founds a monastery and the first church at Canterbury, and is proclaimed its first archbishop. Columba dies on Iona; pilgrims begin to arrive within days.

598 The first English school is founded in Canterbury, probably by St Augustine.

601 Augustine appoints Paulinus as the first Archbishop of York.

604 Augustine appoints Mellitus as Bishop of London and Justus as Bishop of Rochester. King Aethelbert of Kent founds the cathedral church of St Paul in London. King Aethelfrith unites Bernicia and Deira to form the kingdom of Northumbria; he massacres the Britons at Chester.

605 Augustine of Canterbury dies.

606 King Aidan of Dál Riata dies.

614 King Cynegils of Wessex invades Dumnonia (Devon, Somerset and part of Dorset), winning the Battle of Bindon.

616 King Edwin of Deira, supported by East Anglia, conquers Northumbria at the Battle of the River Idle; King Aethelfrith is killed and is succeeded by Edwin.

619 Mellitus becomes Archbishop of Canterbury on the death of Laurentius; when Mellitus leaves London, it reverts to Paganism.

620 Angles, under King Edwin of Northumbria, invade South Rheged, and they expel King Llywarch Hen who flees to Powys; Edwin's army moves north into southern Strathclyde and Gododdin (present-day north-east England and south-east Scotland). The Vikings invade Ireland.

625 Redwald of East Anglia, overlord of England, dies and is buried at Sutton Hoo in a famous ship burial which is uncovered in 1939.

627 Edwin of Northumbria is baptized by Paulinus.

633 Penda of Mercia and Cadwallon of Gwynedd defeat the Northumbrians at the Battle of Hatfield Chase; Edwin of Northumbria and his son, Osfrith, die in the battle; Osric succeeds Edwin and is succeeded by Oswald when he, too, dies.

634 Cadwallon of Gwynedd is defeated and killed by Oswald of Northumbria at the Battle of Heavenfield.

635 Cynegils, King of Wessex, is baptized by Birinius, the first Bishop of Dorchester. Aidan, a monk of Iona, founds the monastery of Lindisfarne in Northumbria.

638   The Northumbrians capture Edinburgh from the Gododdin.

641   The Mercians become a dominant power in Midland Britain. In the Battle of Strathcarron, Eugein I of Alt Clut defeats and kills Domnal Brecc of Dál Riata.

643   Cenwalh becomes King of Wessex.

644   Northumbria is divided in two again – Bernicia and Deira; Oswine, son of Osric, becomes King of Deira, Oswiu, son of Ethelfrith, becomes King of Bernicia.

645   King Cenwalh of Wessex is driven from his kingdom by Penda of Mercia. Famine ravages Wales.

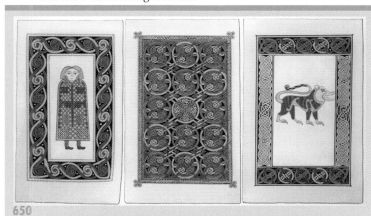

650
The earliest-known example of Celtic Christian art, *The Book of Durrow*, dates from this time.

651   Oswine of Deira dies; Ethelwald, son of King Oswald, becomes king.

654   Penda and 30 other kings and princes, including Aethelhere, are killed by Oswiu of Bernicia in the Battle of Winwaed.

655   Oswiu of Bernicia annexes the kingdom of Deira, becoming overking.

657   Whitby Abbey is founded. Wulfhere becomes King of Mercia and overlord of the southern English.

658   At the Battle of Peonnum, near Wincanton, King Cenwalh of Wessex, defeats the Romano-British Celts; the Saxons advance west through Somerset.

660   The Augustinian monastery at Canterbury is founded.

661   Wulfhere of Mercia takes the Isle of Wight, giving it to Ethelwold, King of Sussex.

664   At the Synod of Whitby, Oswiu abandons the Celtic Christian church and accepts the faith of Rome; it marks the beginning of the decline of the Celtic church. There is an eclipse of the sun and plague sweeps across Britain.

670   King Oswiu dies and is succeeded by Ecgfrith.

673   Author and scholar, the Venerable Bede is born. The convent at Ely is founded.

674   The bishopric of Winchester is founded. Ethelred becomes King of Mercia.

678   A comet appears in the sky and remains visible for three months. Bishop Wilfred of York is driven from his bishopric by Ecgfrith; he leaves for Rome.

682   The West Saxons drive out the British of Dumnonia.

685   Centwine, King of Wessex, is deposed and is succeeded by Caedwalla. At the Battle of Dunnichen, in Angus, the Picts, under

King Bruide mac Bili, defeat the Northumbrians; Ecgfrith is killed and Northumbrian dominance and expansion ends. Aldfrith succeeds him as King of Northumbria.

687 St Cuthbert dies.

688 Caedwalla of Wessex abdicates and travels to Rome; he is baptized and dies seven days afterwards; Ine becomes King of Wessex, controlling Dorset, Hampshire and Wiltshire; he compiles the earliest surviving British code of laws.

692 Brihtwald becomes the first English Archbishop of Canterbury.

697 The set of laws known as the Cáin Adomnáin, is signed by a gathering of Irish, Dál Riatan and Pictish notables at Birr, County Offaly.

c.700 *Beowulf*, the old English poem, is composed sometime between this date and 850.

704 Loingsech mac Óengusso, one of only two kings to be called 'King of Ireland' by Irish historians, is killed while invading Connacht.

710 Ine of Wessex and Nunna of Sussex defeat Geraint, the King of Wales. King Seisyll of Ceredigion invades Dyfed and conquers Ystrad Towi, creating the kingdom of Seisyllwg.

715 At Lindisfarne Priory, the monk Eadfrith copies and illuminates the *Lindisfarne Gospels*.

717 Pictish king Nechtan mac Der-Ilei, expels Ionan clergy from Pictland and adopts Roman practices.

725 Wihtred of Kent dies after reigning for 34 years; he is succeeded by Ethelbert II. Ine of Wessex fights with the south Saxons.

731 Around this date, King Elisedd of Powys expels the Mercians from his kingdom. The British monk the Venerable Bede, completes his history of the church in England, *Historia Ecclesiastica gentis Anglorum*, the first English history.

735 The Venerable Bede dies, marking the end of a golden age of Northumbrian art and learning.

741 York Minster is destroyed by fire.

746 The first Council Of Clovesho is held in Mercia, near London; it uses the first parliamentary system known to have operated in Britain. Kings Aethelbald of Mercia and Ceolred of Wessex unite in an attack on Gwent and Powys.

747 The tithe system is first recorded, whereby a tenth of the profits and stock of parishioners is paid to the church.

749 On the death of Alfwold of East Anglia, his kingdom is divided between Hun, Beorna and Alberht.

750 The Strathclyde Britons under King Teudebur defeat Prince Talorgen of the Picts at the Battle of Mugdock, marking the decline of the Pictish king, Angus I.

752 Cuthred, King of Wessex, defeats Ethelbald of Mercia in the Battle of Burford, securing independence for Wessex.

756 Cuthred is succeeded by Sigeberht as King of Wessex; Wessex falls under the control of Mercia again. Ethelbald of Mercia, overlord of the southern English, who has ruled for 41 years, is killed by his own guards at Seckinton, near Warwick; civil war breaks out in England.

757 Offa seizes the Kingdom of Mercia; around this time he builds Offa's Dyke, the greatest building project of its kind in Europe, to keep out the Welsh and to mark the boundary between England and Wales; he becomes *rex totium Anglorum patriae*, King of all England. Sigeberht of Wessex is deposed and killed; Cynewulf replaces him.

779   Offa defeats Cynewulf of Wessex near Benson in Oxfordshire.

787   The Synod of Chelsea is held; it is the only time in Anglo-Saxon times when papal representatives came to an English church council. Egfrith is crowned King of Mercia.

789   Beorhtric of Wessex marries Offa's daughter Eadburg; as a result there is a dispute between Offa and Charlemagne, the Frankish king; Frankish ports are closed to the English. Constantine I becomes King of the Picts; he is one of the greatest pre-Viking Scottish monarchs.

792   Offa beheads Ethelbert, King of East Anglia; the circumstances are unknown.

793   The Vikings invade Britain for the first time in a surprise attack on the monastic community at Lindisfarne.

The Viking Invasion of Lindisfarne
AD 793

On 8 June 793, Viking pirate raiders landed at a Christian monastery at Lindisfarne in the north-east of England. They plundered the monastery, stealing gold and silver and brutally murdering the older and weaker inhabitants. Stronger men and boys were captured and forced into slavery. This incident was to be the first of many bloody Viking raids which took place all over the British Isles during this period.

795   The Vikings ransack the monastery on Iona.

796   The death of Offa marks the end of Mercian supremacy in England.

797   Welsh forces lose to the Mercians at the Battle of Rhuddlan, when King Coenwulf tries to reassert Mercian domination of North-East Wales.

798   Cenwulf of Mercia stamps out an attempted Kentish coup against him; the Kentish dynasty is ended and Cenwulf governs the kingdom through his brother Cuthred.

c.800 The *Book of Kells* is written and illustrated in Ireland.

800   Vikings attack the monastic settlement on Lambay Island, off Dublin.

825   In the Battle of Ellandon in Wiltshire, Egbert, King of Wessex, defeats the Mercians; Wessex is the dominant kingdom in England, controlling everything south of the Humber; Egbert leads a force against the Northumbrians who submit to him. The Vikings raid Iona again, setting fire to the buildings and killing the bishop.

830   Egbert of Wessex subdues North Wales.

835   The Vikings launch raids on the coast of Kent.

836   Egbert is defeated by the Danes at Carhampton in Somerset.

838   Egbert defeats the Danes and their Cornish allies at Hingston Down in Cornwall.

839   Egbert dies after a 37 year reign; Ethelwulf, his son, becomes King of Wessex. Eóganan mac Óengusa, King of the Picts is killed by the Danes, ending the hundred-year domination of Pictland by the descendants of Óengus I mac Fergusa.

c.840 The Stone of Destiny is moved from Iona to Scone Abbey.

841 The Danes carry out massacres in Kent, East Anglia and Lincolnshire; they found Dublin as a power base in Ireland. Ethelred II becomes King of Northumbria.

844 Kenneth MacAlpin, King Kenneth I of the Picts, establishes a new dynasty; during his reign he unifies Scotland, founding the Kingdom of Alba.

845 The Danes are defeated by a Saxon force at the mouth of the River Parrett, near Bristol.

849 King Alfred is born.

King Alfred
849

King Alfred The Great became ruler of the west-Saxons upon the death of his brother King Aelthelred, whom he had helped to defeat the Danes at the battle of Ashdown. At this time Danish invaders were tightening their grip on East Anglia, Mercia and Northumbria. Alfred is credited with securing the safety of the west-Saxons whilst encouraging a revival of learning and religious faith, the setting up of schools and a basic code of law. He was also responsible for the translation of important texts from Latin into English, ensuring that ordinary people had access to these newly translated texts. He is considered by many to be the first real king of England.

851 350 shiploads of Danes sack London and pillage Canterbury; the Saxons defeat them in a great battle in Surrey.

853 Alfred visits Rome with his father King Ethelwulf. The Mercians defeat the Welsh.

856 Ethelwulf marries Judith, daughter of Charles the Bold – King of the Franks.

858 Ethelwulf dies; his son, Ethelbald, becomes King of Wessex and marries Judith, his stepmother. Kenneth mac Alpin, King of the Scots, dies; Domnall mac Alpin becomes king.

860 Ethelbert, second son of Ethelwulf, becomes King of Wessex.

862 Constantine I (Causantín mac Cináeda) becomes King of the Picts and Scots.

865 Ethelred I, third son of Ethelwulf, becomes King of Wessex. The Danes remain in Thanet and make peace with the Kentish; nonetheless, they ravage eastern Kent. The Danish 'Great Heathen Army', commanded by Halfdan and Ivar the Boneless, lands on the coast of East Anglia; it is unusually large for the time and sweeps across England.

867 The Great Heathen Army takes York and ravages Northumbria and Mercia; Aelle of Northumbria is murdered and Egbert I is installed as a puppet king by the Danes.

870 Edmund, King of East Anglia, resists the Danes and is killed; he is succeeded by Oswald, the last English King of East Anglia. The Danes reach Reading. In the west of Scotland, Alt Clut – Dumbarton Rock – stronghold of the British Kings of Strathclyde, is captured by the Norse-Gael leaders Amlaíb Conung and his brother, Ímar.

871	The Danes attack Wessex and are defeated by Ethelred and Alfred at Ashdown. Ethelred dies of his battle wounds; Alfred 'the Great' becomes King of Wessex and the first King of England.
874	The Danes take Mercia; Burgred is driven out; Ceowulf II becomes king.
875	The Danes attack Wessex again. The Viking kingdom of York is founded by Halfdan. Following the Viking attacks on the east coast, the monks of Lindisfarne leave with the bones of St Aidan, the head of St Oswald and St Cuthbert's coffin, and they wander for eight years in Northumbria and Galloway.
877	120 Danish ships are wrecked at Peveril Point in Dorset. Áed mac Cináeda becomes king of the Picts and Scots.
878	King Alfred defeats the Danes at Edington; in the Peace of Wedmore, England is divided between Wessex in the south and the Danes in the north, the Danelaw; the line of Watling Street is taken as the frontier. Egbert II, the last recorded King of Northumbria, dies. Eochaid, son of Run, King of Strathclyde, becomes King of the Picts. Rhodri Mawr is slain; he is the first Welsh ruler to have united the Welsh tribes and kingdoms under one rule.
880	The Danes settle in East Anglia; their leader, Guthrum, takes the name Athelstan at his baptism.
883	The Lindisfarne monks settle at Chester-le-Street.
886	Alfred takes London from the Danes.
889	Donald II (Domnall mac Causantín) becomes King of the Picts and Scots.
890	The Danish leader, Guthrum, dies. There is an exodus of Strathclyde Britons to Gwynedd in Wales.
895	Alfred captures the Danish fleet; the Danes withdraw to Northumbria and East Anglia or return to the continent.
899	Alfred the Great dies; his son, Edward the Elder, becomes King of Wessex and England.
900	Constantine II becomes King of Alba.
901	Edward the Elder takes the title of King of the Angles and Saxons.
902	Eric, ruler of the Danes in East Anglia, dies in the Battle of the Holme.
903	Monks receive what they believe to be the remains of King Edmund; they bury him at Beodricsworth which is later renamed Bury St Edmunds.
910	The reconquest of the Danelaw begins; at Tettenhall in Mercia, the allied forces of Mercia and Wessex defeat the last major Viking army sent to ravage England. Hywel Dda ('the Good') becomes a king in Wales and eventually rules most of the country; he codifies the laws of Wales.
913	Edward the Elder recaptures Essex from the Danes.
916	In Ireland, the Vikings establish settlements at Dublin and Waterford.
917	King Alfred's daughter, Aethelflaed, takes Derby; England's northern frontier now runs from The Wash to the Dee estuary.
918	Edward takes East Anglia and southern England; he also receives the submissions of the Welsh kings of Dyfed and Gwynedd.
919	Ragnald becomes ruler of the Viking Kingdom of York; he acknowledges the overlordship of Edward. In Ireland, a coalition of the Uí Néill, the Airgialla and the Ulaidh, advance into Leinster and are routed by the Vikings on the outskirts of Dublin.
920	Edward rules England and Scotland as far north as the rivers Forth and Clyde. The Vikings establish settlements at Limerick.

923	The Scottish king, Constantine II, submits to Edward.
924	Edward the Elder dies and is succeeded by his son, Athelstan, who becomes King of Wessex and ruler of most of England.
926	Athelstan annexes Northumbria and forces the kings of Wales, Strathclyde, the Picts and the Scots to submit to him.
927	The River Tees marks the northern frontier of England; Athelstan establishes direct rule over the Danes in York. Welsh kings formally acknowledge the English king as over-king.
937	In the Battle of Brunanburh, Athelstan defeats an alliance of Scots, Celts and Danes; he takes the title of King of all Britain.
939	Athelstan dies; his brother, Edmund, becomes King of England.
940	Dunstan becomes Abbot of Glastonbury. Future High King of Ireland, Brian Boru is born.
943	Malcolm I (Máel Coluim mac Domnail) becomes King of Scots.
945	Edmund I suppresses a rebellion by the Danes in Mercia and Northumbria and forms an alliance with Malcolm I.
946	Edmund is murdered by the outlaw Leofa, when he tries to have him ejected from a party; his brother, Edred, becomes King of England; Dunstan is his chief minister.
948	The Dane, Eric Bloodaxe, becomes King of York, but is driven out.
950	The Welsh king, Hywel Dda, dies.
952	Eric Bloodaxe recaptures York.
954	King Edred invades Northumbria and drives Eric Bloodaxe out of York; he is its last Viking ruler. England is unified from this day on. Idulb mac Causantín, newly crowned King of Scots, takes Edinburgh from the Northumbrians.
955	Edwy, son of Edmund, becomes King of England.
957	The Mercians and Northumbrians rebel against Edwy.
959	Edwy dies; Edgar the Peaceful, his younger brother, becomes king; during the next 16 years, he consolidates his English kingdom. Dunstan leads a movement for monastic reform.
960	Dunstan becomes Archbishop of Canterbury.
962	Dub mac Maíl Coluim becomes King of Scots.
973	Edgar is confirmed as emperor of all England when he is crowned by Dunstan at Bath.
975	Thirteen-year-old Edward the Martyr, son of Edgar, becomes King of England.
976	Brian Boru becomes King of Munster.
978	Edward the Martyr is murdered at Corfe Castle; his younger brother, Ethelred II, the Unready, becomes king.
980	The Danes raid England again, attacking Chester and Southampton. Ethelred is unable to persuade the English to unite against the Danes.
986	Iona is raided once again by the Danes.
988	Dunstan dies.
991	Byrhtnoth of Essex is defeated by Danish invaders in the Battle of Maldon. Ethelred II buys off the Danes with 10,000 pounds of silver (Danegeld).
994	The Danes under Sweyn and the Norwegians under Olaf Trygvesson sail up the Thames and besiege London; they are bought off again by Ethelred.
995	The Lindisfarne community settles in Durham. Constantine III (Causantín mac Cuiléin) becomes King of Scotland.
997	Kenneth III (Cináed mac Duib) succeeds Constantine II as King of Scots.

999 In Ireland, Brian Bóru defeats the Vikings at the Battle of Glen Mama.

1002 Ethelred marries Emma, daughter of Richard, Duke of Normandy. In the St Brice's Day Massacre, Ethelred attempts to wipe out all the Danes in England. Brian Bóru becomes High King of all Ireland.

1003 Sweyn lands in England and takes revenge for the St Brice's Day Massacre in which his sister and her family died.

1005 Sweyn returns to Denmark. Malcolm II (Máel Coluim mac Cináeda) becomes King of Scots.

1006 Sweyn returns, rampaging through Hampshire, Berkshire and Wiltshire.

1007 Ethelred buys two years' peace from the Danes for 36,000 pounds of silver.

1009 A Danish army arrives, led by Hemming and Thorkell the Tall.

1010 Thorkell's army burns Oxford and sweeps into East Anglia.

1012 The Danes raid Kent and sack Canterbury; Alphege, Archbishop of Canterbury is taken and murdered; Thorkell, switches sides and takes his 45 ships into the service of Ethelred; the Danes are bought off for 48,000 pounds of silver.

1013 Sweyn lands in England again and is proclaimed king; Ethelred flees to Normandy.

1014 On the death of Sweyn, the Danish army in England elects his son, Canute, as their king; the English recall Ethelred II as king; Canute retreats to Denmark. In Banffshire in Scotland, the Scots, under Malcolm II, defeat the Vikings in the Battle of Mortlach. In the Battle of Clontarf, the Irish king, Brian Bóru, defeats the Danes, ending Viking political power in Ireland; Bóru is killed in the battle and hopes of a united Ireland under his leadership are dashed.

1015 Canute again invades England.

1016
Edmund Ironside, son of Ethelred II, becomes King of England; he and Canute divide the kingdom, Canute taking the lands north of the Thames and Edmund taking Wessex; Edmund is assassinated; Canute becomes undisputed King of England.

1017 Canute divides England into four earldoms; Wessex, Mercia, Northumbria and East Anglia. Gloucester Abbey is founded.

1018 At Carham, on the River Tweed, Malcolm II and Eogan II of Strathclyde defeat the Northumbrian army; Strathclyde is annexed by the Scots and they gain Lothian; southern and northern Scotland are united. Buckfast Abbey is founded.

1020 The founding of Bury St Edmund's Abbey.

1027 Canute makes a pilgrimage to Rome. William the Conqueror is born.

1028 Canute becomes King of Norway.

1031 Canute persuades Malcolm, King of Scots, to accept his overlordship.

1034 Malcolm II of Scotland dies and is succeeded by Duncan I; Scotland is, largely, a unified country.

1035 Canute dies and his Scandinavian Empire disintegrates; Harold 'Harefoot' becomes regent of England while his half-brother Harthacanute, legitimate heir to the throne, remains in Denmark; England once more becomes a nation of warring kingdoms. William becomes Duke of Normandy.

1037 The Witan, a precursor to parliament, makes Harold I 'Harefoot', Canute's illegitimate son, king.

1039 The last of the Welsh high kings, Gruffydd ap Llywelyn, assumes the throne; his 20 year rule brings unity to Wales.

1040 Harthacanute becomes King of England. Duncan, King of Scotland, is murdered by Macbeth, who becomes king.

1041 Edward the Confessor, Harthacanute's half-brother, enters his household and is treated as Harthacanute's successor.

1042 Harthacanute dies of drink; Edward the Confessor, son of Ethelred II, becomes King of England; the English royal line is restored after 29 years.

1045 Edward marries Edith, daughter of Earl Godwin of Wessex, one of the most powerful English nobles.

1051 Duke William comes to Britain and is promised the English succession by Edward during a quarrel with Earl Godwin. Earl Godwin is exiled.

1052 Edward the Confessor founds Westminster Abbey. Earl Godwin chokes on a crust at a banquet and dies; he is succeeded as Earl of Wessex by his son, Harold, who is in favour with the king.

1055 Harold's brother, Tostig, becomes Earl of Northumbria.

1056 Harold Godwinson launches a campaign against Griffith ap Llewelyn, ruler of Wales.

1057 In Scotland, Macbeth is briefly succeeded by his stepson, Lulach 'the Fool'.

1058 A Norwegian invasion of England is repulsed. After defeating Macbeth and Lulach, Malcolm III (Canmore) is crowned Scottish king; he reigns for 50 years.

1063 Harold and Tostig subdue Wales; Griffith ap Llewelyn is killed by his own troops.

1064 Harold is shipwrecked in Normandy and is taken prisoner by Duke William of Normandy; while there, he is apparently forced to swear a solemn oath to support William of Normandy's claim to England.

1065 Northumbria rebels against Tostig, who is exiled; he is now an enemy of Harold, who failed to support him. Westminster Abbey is completed.

THE NORMAN INVASION

1066 – 1299

1066 Edward the Confessor dies; Harold Godwinson becomes Harold II. Tostig and Harold Hardraada of Norway invade England; they are defeated by Harold II at the Battle of Stamford Bridge, and both are killed; 19 days after the Battle of Stamford Bridge, William of Normandy lands in Pevensey; Harold marches south to meet him; William defeats and kills Harold in the Battle of Hastings; William I, the Conqueror, is crowned King of England, at Westminster Abbey.

> *The English at that time (1066) wore short garments, reaching to the mid-knee; they had their hair cropped, their beards shaven, their arms laden with golden bracelets, their skin adorned with punctured designs; they were wont to eat until they became surfeited and to drink until they were sick. These later qualities they imparted to their conquerors; as to the rest, they adopted their (Norman) manners.*

William of Malmesbury, *Gesta Regum Anglorum* (Deeds of the kings of England) c.1125

1068 William subdues Mercia and Northumbria; the region is laid waste in an action known as the 'Harrying of the North'.

1070 Lanfranc, an Italian lawyer, is chosen as William's Archbishop of Canterbury; he rebuilds Canterbury Cathedral and establishes the primacy of the see of Canterbury over York. Hereward the Wake leads an unsuccessful Saxon revolt in the Fens.

1072 William the Conqueror invades Scotland; Malcolm III pays homage to him.

1077 St Albans Cathedral is begun.

1078 Work begins on the Tower of London and Old Sarum Cathedral.

1079 Robert of Normandy, son of William, attempts to take Normandy for himself; he is defeated but the two are reconciled. The rebuilding of Winchester Cathedral is begun.

1080 Pope Gregory VII demands homage from William; William reminds him that the King of England owes him no allegiance. The present structure of York Minster is begun.

1083 Domhnall MacLochlainn becomes High King of Ireland.

1086 The *Domesday Book* is compiled in England.

1087 William the Conqueror dies after falling from his horse; William II, Rufus, becomes King of England; his older brother, Robert, becomes Duke of Normandy.

1090 William II goes to war with his brother, Robert, in Normandy.

1091 Malcolm Canmore of Scotland invades England, but is opposed by a huge army; he accepts William's overlordship. The Treaty of Caens, between William II and Robert of Normandy, agrees that whichever of the two survives will inherit the domains of his brother.

1093 Donald Bane becomes King of Scots, following the death of his brother, Malcolm III, fighting the English. Work begins on the present structure of Durham Cathedral.

1094 Rebellions by Welsh and English barons are quelled. Donald Bane is deposed in Scotland and Duncan II, son of King Malcolm, becomes king; Duncan is murdered and Donald Bane is reinstated.

1096 The First Crusade is launched.

The Crusades
1096

The Crusades were a series of military offensives waged by Christian Europe against the Muslims of the Middle East. These operations were often sanctioned by the Pope of the Roman Catholic Church, the main objectives being to halt the expansion of the Islamic faith and to recapture the holy land of Jerusalem in the name of Christendom. The Crusades had a far-reaching social and political impact on Britain. Many ordinary men left their homes and families in order to participate in the Crusades, perceiving them as an opportunity for adventure as well as a way to cleanse themselves of sin. The families they'd left behind often struggled to cope in their absence.

1097 The late Duncan's half-brother, Edgar, becomes King of Scotland; William II helps him to defeat Donald Bane. Westminster Hall is begun.

1098 Magnus Barefoot, King of Norway, conquers the Orkney Islands, the Hebrides and the Isle of Man.

1099 The Crusaders take Jerusalem; the First Crusade ends.

c.1100 The Normans begin to build motte and bailey castles. Middle English replaces Old English. Annual trade fairs are held outside city walls and last for days.

1100 Henry I, youngest son of William the Conqueror, becomes King of England.

1101 Duke Robert lands at Portsmouth; he withdraws with the promise of a pension of £2,000 a year, on condition he renounces his claim to the English throne.

1106 Henry I defeats his brother Robert, Duke of Normandy, at the Battle of Tinchebrai, taking Normandy and capturing Robert; Robert remains captive for the rest of his life.

1107 King Edgar of Scotland is succeeded by Alexander I; Scotland is disunited and David I becomes king in Lothian and Strathclyde.

1114 Henry I invades Wales, conquering Gwynedd and Powys. Matilda, Henry's daughter, marries Holy Roman Emperor, Henry V.

1118 Henry I is at war in France throughout the year. The order of the Knights Templar is founded.

1120 William, the only legitimate son of Henry I, drowns in the wreck of the 'White Ship'.

1124 Alexander I of Scotland dies; Scotland is unified again by reforming King David I. The first Scottish coinage is minted.

1128 Henry I's daughter, and only surviving legitimate child, Matilda, marries fourteen-year-old Geoffrey Plantagenet, Count of Anjou; Henry persuades the English barons to agree to make Matilda queen when he dies.

1133   Henry II is born, the son of Geoffrey Plantagenet and Matilda.

1135   Henry I dies; Stephen, son of the Count of Blois and Adela, daughter of William the Conqueror, becomes King of England; there is civil war – known as The Anarchy – between Stephen's supporters and those loyal to Matilda. The Scots invade England.

1136   The Welsh rebel against Stephen; they inflict a crushing defeat on the Normans at the Battle of Crug Mawr. Geoffrey of Monmouth writes *History of the Kings of Britain*.

1138   At the Battle of the Standard, at Northallerton, the Archbishop of York defeats David I of Scotland; 10,000 Scots are killed by the Anglo-Normans.

1139   Matilda lands in England, supported by the Earl of Gloucester, and continues the civil war.

1141   Matilda captures Stephen at the Battle of Lincoln; she is driven out by a popular rising and Stephen is restored. Wales experiences a resurgence under the two Llywelyns of Gwynedd.

1147   The Second Crusade begins.

> ❝ *She at once put on an extremely arrogant demeanour instead of the modest gait and bearing proper to a gentlewoman, began to walk and speak and do all things more stiffly and more haughtily than she had been wont, to such a point that soon, in the capital of the land subject to her, she actually made herself queen of all England and gloried in being so called.* ❞
>
> Anon. *Gesta Stephani* (Deeds of King Stephen) 1148

1148   Matilda leaves England.

1149   Northumbria is ceded to the Scots. The Second Crusade comes to an end. Oxford University is founded around this time.

1152   The marriage of Louis VII of France and Eleanor of Aquitaine is annulled because it is a blood relationship; she marries Matilda's son, Henry of Anjou, allying Aquitaine to Anjou and Normandy.

1153   Henry of Anjou invades England, forcing Stephen to make him his successor in the Treaties of Wallingford, Winchester and Westminster. David I of Scotland dies; Malcolm IV becomes king.

1154   King Stephen dies; Henry of Anjou is crowned Henry II of England, founding the house of Plantagenet, which rules until 1399; he also rules more than half of France. Henry appoints Thomas Becket, as Chancellor. Nicholas Breakspear becomes Pope Adrian IV; the only English pope. The *Anglo-Saxon Chronicle* is completed.

1156   Somerled, King of Kintyre, defeats the Norse King of Man, becoming the first Lord of the Isles. Turloch More O'Connor, king of Connacht, who had become High King of Ireland in 1119 dies.

1157   Henry II recaptures Northumbria from Scotland.

1159   Pope Adrian IV, Nicholas Breakspear, dies.

1160   Galloway becomes subject to the Scottish crown.

1162   Becket is appointed Archbishop of Canterbury; he quarrels with Henry II over the church's rights.

1164   The Constitutions of Clarendon provide a restatement of the laws governing trial of ecclesiastics in England; Becket rejects the

Constitutions and is found guilty of feudal disobedience at the Council of Northampton; he flees to France. Malcolm IV defeats and kills Somerled, 'King of the Hebrides', at the Battle of Renfrew.

> *Know that Thomas who was archbishop of Canterbury has been judged publicly in my court by full counsel of the barons of my realm to be a wicked and perjured traitor to me .... Help me to avenge my dishonour on my great enemy.*

Henry II, proclamation against Becket, 1164

1165 The Welsh revolt against Henry; he invades but is forced to retreat. William I, the Lion, becomes King of Scotland.

1166 With the Assize of Clarendon, Henry establishes a new justice system. Rory O'Connor becomes the last native High King of Ireland.

1169 The deposed King of Leinster seeks help from Strongbow, Earl of Pembroke; Strongbow invades; the beginning of Anglo-Norman rule in Ireland.

1170 Thomas Becket returns to Canterbury but is murdered in the cathedral by four of Henry's knights.

1171 A cult begins around Beckett. Strongbow is crowned King of Leinster; Strongbow surrenders his lands and castles to Henry, who is made Lord of Ireland by the Pope.

1173 Henry's eldest sons rebel against him, supported by their mother, Eleanor of Aquitaine; William the Lion invades the north of England. Thomas Becket is canonized.

1174 Henry defeats his sons' rebellion and captures William the Lion at Alnwick; William signs the Treaty of Falaise, putting Scotland into debt to England; it is only relieved in 1189, when Richard the Lionheart effectively sells southern Scotland back to the Scottish king to fund the crusade. Fire destroys Canterbury Cathedral.

1176 At the Assize of Northampton England is divided into six circuits, each with its own judges. Old London Bridge is built; the first bridge made of stone over the Thames. In Wales, Rhys ap Gruffydd stages the first eisteddfod.

1180 Glass windows begin to appear in English houses.

1185 Lincoln Cathedral is destroyed by an earthquake.

1189 Henry II dies in France; Richard I, Coeur de Lion (Richard the Lionheart), becomes King of England. The Third Crusade begins.

1191 In the crusade, Richard I conquers Cyprus and captures Acre.

1192 Richard I takes Jaffa and makes peace with Saladin, Sultan of Egypt and Syria; on his homeward journey he is captured by his great enemy, Duke Leopold of Austria.

1193 Leopold hands Richard over to Holy Roman Emperor, Henry VI.

1194 Richard is ransomed for 100,000 marks.

1199 Richard I is killed by an arrow fired from a crossbow in the siege of the castle of Chalus-Chabrol; his brother, John Lackland, becomes King of England.

1200 In the Treaty of Le Goulet, the French recognize John's French possessions; in return, John gives up the Vexin region in Normandy, pays 20,000 marks and acknowledges King Philip as his overlord in France.

THE NORMAN INVASION

1202	The Fourth Crusade begins.
1203	John of England orders the murder of his nephew, Arthur, Duke of Brittany, claimant to Brittany, Anjou, Maine and Poitou.
1204	France takes Normandy from England.
1207	Pope Innocent III appoints leading English cleric, Stephen Langton, as Archbishop of Canterbury; John refuses to let him take office.
1208	Innocent III lays England under interdict.
1209	Pope Innocent III excommunicates King John and declares him deposed. Cambridge University is founded.
1210	Llewelyn the Great revolts in Wales, annexing southern Powys and northern Ceredigion.
1213	Innocent III tells Philip of France to invade England to force John from the throne; John surrenders to the pressure and accepts the overlordship of the Pope.
1214	The French win the Battle of Bouvines and open rebellion against King John ensues. William the Lion is succeeded by his son, Alexander II.
1215	The beginning of the First Barons' War; the English barons march to London to meet the king and to demand rights; the *Magna Carta*, one of the most important legal documents in history, is signed by John at Runnymeade. The Fifth Crusade begins.
1216	The barons invite King Philip's son, Louis, to be King of England; Louis lands in England and captures all of the Cinque Ports in the south-east, except for Dover; John dies unexpectedly of a fever at Newark; his nine-year-old son becomes Henry III.
1217	The French lose the Battle of Lincoln and the Battle of Dover and are driven out of England.

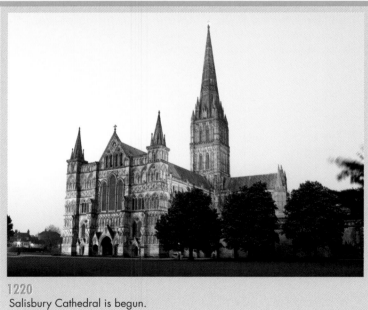

1220
Salisbury Cathedral is begun.

1221	Dominican and Franciscan friars begin to arrive in England. King John's daughter, Princess Joan, marries Alexander II of Scotland.
1222	Alexander II of Scotland conquers semi-independent Argyll.
1227	Henry III of England begins personal rule.
1228	The Sixth Crusade begins.
1230	Bartholomew Anglicus writes *On the Properties of Things*, a popular encyclopedia.

1233	Coal is mined in Newcastle for the first time.
1235	A St Albans monk, Matthew Paris, begins compiling the *Historia Maior*, a book of world history.
1237	The Treaty of York, signed by Henry III of England and Alexander II of Scotland, confirms the border between the two countries.
1238	The Unification of Wales at Strata Florida Abbey; the princes of Wales swear allegiance to Llywelyn the Great.
1240	Around this time, in England, the great council begins to be called 'parliament'.
1242	Henry III launches an unsuccessful campaign to regain the lost English possessions in France.
1245	The rebuilding of Westminster Abbey is begun.
1247	The Treaty of Woodstock makes Wales answerable to the English crown.
1248	The Seventh Crusade begins.
1249	Alexander III succeeds his father, Alexander II.
1250	*The Black Book of Carmarthen*, the oldest Welsh manuscript, is written.
1252	Henry III's daughter, Margaret, marries Alexander III.
1254	Henry III funds funding a war in Sicily on behalf of the Pope, in return for a title for his second son Edmund. Prince Edward, later Edward I, marries Eleanor of Castile.
1256	Llewelyn the Last drives the English from Wales.
1258	The English barons, led by Simon de Montfort, force Henry III to accept the Provisions of Oxford; the crown is forced to recognize the rights and powers of parliament.
1261	In the Treaty of Paris, Henry renounces his claim to French possessions; in return, Louis IX withdraws his support for the barons. The Pope absolves Henry III of his oath to keep the Provisions of Oxford.
1263	King Haaken of Norway and his fleet are beaten by the Scots in the Battle of Largs, ending Norwegian efforts to control the Western Isles.
1264	Henry III is defeated by Simon de Montfort and the English barons at the Battle of Lewes; Henry is captured and de Montfort gains power.
1265	De Montfort's parliament, the first directly elected parliament in medieval Europe; burgesses from the major towns represent boroughs in parliament for the first time; Henry III's son, Edward, defeats, kills and dismembers Simon de Montfort at the Battle of Evesham. Henry's son, Edmund 'Crouchback', is created Earl of Leicester.
1266	The Dictum of Kenilworth restores Henry's full authority and annuls the Provisions of Oxford. Norway cedes the Isle of Man and the Hebrides to Scotland. Philosopher Roger Bacon, writes *Opus Maius*.
1267	In the Treaty of Montgomery, Henry recognizes Llywelyn the Last as Prince of Wales.
1269	The first toll roads are built in England.
1270	The Eighth Crusade begins.
1271	The Ninth Crusade begins.
1272	Henry III is succeeded by his eldest son, Edward, as King of England. In Ireland, the English rule Ulster, east of Lough Neagh, in Meath, as well as most of Connacht and Munster.
1276	Llewelyn the Last leads the Welsh in the First Welsh War.

1277 In the Treaty of Aberconwy, ending the First Welsh War, Llewelyn the Last submits to Edward I. Roger Bacon is imprisoned for heresy.

1279 In the Statute of Mortmain, the church is prohibited from inheriting property without royal licence.

1283 Llewelyn the Last is killed in a Welsh rebellion; Edward I conquers Wales.

1284 The Statute of Wales is enacted at Rhuddlan; Wales is annexed to England and subject to the same laws.

1286 Alexander III of Scotland is succeeded by three-year-old Margaret, 'Maid of Norway', the daughter of Eric II of Norway and Margaret, daughter of Alexander III.

1290 The 'Maid of Norway' dies, aged seven, on her way to marry six-year-old Edward of Caernarvon, a marriage that would have united the crowns of England and Scotland; the first Scottish Interregnum begins; Edward I tries to rule Scotland. Edward expels the Jews from England; there is a massacre of Jews at York Castle.

1292 Edward selects John Balliol from a list of 13 contenders for the Scottish throne.

1294 England goes to war with France. Wales rebels again. The first customs officers are appointed.

1295 The Model parliament of Edward I is held; two knights and two burgesses are summoned from each shire. The Earl of Warwick brings the Welsh uprising to an end. France and Scotland sign an alliance – the start of the Auld Alliance against England.

1296 John Balliol reneges on his homage to Edward; Edward defeats him at Dunbar; Balliol abdicates and a Second Interregnum begins; Edward takes the Stone of Scone to Westminster Abbey; he commissions King Edward's chair, the Coronation Chair, with a space to house the stone.

1297 In the Battle of Stirling Bridge, the Scottish patriot, William Wallace, defeats an English army.

1298 Edward I defeats Wallace at the Battle of Falkirk and reconquers Scotland.

1299 Edward marries Marguerite, daughter of Philip III of France.

THE LATE
MIDDLE AGES

1301 – 1499

1301   Edward I of England invests his baby son Edward as the first
        English Prince of Wales.

1303   Scottish Guardian John Comyn, defeats an English army at Roslin;
        in retaliation,
        Edward conquers Scotland for the third time.

> *The vilest doom is fittest for thy crimes*
> *Justice demands that thou shouldst die three times*
> *Thou pillager of many a sacred shrine*
> *Butcher of thousands, threefold death be thine!*
> *So shall the English from thee gain relief,*
> *Scotland! be wise and choose a nobler chief.*

Anon. *The Chronicle of Lanercost: 1272 – 1346* (1913 trans.)

1305   Sir John Menteith and 60 men capture William Wallace and take
        him to England; Wallace is hung, drawn and quartered in London.
        Edward standardizes the yard and the acre.

1306   Robert the Bruce kills John Comyn in a church in Dumfries; he is
        crowned King Robert I of Scotland at Scone, ending the Second
        Interregnum; Bruce leads a revolt against Edward; he is defeated
        by the English at Methven and becomes a fugitive.

Robert the Bruce
1274–1329

Robert the Bruce was born into an aristocratic Scottish family in 1274. Bruce and his grandfather refused to acknowledge John Balliol as king of Scotland and supported the rebel, William Wallace, in his campaign against English tyranny. When Wallace was eventually defeated and executed, Robert managed to hold on to his land and eventually rose to become king of Scotland, but the following year Edward's army deposed Robert, forcing him to flee the country. Robert I eventually returned to Scotland to lead a successful guerilla war against the English, culminating with the battle of Bannockburn, where his army defeated a much larger English force led by Edward II. Today Robert the Bruce is regarded by many as the Scottish embodiment of bravery and determination against all odds.

1307   Bruce defeats the English in the Battle of Loudon Hill; Edward
        I dies at Burgh-on-Sands, near Carlisle, during a march north to
        face the Scots; his son, Edward II, becomes King of England. Piers
        Gaveston, a favourite of Edward II, is recalled from exile in France
        and created Earl of Cornwall.

1308   Edward II marries Isabella, daughter of Philip IV of France. While
        Edward is in France, Gaveston is made regent; the earls demand
        Gaveston be banished; he is sent to Ireland as lieutenant. In
        Scotland, Robert Bruce consolidates his position against his rivals.

1309   Bruce holds his first parliament at St Andrews; he now controls all
        of Scotland north of the River Tay.

1310   Edward II leads an army into Scotland, but achieves little. English barons appoint 21 peers as the Lords Ordainers, to manage Royal finaces.

1312 Bruce attacks Durham and Hexham. Piers Gaveston is recalled from Ireland but murdered by the Earl of Warwick.

1314 At the Battle of Bannockburn, Robert Bruce defeats Edward's much larger army, securing Scotland's independence. A second failed harvest in a row results in a disastrous famine; millions die across Europe; cannibalism is reported from Poland to Ireland and, in London, many are trampled to death in bread queues.

1316 The famine continues.

1318 The Scots capture Berwick and now threaten to take the whole of the north of England.

1319 A truce is agreed between Scotland and England.

1320 Hugh Despenser and his son rise to positions of influence at the English court. Scottish barons send the Declaration of Arbroath, a declaration of independence and a justification for war with England to the Pope.

1321 Civil war breaks out in England; the Earl of Hereford and Roger Mortimer, Earl of March, take up arms, along with the Earl of Lancaster and his allies, against the Despenser family; the Despensers are sent into exile.

1322 The truce between Scotland and England expires; the Scots launch raids as far south as Preston. Edward defeats his English opponents at Boroughbridge; Lancaster is executed for high treason.

1323 England and Scotland agree a 13 year truce.

1325 Queen Isabella refuses to return from France until Edward II gets rid of the recalled Despensers.

1326 Isabella, heir to the throne, Prince Edward and Roger Mortimer, Earl of March, sail from France with an army to bring down Edward; they land in Suffolk and Prince Edward is declared Keeper of the Realm; the Despensers are captured and hanged.

1327 Parliament proclaims Edward II deposed; his son accedes to the throne as Edward III. Edward II is imprisoned in Berkeley Castle before being murdered, nine months later. The Auld Alliance between Scotland and France is re-established by the Treaty of Corbeil.

1328 The Treaty of Northampton between England and Scotland formally recognizes Robert the Bruce as King of Scotland, and acknowledges Scotland's independence.

1329 Robert the Bruce dies of leprosy and is succeeded by his five-year-old son, David II.

1330 Assuming the government of England, the eighteen-year-old Edward III arrests and hangs Roger Mortimer; he imprisons his mother for the rest of her life.

1332 The first record of the English parliament being divided into two houses. Edward III supports an invasion of Scotland by his protégé, Edward Balliol, seeking to establish him as King of Scotland; unable to consolidate his position, Balliol retreats south.

1333 Edward III launches the Second War of Scottish Independence, openly supporting a renewed attack by Balliol on Scotland; Balliol defeats the Scots at the Battle of Halidon Hill, where English longbowmen win the day for the first time; David II goes into exile in France; Balliol declares himself king.

1335 Edward Balliol's kingship begins to unravel; he flees to England. Edward III, anticipating a French invasion, puts the Channel ports at a stage of readiness.

1336 Edward III invades Scotland again. There are naval skirmishes between England and France in the Channel. Edward embargoes English exports of wool to Flanders.

1337 Philip VI declares Edward's lands in France forfeit and begins raiding the frontiers of Aquitaine; in response, Edward III declares himself King of France; the Hundred Years' War begins. William Merlee attempts the first weather forecast.

1340 England gains control of the English Channel, with a naval victory over the larger French fleet at Sluys; a one year truce is agreed. Edward loses Edinburgh to the Scots. The English parliament passes four statutes providing that taxation can be imposed only by parliament. The writer Geoffrey Chaucer is born.

1341 David II returns to Scotland. In England, it is decided that a peer may only be tried by his peers in parliament.

1346 Edward III of England invades France with a large army, and defeats the larger army of Philip VI, at the Battle of Crécy; Edward begins the siege of Calais. In the Battle of Neville's Cross, near Durham, the Scots are beaten and David II is held prisoner in England for 11 years.

1347 The English capture Calais, which becomes an English colony; a new truce is agreed between England and France.

1348 The Black Death (bubonic plague) arrives in England. Edward III founds the Order of the Garter.

1349 The Black Death ravages England and Scotland; in England, as much as 70% of the population dies. The alliterative romance *Sir Gawain and the Green Knight*, is written by an unknown author around this time.

> **We see death coming into our midst like black smoke, a plague which cuts off the young, a rootless phantom which has no mercy or fair countenance. Woe is me of the shilling in the arm-pit; it is seething, terrible, wherever it may come, a head that gives pain and causes a loud cry, a burden carried under the arms, a painful, angry knob, a white lump. It is in the form of an apple, like the head of an onion, a small boil that spares no one.**

Welsh Poet, Jeuan Gethin, March - April 1349, describing the symptoms of the black death.

1351 With the First Statute of Labourers, the English parliament tries to create a wage freeze. The Statute of Provisors recognizes the king as 'patron paramount' of the English church, a check against papal control. Tennis becomes an open-air sport in England. Edward begins the rebuilding of Windsor Castle.

1353 In the Statue of Praemunire, the English parliament bans appeals to the Pope.

1356 The Third English Campaign begins in France; Edward III's son, Edward, the Black Prince, defeats the French at the Battle of Poitiers, capturing the French king, John II, who is held prisoner for four years.

1360 The Treaty of Bretigny ends the first stage of the Hundred Years' War; Edward III gives up his claim to the French throne but gains territory; a ransom of three million gold crowns is placed on King John.

1361 A second major outbreak of the Black Death lasts for a year.

> *Because of the killing of great beasts, from whose putrid blood running down the streets and the bowels cast into the Thames, the air in the city is very much corrupt and infected, whence abominable and most filthy stench proceeds, sickness and many other evils have happened to such as abode in the said city, or have resorted to it; and great dangers are feared to fall out for the time to come, unless remedy be presently made against it; we, willing to prevent such dangers, ordain, by consent of the present parliament, that all bulls, oxen, hogs and other gross creatures be killed either at Stratford or Knightsbridge (to the east and west of the city respectively).*

Royal proclamation to the mayor and sheriffs of London, 1361

1364 John II dies a prisoner.

1366 The Statutes of Kilkenny forbid Irish-English marriages and prevent the English from using the Irish language or laws.

1367 When civil war breaks out in Castile, England and France, supporting rival candidates renew hostilities; the Black Prince leads an expedition to Spain in support of Pedro the Cruel.

1369 Edward launches his fourth French campaign; Charles V raids the English Channel coast. English replaces French as the official language of parliament and the law courts. Plague breaks out in Britain for the third time. William Langland writes the narrative poem, *Piers Plowman*.

1370 Edward, the Black Prince, sacks Limoges, massacring 3,000 people. Welsh poet Dafydd ap Gwilym, dies.

1371 David II of Scotland is succeeded by Robert II, launching the Stuart dynasty. John of Gaunt, son of Edward III, marries Pedro the Cruel's daughter and takes the title King of Castile and Leon.

1372 French troops recapture Poitou and Brittany. In the naval Battle of La Rochelle, the French regain control of the English Channel. A Castilian fleet destroys an English force on its way to Aquitaine.

1373 John of Gaunt leads an invasion of France, taking his army to the borders of Burgundy. English merchants are obliged by law to use tunnage and poundage weights.

1374 John of Gaunt returns to England and takes charge of the government; Edward III is in his dotage and the Black Prince is ill.

1375 The Truce of Bruges halts hostilities between England and France for a year. Robin Hood appears in English literature for the first time.

1376 Government reforms are introduced by the Good parliament. The Black Prince dies. The Truce of Bruges is extended for another year. John Wyclif, an Oxford theologian, calls for church reforms.

1377 Edward III dies and is succeeded by his grandson, ten-year-old Richard II, son of the Black Prince. The war between England

and France resumes; Rye and Portsmouth are sacked. The spring parliament levies a poll tax of 4d per head on everyone in England between twelve and sixty.

1379 The spring parliament announces another poll tax, according to rank this time.

1380 Another poll tax is levied, a shilling a head for the entire male population, to be collected in two instalments; there are demonstrations across England. The French continue to raid England's south coast. John Wycliffe begins to translate the Bible into Middle English.

1381 The first instalment of the poll tax in England results in mass evasion; the government decides to collect the second instalment immediately; the Peasants' Revolt begins, led by Wat Tyler; rebels enter London; the king withdraws to the Tower; the rebels demand the abolition of serfdom, the limiting of rents and the heads of Chancellor Sudbury, Treasurer Hales, John of Gaunt and others; Richard agrees to everything except the executions; he summons the rebels to Smithfield; Mayor Walworth kills Wat Tyler when he becomes abusive to the king, and the rebellion ends.

1382 John Wycliffe is expelled from Oxford because of his opposition to church doctrines.

1384 Wycliffe dies; the Lollards, the religious movement inspired by him, are expelled from Oxford.

1385 Richard II leads an army into Scotland, but the Scots are not drawn into battle. Geoffrey Chaucer writes *Troilus and Criseyde*.

1386 The king dispenses with the services of a number of nobles, who become known as the Lords Appellant; parliament forces him to remove the unpopular councillors he replaced them with.

1387
Richard agrees to hold a parliament to settle the Lords Appellants' grievances. Geoffrey Chaucer writes *The Canterbury Tales*.

1388 The Merciless parliament meets and demands the impeachment of a number of the king's favourites for high treason; a number are executed and the rest flee the country.

1389 At 22, Richard II declares himself of age to rule. A three-year truce is agreed between England and France.

1390 Plague breaks out in England for the fourth time. Robert II of Scotland is succeeded by his son, Robert III.

1392 John of Gaunt leads the English side in peace negotiations with the French at Amiens. Foreigners are forbidden from selling goods in England.

1393 Winchester College is founded by William of Wykeham.

1394 Richard II leads an expedition to subdue Ireland; he tries to create an alliance with the Gaelic Irish by recognizing their grievances against absentee Anglo-Irish landowners; he returns to England in 1395.

1395 Geoffrey Chaucer is granted a pension of £20 a year for life by the king.

1396 When his first wife, Anne of Bohemia, dies, Richard II marries the seven-year-old Princess Isabella, daughter of Charles VI of France; a peace treaty is agreed between England and France.

1397 Richard II proclaims himself absolute monarch, ridding himself of the Lords Appellants; the Earl of Arundel is executed, Warwick is exiled and Gloucester is murdered in captivity at Calais.

1398 In the Shrewsbury parliament, all the acts passed by the Merciless parliament are annulled. Richard Whittington is elected Lord Mayor of London.

1399 John of Gaunt dies; his eldest son, Henry Bolingbroke, banished by Richard for 10 years, lands in Yorkshire, gathering 60,000 supporters; the unpopular Richard II is deposed and Bolingbroke becomes Henry IV of England, founding the House of Lancaster. The Wilton Diptych, a portable altarpiece, is painted for Richard II around this time.

The War of the Roses
1455 – 1487

The War of the Roses was a series of civil wars fought from 1455 to 1487 between supporters of the House of Lancaster and affiliates of the House of York so named because each rival house was represented by a rose – red for the Lancastrians and white for the Yorkists. Both houses were branches of the Plantagenet Royal family descending from Edward III. The antagonism began when Henry Bolingbroke, the duke of Lancaster, overthrew his cousin King Richard II. Bolingbroke's claim to the throne was weak, the crown should have been passed to a descendent of Lionel of Antwerp, the Duke of Clarence. Despite this, Bolingbroke was crowned Henry IV, and was tolerated by the people because Richard's rule had been an unpopular one. Needless to say, the descendents of the House of York were not satisfied and violence broke out between the rival houses. The fighting was fuelled because during this period many aristocrats could afford to employ private armies to fight battles on their behalf.

1400 The Earls of Huntingdon, Kent, Rutland and Salisbury fail in an attempt to restore Richard to the throne; they are executed. Richard II is murdered while held captive in Pontefract Castle. Owain Glyn Dwr is proclaimed Prince of Wales and raises a rebellion; Henry IV leads a punitive force into Wales but achieves little. The first known literature in the Cornish language is written. Geoffrey Chaucer dies.

1401 The persecution of the Lollards begins; a new act permits the burning of heretics. A Scottish army, led by the Duke of Albany, invades England; it is decisively beaten at Homildon Hill and many Scottish nobles are captured.

1402 Henry IV puts down a rebellion in Wales led by Owain Glyn Dwr.

1403 The Percy family revolts, allying itself with Owain Glyn Dwr, the Mortimers and the Scottish Earl Douglas; in the Battle of Shrewsbury, Henry IV defeats and kills Harry 'Hotspur' Percy, son of the Earl of Northumberland.

1404 Glyn Dwr presides over the first Welsh parliament. William of Wykeham dies.

1405 Rebellion continues in North Wales, against Henry IV; the French fight alongside Glyn Dwr in a large-scale raid into England; a second rebellion is led by Northumberland in favour of the Earl of March, who is being held prisoner by Henry; the Welsh are routed by Henry at Usk; Northumberland's rebellion is crushed and he flees to Scotland. Henry IV's increasing ill health leads to his son, Prince Henry, becoming increasingly influential.

1406 James, son of the King of Scotland, is taken prisoner by the English; his father dies and he becomes James I; the Duke of Albany is regent. Richard Whittington is elected Lord Mayor of London for a second time.

1407 England is struck by plague for a fifth time.

1408 The Earl of Northumberland rebels against Henry IV for a third time. He is defeated, captured and executed at the Battle of Bramham Moor. John Gower, the last of the Anglo-Norman poets, dies.

1410 Owain Glyn Dwr's revolt in Wales comes to an end.

1413 Henry V becomes King of England. Scotland's first university is founded at St Andrews around this time.

1414 Henry V adopts Edward I's claims on the French crown. Lollards attempt to capture Henry and take the City of London, but are arrested by the king's troops; around 40 are hanged.

1415 Henry V invades France in an attempt to recover his heritage; he takes Harfleur after a five-week siege; he famously defeats a French army three times the size of his own at Agincourt, and he returns in triumph.

1416 The death of Owain Glyn Dwr.

1417 An English army leaves for France and is victorious in the Battle of Caen; it takes Pontoise.

1418 The English take Louviers, Compiègne and Cherbourg; Rouen is besieged.

1419 The starving inhabitants of Rouen surrender their city; Henry takes Mantes and Dieppe; he now controls all of Normandy, apart from Mont St Michel. Richard Whittington is voted Lord Mayor of London for a third time.

1420 The Treaty of Troyes agrees that Henry will inherit the French throne on the death of Charles VI; he marries Catherine de Valois, the French king's daughter; he takes Melun and marches into Paris in triumph.

1421 An upsurge of French resistance forces Henry to return to France.

1422 Henry takes Meaux but dies of dysentery, to be succeeded by his nine-month-old son, Henry VI; John, Duke of Bedford, becomes regent; the third stage of the Hundred Years' War begins. Charles VI of France also dies; Charles VII succeeds him.

1423 At the Battle of Verneuil, in the Hundred Years' War, English and Burgundian forces defeat a Franco-Scottish army. In prison, James I of Scotland writes the poem, the *Kingis Quair*.

1424 Regent, the Duke of Bedford, defeats the French at Cravant. James I returns to Scotland after being held captive for 18 years.

1425 Civil war looms in England; the Chancellor, Henry Beaufort, raises an army and a skirmish takes place on London Bridge between his force and the Duke of Gloucester's. The Parliament of Bats is held; members are forbidden to carry weapons and carry sticks and bats instead.

1428	English troops, under Salisbury, lay siege to Orleans; Salisbury is killed.
1429	Military commander, Joan of Arc (Jeanne d'Arc), relieves the siege of Orleans, saving not only the city, but France, itself; Charles VII is crowned King of France at Rheims.
1430	The Burgundians capture Joan of Arc at Compiègne and sell her to the English. Henry VI, now eight, spends two years in France; Humphrey, Duke of Gloucester, is regent. Around this time, Middle English gives way to Modern English.
1431	Joan of Arc is burned as a witch at Rouen; Henry VI of England is crowned King of France, in Paris. Marjory Kemp dictates the first autobiography in English.
1432	Henry VI returns to England.
1435	At the Congress of Arras, the French agree to cede Normandy and Guienne if Henry renounces his claim to Charles's throne; the offer is rejected.
1436	The French retake Paris.
1437	John, Lord Talbot, captures Pontoise and threatens Paris. Henry VI is declared to be of age. The unpopular James I of Scotland is assassinated and succeeded by his son, James II.
1440	Eton College is founded by Henry VI as a charity school, to provide free education to poor students.
1444	Henry VI is to marry Margaret of Anjou in return for a two-year truce between England and France.
1445	The French hint that if Maine was returned to France, there could be a peace settlement.
1446	There is resentment in England about Maine being ceded to France. The London Guildhall is completed.
1447	The spring parliament is summoned to Bury; Humphrey, Duke of Gloucester, is arrested and is murdered, probably on the orders of the Duke of Suffolk.
1450	The Duke of Suffolk is impeached by parliament for mismanaging the war in France and for fraud; Henry intercedes and banishes him for five years; Suffolk is intercepted en route and beheaded. England loses Caen and Cherburg; Normandy is now under French control, leaving the south coast of England exposed to attack.
1451	The French take Guienne. Glasgow University is founded.
1453	The English lose the Battle of Chatillon, the last of the Hundred Years' War; the English withdraw from France, their only remaining French possessions being the Channel Islands and Calais. The Battle of Heworth between the supporters of the Nevilles and the Percies marks the beginning of the feud between the royal houses of York and Lancaster that leads to the War of the Roses. Henry VI becomes insane.
1454	Richard, Duke of York, rules as regent.
1455	Henry VI recovers from his illness; Richard of York is replaced by Somerset and excluded from the Royal Council; Somerset is defeated and killed in the Battle of St Albans.
1457	Henry VI unsuccessfully tries to broker peace between the Yorkists and the Lancastrians. The French raid the port of Sandwich.
1459	Queen Margaret, Henry's consort, and leader of the Lancastrians, prepares for war, raising troops in Cheshire; at the Battle of Blore Heath, a force led by the Earl of Salisbury, defeats a Lancastrian army; the Lancastrians again defeat the Yorkists at Ludford Bridge at Ludlow; the Duke of York and his son, the Earl of Rutland, escape to Ireland and the Earls of Warwick and March make for Calais.

1460 Richard of York is defeated and killed at the Battle of Wakefield; the Yorkists, under the Earl of Warwick, take London; at the Battle of Northampton, Henry VI is captured by Yorkists and taken to London; it is agreed by parliament and Henry VI that, on Henry's death, York should become king. King James II of Scotland is succeeded by his son, James III.

1461 The Yorkists win the Battle of Mortimer's Cross; Queen Margaret marches her army south with promises of help from Scotland and France; she defeats the Earl of Warwick at the second Battle of St Albans and frees her husband, Henry VI; Henry is deposed and succeeded by Edward, Earl of March, son of the late Duke of York, founding the House of York; Edward defeats Margaret at the bloody Battle of Towton, featuring the largest armies ever to have met on an English battlefield 28,000 men lose their lives; Edward is confirmed as King Edward IV of England; Henry VI and Margaret flee to Scotland.

1462 Queen Margaret sails to north-east England from Boulogne with 800 French troops.

1463 The Duke of Somerset changes sides, deserting Edward IV.

1464 Somerset is taken prisoner and executed. Edward IV negotiates a 15-year truce with Scotland, depriving the Lancastrians and Henry VI of safe refuge. There is an outbreak of Bubonic Plague in Britain. The composer Robert Fayrfax is born.

1465 Henry VI is captured by Edward IV; he is held prisoner until 1470. France declares war on England, but takes no action.

1468 King Christian I of Norway, in need of money for his daughter's dowry, pawns the Orkneys to Scotland for 50,000 Rhenish gilders and the Shetlands for 8,000 Rhenish gilders.

1469 The Earl of Warwick and Duke of Clarence rebel against Edward IV; at the Battle of Edgecote, Warwick defeats Edward; Edward is taken prisoner for several months before being released; Warwick and Edward are reconciled.

1470 There is a rebellion in Lincolnshire against royal tax gatherers, led by Sir Robert Wells; Edward defeats the rebels near Empingham, in the Battle of Lose Coat Field. Warwick changes sides again; with Queen Margaret, and Clarence, he defeats Edward IV and restores Henry VI.

1471 In the Battle of Barnet, Edward IV defeats and kills Warwick as he tries to escape from the battlefield; Prince Edward, Henry VI's son, is stabbed to death by Clarence and Gloucester after the Battle of Tewkesbury, in which the Lancastrians are routed; Henry VI is deposed again and then dies, probably murdered, in the Tower of London; Edward IV marches triumphantly into London; Edward's son, also Edward, is created Prince of Wales.

1474 William Caxton prints the first book in English, *The Recuyell of the Historyes of Troye*, in Bruges.

1475 Edward IV revives the old claim to the French throne and invades France; the Treaty of Piequigny between England and France forces Louis XI to pay a yearly pension to Edward and a ransom for Queen Margaret.

1476 William Caxton sets up a printing press at Westminster.

1477 Caxton prints his first book, *The Dictes or Sayings of the Philosophers*; it is written by Earl Rivers, the king's brother-in-law; he also prints Chaucer's *Canterbury Tales*.

1478 The Duke of Clarence is executed for high treason.

1479 There is an outbreak of plague.

1480 Caxton prints *The Chronicles of England*.

1483 Edward IV dies; twelve-year-old Edward V becomes King of England; he is declared illegitimate and deposed by his uncle, Richard Duke of Gloucester, who becomes King Richard III; Edward V and his brother are murdered in the Tower of London.

> *He was little of stature, deformed of body, the one shoulder being higher than the other, a short and sour countenance, which seemed to savour of mischief, and utter evidently craft and deceit. The while he was thinking of any matter, he did continually bite his nether lip, as though that cruel nature of his did raise itself in that little carcass. Also he was wont to be ever with his right hand pulling out of the sheath to the middle, and putting in again, the dagger, which he did always wear.*

Polydore Vergil, 1534, about Richard Duke of Gloucester (who would become Richard III)

1484 Richard III's son, Edward, dies.

1485 Lancastrian contendor, Henry Tudor, lands at Milford Haven with a force of 1,800 French troops provided by Charles VIII of France; in the Battle of Bosworth Field, Henry defeats and kills Richard III, ending the Wars of the Roses; Henry becomes Henry VII, establishing the Tudor dynasty. William Caxton prints *Morte d'Arthur*, Sir Thomas Malory's collection of Arthurian romances.

1486 The houses of York and Lancaster are united by the marriage of Henry VII to Elizabeth of York, daughter of Edward IV.

1487 The Battle of Stoke Field is the final engagement of the Wars of the Roses; Henry VII defeats a Yorkist army, led by the impostor, Lambert Simnel, who is impersonating the late Earl of Warwick. Henry creates the Star Chamber.

1488 James III of Scotland is defeated and murdered at the Battle of Sauchieburn; his son becomes James IV.

1489 James IV of Scotland suppresses rebellions by the Earl of Lennox in the west and Lord Forbes in the east of Scotland.

1491 When Charles VIII annexes Brittany by marrying Anne, Duchess of Brittany, Henry VII lays siege to Boulogne. Perkin Warbeck, pretender to the throne of England, arrives in Cork, calling himself Richard, Duke of York and seeking support for his plot against Henry VII. William Caxton dies, having printed and published 80 books.

1492 In the Treaty of Etaples, Henry VII agrees to withdraw from his siege of Boulogne for a payment of £149,000.

1493 Perkin Warbeck is received as her nephew by Margaret, Duchess of Burgundy.

1494 Sir William Stanley and other nobles are executed for their parts in the Perkin Warbeck plot. Poynings' Law (the Statute of Drogheda), passed by Sir Edward Poynings, the king's deputy in Ireland, states that no Irish parliament may be held or legislation passed without the consent of the English parliament.

1495 Perkin Warbeck lays siege to, but fails to take Waterford in Ireland; he is warmly received in Scotland.

1496 Accompanied by Perkin Warbeck, James IV leads an unsuccessful raid into northern England. Henry VII signs the Magnus Intercursus trade treaty with the Netherlands; the Netherlands is the key market for woollen textiles, England's main export at the time.

1497 The people of Cornwall rebel against paying taxes for a war against Scotland; 15,000 rebels march on London; they are defeated and the leaders are executed. Perkin Warbeck returns to Cork and then, to Cornwall; he fails in an attempt to take Exeter, flees to Beaulieu Abbey and is captured. John Cabot discovers Newfoundland.

1499 The truce between England and Scotland is renewed at Stirling. Perkin Warbeck is hanged in the Tower of London; the Earl of Warwick is also executed, ending the male line of Edward IV. Scotland is ravaged by plague.

REFORMATION & RESTORATION

1500 – 1759

1500 Around this time, the English navy begins building ships with double-gun decks, carrying up to 70 guns. A printing press is set up in Fleet Street, in London, by Wynkyn de Worde, establishing the connection between that street and printing.

1501 Catherine of Aragon marries Arthur, Prince of Wales, son of Henry VII.

1502 Margaret, daughter of Henry VII, marries James IV of Scotland. The Prince of Wales dies; papal dispensation allows his widow, Catherine of Aragon, to marry Arthur's eleven-year-old brother, Henry, later Henry VIII; they become engaged.

1503 In an effort to resolve the ongoing problems between the English and Scottish crowns, James IV of Scotland marries Margaret, Henry VII's daughter; the marriage gives James IV's descendents a claim to the English throne.

1504 Coins are minted bearing an accurate likeness of the king.

1505 James IV threatens an invasion of England. The composer Thomas Tallis is born.

1507 An epidemic of 'sweating sickness', similar to the plague, sweeps through London.

1508 James IV refuses to promise Henry VII that he will not renew the Scottish alliance with the French. The first book to be printed in Scotland is a volume of Chaucer.

1509 Henry VII's death is greeted with rejoicing by the population; his seventeen-year-old son becomes Henry VIII of England; he marries his brother's widow, Catherine of Aragon. Dutch humanist Erasmus, visits England and lectures at Cambridge.

1510 In a bid for popularity, Henry VIII executes Henry VII's tax-gatherers and the House of Commons Speakers. Erasmus becomes Professor of Greek at Cambridge. The morality play, *Everyman*, is performed for the first time.

1511 Henry VIII joins the Holy League against the French and launches reforms of the Royal Navy. All men under the age of 40 are required to possess bows and arrows and to practise archery.

1512 Henry VIII claims the French throne; England goes to war with Scotland and France. Doctors and surgeons have to apply for licences to practise in London.

1513 In the Battle of Flodden Field, in Northumberland, the invading Scots are defeated by the English; James IV is one of the thousands of Scots killed; James V becomes king with Queen Margaret as his Guardian. Henry VIII withdraws from the Holy League.

1514 England makes peace with Scotland and France. Henry VIII's sister, Mary Tudor, marries Louis XII of France; he dies three months later and she marries the Duke of Suffolk. Thomas Wolsey becomes Archbishop of York and orders work to begin on Hampton Court Palace. Queen Margaret Tudor, Regent of Scotland, marries Archibald Douglas, Earl of Angus.

1515 Thomas Wolsey, Archbisop of York, is made Lord Chancellor of England and Cardinal. Laws are passed in England against the enclosure of common land. The young James V of Scotland is captured by the Duke of Albany; he proclaims himself Protector of Scotland; Queen Margaret flees to England. There is anarchy in Ireland. Alexander Barclay writes *Eclogues*, the earliest English pastoral poems.

1516 Sir Thomas More writes *Utopia*.

1517 The Duke of Albany leaves for France, and Queen Margaret returns to Scotland where she quarrels with her husband, Angus. Wolsey is made papal legate to England. Riots in London against foreigners living in the city are brutally suppressed. 'Sweating sickness' sweeps England again. The Protestant Reformation begins; Martin Luther nails his *95 Theses* on the church door at Wittenberg.

1518 Wolsey devises peace between England, France, the Pope and Spain in the Peace of London.

1519 Queen Margaret of Scotland forms an alliance with the Earl of Arran, sworn enemy of her husband.

1520 The Field of Cloth of Gold; Francois I of France meets Henry VIII but fails to gain his support against Charles V, Holy Roman Emperor. The Duke of Albany returns to Scotland. Robert Fayrfax composes *Music for the Field of the Cloth of Gold*.

1521 For showing opposition to Martin Luther, Henry VIII receives the title 'Defender of the Faith' from Pope Leo X. Foreign Lutheran books are burned in London.

1522 England declares war on Scotland and France; in the Treaty of Windsor, Henry VIII and Emperor Charles V of the Holy Roman Empire agree to the invasion of France. Opposition builds to the increasing power of Wolsey.

1523 An English army invades Scotland.

1524 Scotland is governed by Queen Margaret and the Earl of Arran. English courtiers eat turkeys brought from South America.

1525 Wolsey signs a peace agreement with France. Hops are introduced to England. Hampton Court Palace is completed. William Tyndale publishes *The New Testament* in English.

1526 The Earl of Kildare, Lord Deputy of Ireland, is imprisoned in the Tower of London; Sir William Skeffington takes his place. The authorities in England try to suppress the distribution of Tyndale's Bible. Hector Boece writes the *History of Scotland*.

1527 The Royal Divorce crisis begins; Henry seeks the Pope's permission to divorce Catherine of Aragon. Henry's sister, Queen Margaret of Scotland, divorces Angus and secretly marries Henry Stuart, Lord Methven. Copies of Tyndale's English translation of the *New Testament* are burned at St Paul's Cathedral. Bavarian portrait painter Hans Holbein, paints *Sir Thomas More*.

1528 England and France go to war with Spain. The Scottish Reformation begins; Patrick Hamilton is burned at the stake at St Andrews, Scotland's first Protestant martyr. James V concludes a five-year truce with England. There is an outbreak of plague.

1529 Henry VIII dismisses Wolsey and strips him of his property and official positions, for failing to obtain the Pope's consent to his divorce from Catherine of Aragon, but Wolsey remains Archbishop of York; Sir Thomas More is appointed Lord Chancellor; Henry VIII convenes the Reformation parliament and begins the process of cutting England's ties with the church of Rome. A 'Sweating sickness' epidemic rages in England.

1530 22 abbots sign a petition to the Pope in support of Henry VIII's divorce. Wolsey is accused of treason and summoned to London; he dies en route.

1531 The English clergy recognize Henry VIII as Supreme Head of the English church. Thomas Cromwell joins the Privy Council. An appearance in the sky of Halley's Comet creates widespread panic. The building of sewers in London is to be regulated by law.

1532 The Act of Annates further erodes papal authority in England; Sir Thomas More resigns his post as Chancellor in protest; Thomas Cromwell takes over. Sir William Skeffington is replaced in

Ireland by Kildare, who has been released from the Tower; there is increasing disorder. The building of St James's Palace is begun.

1533 The Act of Appeals makes the king, not the Pope, the final legal authority; it claims that England is an Empire and the English crown is an imperial crown; Henry VIII's marriage to Catherine of Aragon is annulled; he marries Anne Boleyn and is excommunicated by Pope Clement VII; Thomas Cranmer is appointed Archbishop of Canterbury. The truce between England and Scotland is extended.

1534 In the Act of Supremacy, Henry VIII is declared Supreme Head of the Church of England; a series of acts removes power from Rome and places it in Henry's hands; the Anglican Church becomes the established church in England and Wales, the Channel Islands and the Isle of Man. Anne Boleyn bears Henry a son, who dies in infancy. The Treason Act extends the definition of treason to include verbal attacks on the king. England and Scotland sign a peace treaty. English farmers are forbidden by law from owning more than 2,000 sheep. The Court of the Council of Wales and the Marches is established by Edward IV 'to restrain the wild Welchmanne'.

1535 Sir Thomas Cromwell is appointed vicar general and devises plans for seizing the church's wealth. Sir Thomas More is beheaded at the Tower of London for failing to take the Oath of Supremacy. Wales is formally united with England; Welsh law is fully replaced by English law under the Laws in Wales Acts 1535 – 1542; Welsh can no longer be used for official or legal purposes. Henry VIII authorizes the printing of Miles Coverdale's translation of the *Bible* in London.

Catherine of Aragon
1485–1536

Catherine was the youngest daughter of Ferdinand and Isabella of Spain. By the time she was three years-old she was betrothed to Arthur, the son of Henry VII. In 1501, when she was sixteen years old Catherine travelled to England. The marriage took place as planned, but within six months Arthur was dead. It is most likely he contracted the sweating sickness which was sweeping England at the time. Henry VII was keen to hang on to the princess's dowry and so, when his younger son Henry came of age, he was duly married to his brother's widow. For a while the newlyweds were happy together, but Catherine's inability to produce a healthy, male heir began to trouble Henry. He fell in love with Ann Boleyn, one of his wife's attendants, and began to petition the Pope for the annulment to his marriage with Catherine. When this did not work, he turned to the archbishop of Canterbury for help. Catherine was determined to hang on to her title, for her own sake and that of her daughter, Mary. She refused to give up the title of Queen of England until her death in 1536, when she was buried according to her new title; Princess Dowager of Wales.

1536 Henry VIII's marriage to Anne Boleyn is declared invalid and she is beheaded; Henry marries Jane Seymour 11 days after the execution. The dissolution of the monasteries begins under Cromwell direction. The Pilgrimage of Grace, a popular rising by Roman Catholics in the north of England, ends with 216 people being hanged. Sir William Skeffington, again Lord Deputy of Ireland, is replaced by Lord Leonard Grey. William Tyndale is burned at the stake as a heretic in Vilvoorde, in Belgium. Hans Holbein is appointed court painter to Henry VIII. Catherine of Aragon dies.

1537

Jane Seymour dies after the birth of a son, the future Edward VI. James V of Scotland marries Madeleine, daughter of the Francis I, King of France, but she dies shortly after. Hans Holbein paints *Henry VIII (left)*.

1538 James V marries Mary of Guise. Parish registers are formally started. Thomas Elyot writes his *Latin Dictionary*, the earliest comprehensive dictionary of the language.

1539 Parliament passes the Act for the Dissolution of the Greater Monasteries; all remaining abbeys and monasteries are dissolved; the abbots of Colchester, Glastonbury and Reading are executed for treason. The *Great Bible* in English is published with Henry's approval.

1540 Henry VIII marries Anne of Cleves; six months later he divorces Anne and marries Catherine Howard; Thomas Cromwell is executed for treason. Edmund Campion, English Jesuit and martyr, is born. The first recorded horse-race meeting in Britain takes place at the Roodeye Field, now the Roodee, at Chester.

1541 The beginning of the Reformation in Scotland, led by John Knox. The Irish parliament elects Henry VIII a King of Ireland and head of the Irish church; Irish lords are forced to renounce their traditional Gaelic titles and give up their lands, receiving them back from Henry VIII only if they accept English titles. Wales is permitted representation in the English parliament.

1542 Catherine Howard is executed for treason. Border raids by the Scots force Henry VIII to declare a second war with Scotland; the Duke of Norfolk invades Scotland; the English win the Battle of Solway Moss; the Scots defeat the English at Hadden Rigg. James V's daughter, Mary Queen of Scots, is born; James dies and is succeeded by six- day-old Mary.

1543 Henry VIII marries his sixth wife, Catherine Parr. England goes to war with France; an alliance is formed between Henry and Charles V against Scotland and France. The Treaties of Greenwich between England and Scotland provide for the marriage of Mary Queen of Scots, to Prince Edward Tudor; the Scottish parliament repudiates them six months later and renews the alliance with France. The Act for the Advancement of True Religion bans the labouring classes from reading scripture. William Byrd, the composer, is born. Hans Holbein dies.

1544 Henry VIII and Charles V invade France; Henry also invades Scotland; Leith is captured and Edinburgh is sacked and burned. An Act of parliament releases Henry VIII from his debts.

1545 The Scots defeat an English force at Ancrum Moor; the English parliament meets to raise funds for the Scottish war. French troops land on the Isle of Wight. Watched by Henry, the warship, the Mary Rose, sinks in the Solent.

1546 The Peace of Andres brings hostilities between France and England to a close. Henry VIII becomes ill with syphilis and cirrhosis; he appoints a Council of Regency for his heir. The first book printed in Welsh, *Yng Lhyvyr Hwnn*, is published. The population of England is more than 4 million. A succession of poor harvests brings famine.

1547 Henry VIII dies at the age of 55; his son by Jane Seymour, nine-year-old Edward VI, becomes King of England; the Duke of Somerset is protector. St Andrews is captured by the Earl of Arran, the Scottish regent. In the Battle of Pinkie, the Duke of Somerset's English army defeats the Scots, capturing Edinburgh.

1548 6,000 French troops land at Leith and take Mary Stuart, six years old and engaged to the French dauphin, to France. The heresy laws in England are abolished. The Treaty of Haddington seals the Franco-Scottish alliance. John Bale writes the first historical drama in English, *King Johan*. The first Welsh-English dictionary is published by William Salesbury.

1549 The Act of Uniformity authorizes the use of the English *Book of Common Prayer*, compiled by Thomas Cranmer. The Duke of Somerset falls from favour and is imprisoned in the Tower; the Earl of Warwick succeeds as protector.

1550 Somerset, released from the Tower, plots to regain his power and influence; he is arrested by the former Earl of Warwick, now Duke of Northumberland, and condemned to death for treason.

1551 Archbishop Cranmer publishes the *42 Articles*, the basis of Anglican Protestantism. The first civil divorce on the grounds of adultery is granted in England.

1552 The Second Act of Uniformity dismantles the Mass. The Duke of Somerset is executed.

1553 On the death of Edward VI of tuberculosis, Lady Jane Grey is proclaimed Queen of England by the Duke of Northumberland; her reign lasts nine days; Mary I, daughter of Henry VIII and Catherine of Aragon, becomes Queen of England; she is an ardent Catholic; the Mass, holy days, celibate clergy and Roman Catholic bishops are restored in England; Northumberland is executed. Thomas Cromwell becomes Lord Chancellor. Parish registers are started in Scotland. Sir Hugh Willoughby and Richard Chancellor attempt to discover the North-East Passage to Asia; they establish trade relations between England and Russia.

1554 Lady Jane Grey is executed. The Corn Law of 1436 is re-enacted in an attempt to relieve food shortages caused by poor harvests. Sir Thomas Wyatt raises a rebel army of 4,000 in Kent, in opposition to Queen Mary's forthcoming marriage; he surrenders and is executed; Princess Elizabeth, suspected of involvement in Wyatt's rebellion, is sent to the Tower. Mary marries King Philip of Naples and Jerusalem who, in 1556, becomes Philip II of Spain; the English parliament refuses to allow Philip to be crowned King of England. The Pope becomes head of the English church.

Lady Jane Grey
1537–1554

Lady Jane Grey was born in October 1537 to Henry Grey and Frances Brandon, the niece of Henry VIII. Her arrival was overshadowed by that of her cousin Edward, the only male heir to Henry VIII. As a nine-year-old, Jane was admitted to court under the guardianship of Catherine Parr, who she became very close to. Upon Catherine's death, Jane's guardianship was eventually passed to John Dudley who – together with Jane's parents – conspired to have her marry his son Lord Guildford Dudley, and ascend to the throne of England. By this time Edward, who had always been weak and sickly, was very ill and fading rapidly. When Edward died, Dudley bullied the council into accepting Lady Jane Grey and her husband as king and queen of England. At this point Jane still did not know that Edward had died, and had no idea of the plans her family had made on her behalf. She was horrified, and the British public were equally displeased. Jane was on the throne for a total of nine days, all of which she spent imprisoned within the confines of the Tower of London. The people began to revolt, calling for the Lady Mary to be crowned queen of England. Eventually this is exactly what happened. Jane was sentenced to death and beheaded within the confines of the Tower on 9 February 1554.

1555 Protestants are persecuted and around three hundred, including Thomas Cranmer, are burned at the stake; monasteries are reopened. Princess Elizabeth is released.

1556 John Knox travels to Geneva.

1557 Philip II persuades Mary to declare war on France; English and Spanish armies win the Battle of St Quentin. *The Sack-full of Newes* becomes the first English play to be censored.

1558 England loses Calais. Mary I dies; Elizabeth I, daughter of Henry VIII and Anne Boleyn, becomes Queen; all Catholic legislation in England is repealed. The last of the Scottish Protestant martyrs, Walter Milne, is burned at the stake; there is Protestant rioting in Edinburgh. Mary Stuart marries the dauphin, later King Francis II of France. John Knox writes *The First Blast of the Trumpet Against the Monstrous Regiment of Women*.

1559 Elizabeth suppresses the refounded religious houses; the Act of Supremacy makes Elizabeth Supreme Governor of the English church; the Act of Uniformity orders the use of the 1552 *Prayer Book*. Mary, Queen of Scots, declares herself Queen of England and Scotland when her husband becomes King of France. A fiery sermon by John Knox at Perth incites a rebellion; the Protestant lords capture Edinburgh and pillage religious houses.

1560 The Treaty of Berwick is signed between Elizabeth I and Scottish reformers. The Treaty of Edinburgh is signed between England, France and Scotland; French troops are to be withdrawn from Scotland, and French involvement in Scottish affairs is to end. The church of Scotland is founded. Mary Queen of Scots, widowed, returns to Scotland. Shane O'Neil, the most powerful man in Ireland, is subjugated by Elizabeth.

1561 John Knox publishes a *Book of Discipline*, a constitution for the Scottish church. St Paul's Cathedral in London is badly damaged by fire. Thomas Sackville and Thomas Norton write *Gorboduc*, the earliest known English tragedy.

1562 The Treaty of Hampton Court is signed by Elizabeth and Louis de Bourbon, the Huguenot leader, calling for English troops to occupy Dieppe and Le Havre. In Ireland, the Earl of Tyrone leads two failed rebellions. John Hawkins begins British participation in the slave trade when he takes 300 African slaves from a Portuguese ship bound for Brazil. Milled coins are introduced in England.

1563 The *Thirty-nine Articles* are published, completing the establishment of the Anglican church. English troops bring the plague back from Le Havre; it kills 20,000 in London alone. The first children's book is published; *A Booke in English Metre of the Great Marchante Man Called Dives Pragmaticus, Very Preaty for Children to Read.*

1564 In the Peace of Troyes, England renounces its claim to Calais in exchange for a substantial sum of money. Elizabeth loans John Hawkins a ship in exchange for a cut of the profits form his slave trading. Poet and dramatist Christopher Marlowe is born. William Shakespeare is born.

1565 Mary, Queen of Scots, marries her cousin, Lord Darnley. The Royal College of Surgeons is given permission to carry out dissections. The Royal Exchange in London is founded. Tobacco and sweet potatoes arrive in Britain.

1566 David Rizzio, Mary Queen of Scots' private secretary, is murdered on the orders of Lord Darnley; James VI of Scotland is born, the son of Mary and Darnley.

1567 Lord Darnley is murdered, probably by the Earl of Bothwell; Mary marries Bothwell, is imprisoned at Loch Leven Castle and forced to abdicate; James VI becomes King of Scotland; the Earl of Moray is named as regent.

1568 Mary Queen of Scots escapes and loses the Battle of Langside; she crosses into England and is imprisoned at Carlisle Castle.

1569 A rebellion in England of the Catholic northern Earls fails to restore Catholicism and release Mary. The Revolt of the Desmonds takes place in Ireland.

1570 Elizabeth is declared deposed by Pope Pius V, who describes her as a heretic. The Scottish regent, the Earl of Moray is assassinated by the Hamiltons; the Earl of Lennox becomes regent. The forfeiture of lands belonging to Shane O'Neill, chief of Ulster's O'Neill clan, leads to the opening up of Ulster to English colonization. Nicholas Hillyard paints *Elizabeth I.*

1571 The Earl of Lennox dies, and is succeeded as regent by the Earl of Mar.

1572 On the death of the Earl of Mar, the Earl of Morton becomes regent. John Knox dies. Poet and dramatist Ben Jonson is born.

1573 The Pacification of Perth ends fighting in Scotland; Edinburgh Castle surrenders to the English, freeing Elizabeth from all threats from Scotland; support for Mary in Scotland collapses. The Revolt of the Desmonds is crushed in Ireland. John Donne, the poet, is born. The architect Inigo Jones is born.

1576 The Theatre, in Shoreditch, is the first purpose-built theatre in Britain.

1577 An alliance is formed between England and the Netherlands. The institution later to become the Royal Society is established. Francis Drake sets out on the *Golden Hind* on a voyage around the world. London's second theatre, The Curtain, opens. Ralph Holinshed publishes *Chronicles of England, Scotland and Ireland.*

1578 James VI of Scotland assumes personal rule. English adventurer, Sir Humphrey Gilbert, is granted a patent to settle North America.

1579 James Fitzmaurice Fitzgerald lands in Ireland and launches the Second Desmond Revolt against the English; he is killed, but the English become engaged in an expensive conflict lasting until 1583; it is the first rebellion to use Catholicism as its justification. Francis Drake claims Nova Albion (California) for Elizabeth. Father Thomas Stephens is the first Englishman to settle in India.

1580 Drake returns from his round the world voyage.

1581 The *Ark Royal* is built for Sir Walter Raleigh as *Ark Raleigh* before being sold to Elizabeth. Francis Drake is knighted on the deck of the *Golden Hind* at Deptford. The former regent of Scotland, the Earl of Morton, is executed for complicity in the murder of Mary Stuart's husband, Lord Darnley. Sedan chairs come into use in Britain.

1582 3,000 people die of starvation in Munster. Sir Humphrey Gilbert reaches Newfoundland. Edinburgh University is founded.

1583 A conspiracy devised by Francis Throckmorton against Elizabeth I implicates Mary Queen of Scots; Throckmorton is executed. Gerald, Earl of Desmond, dies; the Plantation (colonization) of Munster begins. Sir Walter Raleigh travels to Virginia. Life insurance policies are first issued in London.

1584 Raleigh founds a colony on Roanoke Island and is knighted.

1585 The English intervene in the Spanish-Dutch war, attacking Spanish ports. James VI of Scotland signs a peace agreement with England. English navigator, Edward Fenton, devises a scheme for repopulating Munster. William Shakespeare leaves Stratford for London. The composer Thomas Tallis dies.

1586 The Babington Plot to kill Elizabeth and to replace her with Mary is uncovered by Elizabeth's private secretary, Sir Francis Walsingham; Babington and the other conspirators are executed; Mary is implicated, but Elizabeth delays her sentencing. The English and the Dutch defeat the Spanish at the battle of Zutphen. Sir Thomas Hariot brings the first potatoes to England from Colombia.

1587 Mary Queen of Scots is executed at Fotheringay Castle. England goes to war with Spain; Drake destroys the Spanish fleet at Cadiz.

1588 The Spanish Armada is defeated by the English fleet under Lord Howard of Effingham, Sir Francis Drake and Sir John Hawkins, opening the world to English trade and colonization. The first shorthand manual, *Characterie, An Arte of Shorte, Swifte and Secrete Writing by Character* is published by Timothy Bright. Christopher Marlowe writes *Dr Faustus*. William Morgan, Bishop of Llandaff and St Asaph, publishes a Welsh translation of the *Bible*; it saves the Welsh language from extinction.

> ## I know I have the body of a weak and feeble woman, but I have the heart and stomach of a king.

Elizabeth 1, Tilbury Speech, 1588

1589 James VI of Scotland marries Anne of Denmark. William Lee invents the first knitting machine, the stocking frame; it remains in use for centuries, and its principle of operation is still used. Sir John Harrington, Elizabeth I's godson, invents the first flushing toilet at his house at Kelston, near Bath; he calls it 'Ajax'.

1590 Edmund Spenser publishes *The Faerie Queene*, Books 1 – 3. Christopher Marlowe writes *The Jew of Malta*. William Shakespeare's career as a playwright begins.

1591 Trinity College, Dublin, is founded. Shakespeare writes *Henry VI*.

1592 Queen Elizabeth orders an 'Ajax' flushing toilet. John Davis discovers the Falkland Islands. 15,000 Londoners die of plague.

The Duke of Buckingham
1592

George Villiers, the first Duke of Buckingham, is claimed by some to have been the lover of King James I. As a young man he was known as 'the handsomest-bodied man in all of England', he was also very charming and it is thought that he was brought to court deliberately in the hope that the king would take a shine to him and withdraw from Robert Carr – the first Earl of Somerset – who was the king's favourite until that time. George and James became very close indeed, and Villiers climbed the ranks of the peerage quickly. In 1615, he was made a gentleman of the Bedchamber, and in 1616 he rose to the rank of baron and then viscount before becoming an earl, a marquess and finally the Duke of Buckingham. When the peerage was stripped-back during the Tudor period, Villiers remained the highest ranking man outside of the royal family, and so was able to use his position to grant wealth and status to his friends and family. His corrupt behaviour did not go down well with the rest of the aristocracy. He continued to be protected by the establishment until 1628, when he was stabbed to death in the Greyhound Inn, in Portsmouth. His murderer was John Felton, a disgruntled lieutenant who had been passed-over for promotion by the duke one too many times.

1593 The plague closes London's theatres for a year. Admiral Sir Richard Hawkins recommends the drinking of orange juice and lemon juice as a means of preventing scurvy. Shakespeare writes the plays *Richard III* and *The Comedy of Errors*. Playwright Christopher Marlowe is murdered in mysterious circumstances.

Scurvy
1593

Scurvy is a condition characterized by general weakness, anaemia, gum disease and skin haemorrhages resulting from a lack of vitamin C and vitamin B in the diet. Scurvy was a serious problem in Britain during the winter months, when fresh fruit and vegetables were not readily available. However, the most dramatically affected were seafarers in the days when only non-perishable food could be stored on-board a ship. Sir Richard Hawkins called the disease 'the plague of the sea, and the spoyle of mariners'. It is likely that the symptoms of the disease were exacerbated by an overdose of vitamin A which came from eating seal's livers (a popular food while at sea). It was not until 1795 that the British Navy began providing sailors with rations of lime juice. This would prove to be an effective treatment for scurvy, but earned British seamen the popular nickname 'Limey'.

1594 Economic recession begins in England with the first of five disastrous harvests. The Scottish Highlanders under the Duke of Argyll are beaten by the Catholic Earl of Huntly at Glenlivet. Hugh O'Neill, Earl of Tyrone, leads a rebellion in Ulster, asking the Spanish for support and beginning the Nine Years' War; he defeats a small English force at the Ford of Biscuits near Enniskillen. Shakespeare writes the plays, *Titus Andronicus* and *The Taming of the Shrew*.

1595 Raleigh explores 300 miles (480 km) of the Orinocco, searching for El Dorado. Sir John Norris fails to quell the Earl of Tyrone's revolt. Londoners riot for bread. The longbow is abandoned by the English army. Sir Francis Drake and Sir John Hawkins both die during an expedition to the West Indies. Shakespeare writes the plays, *Two Gentlemen of Verona* and *Love's Labours Lost*.

1596 The English fleet sacks Cadiz in Spain; the Spanish take Calais. The Earl of Tyrone refuses to abide by a peace agreement in Ireland. Shakespeare writes *A Midsummer Night's Dream*. Edmund Spenser publishes Books 4 – 6 of *The Faerie Queene*.

1597 A second Spanish Armada, heading for Britain, is dispersed by stormy weather. Transportation is authorized by Act of parliament as a punishment for criminals. Shakespeare writes the *Sonnets* and the plays *Romeo and Juliet*, *Richard II*, *King John* and *The Merchant of Venice*.

1598 In the Poor Law Act, the English parliament provides for the establishment of workhouses and the punishment of beggars. The Gaelic native Irish army, under Hugh O'Neill, defeats an English expeditionary force in the Battle of the Yellow Ford. The Bodleian Library at Oxford is founded by Sir Thomas Bodley. Francis Bacon is arrested for debt. Shakespeare writes *Henry IV*. Ben Jonson writes *Every Man in his Humour*.

1599 The Earl of Tyrone leads a rebellion against the English in Ireland; Robert Devereaux, Earl of Essex, is appointed Lord Lieutenant in Ireland; Essex is defeated at Arklow and signs a truce with the Earl of Tyrone; Essex is arrested and banished. The Globe Theatre opens in Southwark. Shakespeare writes *Julius Caesar*. Oliver Cromwell is born.

1600 Elizabeth I grants a charter to the East India Company. The Earl of Tyrone invades Munster. Shakespeare writes *Hamlet, As You Like It* and *Much Ado About Nothing*.

1601 The parishes are charged with providing for the needy. Essex attempts rebellion and is executed. Spain sends two fleets in support of the Irish in their rebellion against the English; Mountjoy defeats them at the battle of Kinsale. Shakespeare writes *Troilus and Cressida*.

1602 Mountjoy's forces defeat and capture a Spanish army in Ireland. Shakespeare writes *The Merry Wives of Windsor* and *Othello*.

1603 Elizabeth dies, aged 69; the Union of the Crowns; James VI of Scotland becomes James I of England, uniting the kingdoms of England and Scotland. Sir Walter Raleigh is suspected of a plot to put Arabella Stuart, daughter of the Earl of Lennox, on the throne; he is imprisoned in the Tower. In Ireland, Hugh O'Neill surrenders, bringing the Nine Years' War to an end. Plague ravages Britain. Shakespeare writes *All's Well That Ends Well*.

1604 England and Spain make peace in the Treaty of London. Shakespeare writes *Measure for Measure*. Robert Cawdrey compiles the first dictionary, *Table Alphabeticall*.

1605
The Gunpowder Plot (above); Guy Fawkes and other Roman Catholic dissidents fail to blow up parliament and James I. The new Lord Deputy of Ireland, Arthur Chichester, begins to restrict the authority of the Earl of Tyrone and Rory; they flee to the continent, marking the end of Ireland's ancient Gaelic aristocracy. Shakespeare writes *King Lear*.

1606   The Gunpowder Plot conspirators are hung, drawn and quartered. The Union Jack is adopted as the British flag. Scots settle in the Ards Peninsula in Ireland. 120 colonists set sail for America. Shakespeare writes *Macbeth* and *Anthony and Cleopatra*. Ben Jonson writes *Volpone*.

1607   The lands of the rebellious Irish earls are confiscated, preparing the way for the plantation (colonization) of Ulster. The colony of Virginia is founded at Jamestown by John Smith. Shakespeare writes *Timon of Athens*.

1608   The first municipal library is opened in Norwich. Shakespeare writes *Coriolanus*.

1609   Scottish and English Protestants are encouraged to settle in Ulster.

1610   In the Great Contract, James offers to give up some feudal rights in return for an annual allowance of £200,000; parliament rejects it; James dissolves parliament. Hudson Bay is discovered by Henry Hudson.

1611   The order of the Baronets is created by James to raise cash. The King James Version of the *Bible* is completed. Shakespeare writes *A Winter's Tale* and *The Tempest*.

1612   Bartholomew Legate and Richard Wightman are the last two people to be burned for heresy in England.

1613   James I's daughter, Elizabeth, marries Frederick V, Elector of Palatine; through her descendents the House of Hanover will inherit the British throne in 1714. Shakespeare writes *Henry VIII*.

1614   James I dissolves the Addled Parliament; he does not call another parliament for seven years. John Webster writes *The Duchess of Malfi*. John Napier publishes the first logarithm tables.

1616   Sir Walter Raleigh is released from the Tower on parole to search for El Dorado. William Shakespeare dies.

The Search for El Dorado
1616

In 1616, Sir Walter Raleigh sailed for South America for the second time. His expedition had two main objectives. The first was to search for the lost city of El Dorado, described by the Spanish conquistadors as a land of gold which they believed lay at the heart of the Amazon jungle. His second objective was to secure a foothold for an English settlement in South America, so that they could mine the abundant reserves of precious metals there. Sir Walter bought his way out of prison in order to embark upon this quest, and James I (who disliked Raleigh intensely) agreed to the expedition on the condition that no offence was given to the Spanish settlers in the region.

When they arrived in Guiana, Sir Walter sent his own son and a trusted aide on the trail for El Dorado, during which they stumbled across and attacked a Spanish settlement. Sir Walter's son was killed in the attack, El Dorado was never found and Sir Walter was forced to return home a failure. Having disobeyed the king's instructions, he was imprisoned and finally executed.

1617   James I meets the Scottish parliament. One-way streets are introduced in London.

1618   The Thirty Years' War, involving most of the major continental powers. Francis Bacon becomes Lord Chancellor. Sir Walter Raleigh is executed.

1620   The Pilgrim Fathers land at Plymouth Rock on Cape Cod, Massachusetts, in the *Mayflower*, captained by Miles Standish; they found New Plymouth.

1621   James I's Third parliament. The Commons produce a declaration of parliamentray rights, the 'Great Protestation'. Francis Bacon is impeached for accepting bribes; he is fined £40,000 and banned from parliament and the Royal court.

1622   James I dissolves parliament. William Oughtred invents the slide rule.

1623   A patents law is introduced, providing protection for inventors.

1624   James I's Fourth parliament; parliament refuses to declare war on Spain. Virginia becomes a crown colony.

1625   Charles I becomes King of England and marries Henrietta Maria, sister of Louis XIII of France. England, Denmark and France form an alliance against the Hapsburgs. The Treaty of Southampton unites England and the Netherlands against Spain. Parliament taxes tobacco. In London alone, 41,000 people die of the plague.

1626   Charles convenes his second parliament, but when the Duke of Buckingham, his chief advisor, is impeached, he dissolves it.

1627   England declares war on France; Charles sends a fleet in a doomed attempt to help French Huguenots defend La Rochelle. Francis Bacon's *New Atlantis* is published.

1628 Charles I's Third parliament; the Petition of Right, forces him to accept parliament's statement of civil rights in return for finances. Buckingham is murdered. William Harvey publishes his work on the circulation of blood.

1629 Charles I has several MPs arrested, dissolves parliament and rules personally until 1640.

1630 The colony of Massachusetts is founded in America. England makes peace with France and Spain.

1631 William Oughtred invents the multiplication sign, 'x'. John Donne dies. Kew Palace is built.

1632 The colonies of Maryland and Antigua are founded. The writer George Herbert dies. Flemish artist, Anthony van Dyck, becomes court painter.

Sir Christopher Wren
1632–1723

Sir Christopher Wren was a designer and mathematician, an astronomer and the greatest architect of his era. As a child Wren was sickly, but showed an early talent for maths as well as a passion for inventing things. In 1662 he became one of the founding members of the Royal Society alongside many other eminent mathematicians and scientists. The great fire of London provided Wren with an opportunity to redesign the London landscape. His radical plans for the city were rejected, but he was commissioned to design and build as many as 51 London churches including the magnificent St Paul's Cathedral (left), which continues to stand as an impressive monument to Sir Christopher Wren's religious fervour and formidable talent.

1634 Charles I introduces Ship Money, a tax on ports and maritime counties dressed up as an attempt to raise money for a defensive fleet. Parish registers are started in Ireland. Covent Garden Market opens. The fens are drained by Dutch engineer, Sir Julius Vermuyden. Rubens paints the Banqueting House ceiling in London.

1635 Charles extends Ship Money to inland towns and counties. The colony of Rhode Island is founded in America. A postal service is established between Edinburgh and London. A speed limit for hackney coaches of 3mph (4.8 kph) is imposed in London.

1636 Connecticut is founded in America. Van Dyck paints *Charles I in Three Positions*.

1637 Charles tries to force the English liturgy and a new prayer book onto the Scottish church; there is rioting in Edinburgh.

1638 In Scotland, the Solemn League and Covenant is signed as a display of support for the reformed religion and to protest against Charles's new prayer book; when Charles threatens to get his way by force, the Covenanters form an army; a general assembly at Glasgow abolishes episcopacy, creating the structure of the church of Scotland. Torture is abolished in Britain.

1639 The First Bishops' War between Charles I and the Scottish church ends with the Pacification of Dunse. Thomas Wentworth, Lord Deputy of Ireland, ruthlessly subdues the country. The independent chapel at Llanfaches in Monmouthshire is the first Welsh nonconformist church.

1640 Charles I convenes the short parliament; it is dissolved for its refusal to grant him money. The Second Bishops' War; the Scots defeat the English at Newburn; the war ends with the Treaty of Ripon. The Long parliament begins; it can only be dismissed with consent of its members. The first stagecoach routes are opened.

1641 The Triennial Act requires parliament to be summoned every three years. The Grand Remonstrance, a list of grievances, is presented to Charles I by parliament; the king's minister, the Earl of Strafford, is executed; the Star Chamber and the High Commission are abolished. Catholics in Ireland revolt; 30,000 Protestants are massacred; English settlers are driven out of Ulster. Charles's daughter, Mary, marries William II, Prince of Orange. In Manchester, the first cotton factories open.

1642 **January** Charles I fails in an attempt to arrest five members of parliament; Hollis, Hampden, Strode, Haselrigg and Pym; Bills are introduced excluding bishops from the Lords and giving control of the army to the Commons. **March** Charles rejects the Bills. **July** A committee of public safety is appointed by parliament; theatres close until 1660. **August** The English Civil War begins when Charles raises his standard at Nottingham. **October** The first battle of the war between the Cavaliers (royalists) and Roundheads (parliamentarians) is fought at Edgehill and is indecisive. **November** Charles's defeat at Turnham Green halts his advance on London.

> ## You lost a great deal of blood for me that day and I shall not forget it. For a lawyer, a professed lawyer to throw off his gown and fight so heartily for me, I must need think very well of it.

Charles I to Sir Edward Lake, who had just fought at Edgehill

1643 The Second Campaign of the English Civil War begins; the parliamentarians win at Bradford, Gainsborough, Grantham and Winceby; the English parliament agrees to the Solemn League and Covenant, securing the support of the Scottish army, which invades England. **June** The royalists win at Chalgrove Field. **July** Royalist forces take Bristol. **September** The royalists organize a ceasefire in Ireland so that English Protestant soldiers can be sent home to fight the parliamentarians. **October** The first Battle of Newbury proves indecisive.

1644 The Third Campaign of the English Civil War brings the 'Clubmen' risings of armed neutrals; the Commons passes the Self-denying Ordinance, removing all MPs, apart from Oliver Cromwell, from military commands. **January** The royalists lose the Battle of Nantwich. **April** York is besieged by Roundhead troops. **July** Prince Rupert relieves York; in the Battle of Marston Moor, the decisive battle of the war, Oliver Cromwell defeats Prince Rupert. **August** The Highland clans rise in support of Charles. **September** The Highlanders beat the Covenanters at the Battle of Tippamuir. **October** The Second Battle of Newbury is indecisive.

1645 **February** Cromwell's New Model Army is formed; Sir Thomas Fairfax is its lord general and Cromwell is second-in-command. The royalist Highlanders defeat the Covenanters at the Battle of Inverlochy. **May** The royalists again defeat the Covenanters at the Battle of Auldcarn. **June** The royalists are crushed at the Battle of Naseby, effectively bringing the civil war to an end. **July** The Royalist army defeats the Covenanters at the Battle of Alford. **September** The Marquess of Montrose, supporting Charles in Scotland, flees to Europe after losing to General Leslie in the Battle of Philiphaugh.

1646 Charles I surrenders to the Scots at Newark; parliament demands that the king surrenders control of parliament for 20 years and agrees to religious reforms in favour of the Protestants; Charles rejects them and tries to escape.

1647 The army refuses to disband. **January** The Scots agree to hand Charles over for £400,000. **June** The army seizes Charles in Northamptonshire. **November** Charles escapes to the Isle of Wight, but is captured. **December** Parliament presents four Bills to the king; these hand control of the army to parliament for 20 years, require that all declarations against parliament be annulled, banish all peers created by Charles from the House of Lords and allow the Lords and the Commons to adjourn as and when they want.

1648 **January** Parliament renounces its allegiance to the king; the Scots support Charles in a second civil war. **August** Rebellions in support of the king break out. royalist hopes end with defeat at Preston. **December** The parliament known as the Rump Parliament decides to bring Charles to trial.

> ## *I tell you we will cut off his head with the crown upon it.*
>
> Oliver Cromwell to one of the judges at the trial of King Charles I, 1648

1649 **January** Charles is found guilty of high treason and executed in front of the Banqueting House in Whitehall. **February** In Edinburgh, Charles II is proclaimed king; the Irish rise in support of Charles II. **March** Parliament abolishes the monarchy and the House of Lords; it establishes a Commonwealth run by a Council of State.

1650 **April** Montrose is defeated at the Battle of Corbiesdale and executed. **June** Charles II arrives in Scotland and takes the Covenant; Cromwell invades Scotland and defeats an army twice the size of his at Dunbar.

1651 Charles II is crowned King of Scotland at Scone; he marches into England; Oliver Cromwell captures Perth; Charles loses at Worcester and flees to France. Thomas Hobbes writes *Leviathan*. The *Mercurius Scoticus*, Scotland's first newspaper, is published.

1652 The English navy defeats the Dutch at the Battle of the Downs; the First Anglo-Dutch War begins.

1653 Cromwell dissolves the Rump Parliament and becomes Lord Protector; the Bare Bones Parliament meets. The English defeat the Dutch off Portland and in the naval Battle of Texel. Isaak Walton writes *The Compleat Angler*.

1654 The Treaty of Westminster ends the First Anglo-Dutch War. The First Protectorate Parliament meets, formed of MPs from the three kingdoms; Cromwell is opposed and dissolves it as quickly as possible.

1655 Parliament votes that the position of protector should be elective rather than hereditary; Cromwell favours military rule and dissolves parliament. England captures Jamaica from Spain.

1656 Britain goes to war with Spain. The Second Protectorate Parliament meets.

1657 Parliament offers Cromwell the title of King; he rejects the offer, but claims the right to personally elect the members of the House of Lords.

1658 The Third Protectorate Parliament meets; it is dissolved after 16 days. Cromwell dies of pneumonia and is buried in Westminster Abbey; he is succeeded by his son, Richard. The population of Ireland, at 1,500,000 before Cromwell, is reduced by two-thirds, to 500,000, at his death. France joins Britain against Spain; Britain and France defeat Spain in the Battle of the Dunes.

1659 The army forces Richard Cromwell to resign; the Rump Parliament is restored, but is expelled by the army and a military committee of safety rules the country; the unpopularity of military rule results in the restoration of the Rump Parliament.

1660 General Monk assumes control of government; he reconvenes the Long Parliament. In the Declaration of Breda, Charles II promises a parliamentary settlement; the Convention Parliament restores Charles II to the throne; the bodies of Cromwell and others are taken from Westminster Abbey and hanged at Tyburn. War with Spain comes to an end. Samuel Pepys begins to write his diary.

1661 The coronation of Charles II. The Cavalier Parliament passes a series of repressive laws against the Nonconformists, collectively known as the Clarendon Code, and establishes the Anglican church. The Treason Act makes it treason to merely plan a rebellion. England takes Bombay. Postmarks are introduced by English Postmaster general, Henry Bishop.

1662 The Act of Uniformity requires the use of all the rites and ceremonies in the *Book of Common Prayer* in Church of England services; 2,000 clergymen leave the church. The Quaker Act imposes severe penalties on Quakers meeting for worship. Christopher Wren designs his first building. Thomas Fuller writes *Worthies of England*, the first attempt at a dictionary of national biography.

1663 England siezes New Amsterdam from the Dutch and changes its name to New York. A hearth tax is introduced. The first turnpike toll is established.

1664 New Jersey is founded in America.

Witchhunts in Britain
1644

In the difficult years following the English civil war, paranoia surrounding the practice of witchcraft was rife in British towns and cities – particularly in the East of England. These tensions were exploited by self-appointed witchhunters such as Matthew Hopkins and John Stearne, who travelled the region staging interrogations and trials. Mass trials took place in Essex and Suffolk (interestingly two counties that had found themselves at the heart of the violence during the civil war), and as a result almost 40 people were executed. The hysteria spread to parts of Norfolk and eventually to counties further west. In all approximately 150 men and women were placed under interrogation, suspected of dabbling in the occult, and up to 100 people were eventually executed.

1665 The Second Anglo-Dutch War begins; the Duke of York defeats the Dutch off Lowestoft. Sir Isaac Newton conceives gravitation after watching an apple fall. The Great Plague breaks out in London in March; by October, 70,000, a quarter of the capital's population, will be dead. The *London Gazette* is first published.

> *It was dark before I could get home, and so land a churchyard stairs, where to my great trouble I met a dead corps of the plague in a narrow alley just bringing a little pair of stairs.*

Samuel Pepys, 1665

1666 France declares war on Britain. A British fleet is defeated by the Dutch. Scottish Covenanters revolt, but lose the Battle of Pentland Hills. The Great Plague ends. The Great Fire of London breaks out on 2 September; St Paul's Cathedral and two-thirds of central London are destroyed, and 65,000 people are left homeless.

1667 The Dutch fleet defeats the English in the Medway estuary; there is widespread panic throughout Britain. The Treaty of Breda, between the Netherlands, England, France and Denmark, ends the Second Anglo-Dutch War. The Cabal Ministry is formed to conduct the government; it is named after the first letter of the surnames of its members: Clifford, Arlington, Buckingham, Ashley and Lauderdale.

Robert Hooke proposes systematic weather recording; the start of the science of meteorology. John Milton writes *Paradise Lost*.

1668　The Triple Alliance of England, the Netherlands and Sweden is formed against France. The East India Company takes control of Bombay. Sir Isaac Newton invents the reflecting telescope. John Dryden becomes the first poet laureate.

1669　Samuel Pepys' diary ends.

1670　The Secret Treaty of Dover is signed between Charles II of England and Louis XIV of France to restore Roman Catholicism to England. North and South Carolina are founded. The Hudsons Bay Company is founded. Wren begins the rebuilding of London's churches.

1671　Aphra Behn, one of the first female English professional writers, writes *The Forc'd Marriage*. John Milton writes *Paradise Regained* and *Samson Agonistes*.

1672　In the Declaration of Indulgence, Charles II permits freedom of worship. The Third Anglo-Dutch war breaks out.

1673　An Anglo-French attempt to invade Holland fails. The Test Act deprives Roman Catholics and Nonconformists of public office. John Dryden writes *Marriage a la Mode*. The first metal dental fittings are fitted.

1674　The Treaty of Westminster is signed between England and the Netherlands, ending the Third Anglo-Dutch War; in the treaty, New Amsterdam is formally recognized as British and becomes New York. There are moves to exclude the Duke of York from the succession due to his Catholicism. John Milton dies.

1675　John Ogilby's *Britannia*, the first British road atlas, is published. Work begins on Sir Christopher Wren's new St Paul's Cathedral; Wren also designs the Royal Observatory at Greenwich.

1676　It becomes a legal requirement to observe the Sabbath. Britain is hit by an influenza epidemic. In the City of London, The Monument, commemorating the Great Fire of London, is completed.

1677　William III, ruler of the Netherlands, marries Mary, daughter of James, Duke of York, the heir to the throne.

1678　Charles II concludes an alliance with the Dutch against the French. Catholics are disqualified from being MPs; the Duke of York is excepted. There are eclipses of the sun and moon; the country is gripped by hysteria. John Bunyan writes *The Pilgrim's Progress, Part 1*.

1679　The Act of Habeas Corpus is passed. Parliament's Bill of Exclusion against the Duke of York is blocked by Charles II; the Cavalier Parliament is dismissed; the supporters of the bill become known as Whigs, their opponents, the Abhorrers, become known as Tories. The Scottish Covenanters rebel; they defeat Viscount Dundee at Drumclog; the Duke of Monmouth defeats the Covenanters at Bothwell Bridge. Edmund Halley publishes his *Catalogue of the Southern Stars*.

1680　The Penny Post is launched in London. New Hampshire is founded in America.

1681　Charles II's Fifth Parliament; the Test Act, designed to repress Presbyterians, is rejected by Charles; he dissolves parliament and rules without it.

1682　Edmund Halley observes the bright comet that becomes known as Halley's Comet. Elias Ashmole founds Britain's first museum, the Ashmolean, in Oxford.

1683　Sir Isaac Newton explains the connection between tides and gravitation. Britain's first museum, the Ashmolean, is open to the public.

1684 The Duke of Monmouth is banished to Holland for his part in the Rye House Plot to assassinate Charles. London's first street lighting is introduced. John Bunyan writes *The Pilgrim's Progress, Part 2*.

1685 Charles II dies, converting to Catholicism on his deathbed; his brother becomes James II of England and VII of Scotland; he holds his first Parliament; a rebellion by Charles II's illegitimate son, the Duke of Monmouth, is quelled. The Pennsylvania colony is established in America.

1686 James II disregards the Test Act; Roman Catholics are appointed to public office.

1687 James II issues the Declaration of Liberty of Conscience, extending toleration to all religions, but favouring Catholics.
Isaac Newton publishes *Philosophiae naturalis principia mathematica*.

1688 The 'Glorious Revolution' begins when a son, James Stuart (the Old Pretender), is born to James II, sparking outrage at the prospect of a succession of Catholics; William III of Orange is invited to save England from Roman Catholicism; he lands at Torbay; James II flees to France.

1689 The Convention Parliament issues the Bill of Rights, establishing a constitutional monarchy in Britain; it bars Catholics from the throne; election of MPs is to be free; William III and Mary II become joint monarchs of England, Scotland and Ireland; the Convention Parliament becomes a regular parliament. Freedom of worship is granted to dissenters in England. The Grand Alliance is formed between England, the Netherlands and others. James II lands in Ireland with 20,000 French troops; Northern Irish Protestants retreat to the city of Derry and are besieged by James's army. James II's parliament restores all lands confiscated in Ireland since 1641. The Highlanders rise in support of James; he defeats the Whig General Mackay at the Battle of Killiecrankie, but dies in the battle; the Highland revolt is over. War breaks out with France.

1690 James II controls much of Ireland; William of Orange (William III) lands at Carrickfergus and defeats James's Irish-French army at the Battle of the Boyne; James retreats to France; William reconquers Ireland. The French defeat an Anglo-Dutch naval force at Beachy Head; there is fear of a French invasion.

1691 William orders the Scottish clan chiefs to take the oath of allegiance. In Ireland, the Catholics are defeated at Aughrim and surrender at Limerick. Lloyd's Coffee House in London becomes the home of maritime insurance.

1692 Exclusion of Catholics from parliament and all professions. The massacre of Glencoe takes place; every member of the MacDonald clan under the age of seventy is murdered by the Campbells for refusing to take the oath of allegiance.

1693 William borrows a large sum of money at 10 per cent to pay for the war with France; the beginning of Britain's National Debt. William loses the Battle of Landen in Flemish Brabant to the French; 19,000 allied troops die.

1694 Queen Mary dies. The Royal Navy bombards Dieppe, Le Havre and Dunkirk. Scotsman William Paterson founds the Bank of England. Censorship of the press ends.

1695 William's Third Parliament; anti-Catholic laws are introduced. The Bank of Scotland is founded.

1696 The Second Treason Act permits the accused to have a copy of the indictment and a list of jurors before the trial. The Window Tax is introduced, influencing British architecture for the next 50 years.

Henry Winstanley begins work on the first Eddystone Lighthouse.

1697 William III and Louis XIV sign the Treaty of Ryswyck, ending the War of the Grand Alliance and acknowledging William as King of England and Anne as his successor. The rebuilt St Paul's Cathedral reopens.

1698 William III's Fourth Parliament officially sanctions the slave trade. The London Stock Exchange is founded.

The Slave Trade in Britain
1698

It is a sad fact that many British families, businesses, towns and cities owe their existence to the transatlantic slave trade which thrived from the end of the 14th century until it was outlawed in 1807. British merchants were responsible for transporting thousands of African people across the Atlantic ocean in squalid and dangerously overcrowded slave ships such  as *The Jolly Bachelor* and *The Adventure*. Those who survived the middle passage were sold to wealthy landowners in the Caribbean and North America. British cities such as London, Bristol and Liverpool became major slaving ports. By the end of the 17th century, one in every four ships leaving Liverpool was a slave ship, and the industry's movers and shakers were becoming some of the richest people in the world. The passing of The Slavery Abolition Act meant that the slave trade was eventually banned in Britain and its colonies in 1834, but unfortunately trade in human traffic still exists in various forms.

1699 80 per cent of the inhabitants of the Caribbean are slaves. William Dampier explores the west coast of Australia. The Darien Scheme is launched in Scotland, an attempt to establish a settlement on the Isthmus of Darien in Panama; fortunes and lives are lost. Billingsgate Market opens in London.

1700 The Duke of Gloucester, only surviving child of Queen Anne, dies.

1701 William's Fifth Parliament, the Act of Settlement settles the succession to the throne on the Protestant descendents of Sophia of Hanover. Former King James II dies in France; Louis XIV proclaims his son, James Edward (the Old Pretender), King of Great Britain and Ireland. William's sixth Parliament agrees an attainder on James Edward Stuart. Jethro Tull invents the seed drill.

1702 William III dies after a fall from his horse; William's sister-in-law becomes Queen Anne. The government is controlled by a Whig-Tory Ministry, led by John Churchill and Godolphin; Churchill becomes Captain-General of England's land forces; he captures Kaiserworth, Venloo and Liege, and is made Duke of Marlborough. Delaware is founded in America. The first English daily newspaper, the *Daily Courant*, is published.

1703 Marlborough captures Bonn, Huy, Limoges and Guelders. England and Portugal sign the Methuen Treaty. A hurricane devastates England; the Eddystone lighthouse is destroyed.

1704 Marlborough and Prince Eugene defeat the armies of France and Bavaria in the Battle of Blenheim. Gibraltar is captured from the Spanish. After a quarrel on board ship, Alexander Selkirk is put ashore on an uninhabited island at his own request; he is marooned for four years; his story becomes the basis for Daniel Defoe's *Robinson Crusoe*.

1705   Lord Peterborough captures Barcelona. Edmund Halley accurately predicts the return of the comet that now bears his name. Sir John Vanburgh and Nicholas Hawksmoor begin Blenheim Palace.

1706   The Earl of Galway and allied forces enter Madrid; British, Dutch and Danish forces under Marlborough defeat the Spanish and French at Ramillies in Belgium. Parliament creates a Turnpike Trust; local gentry are encouraged to maintain roads by raising tolls. Work begins on the second Eddystone Lighthouse.

1707   The Act of Union unites the parliaments of England and Scotland at Westminster; Scotland is to send 16 member peers to the House of Lords and 45 to the House of Commons; legal systems and churches remain independent.

1708   Marlborough defeats the French Oudenarde in Belgium; he captures Lille after a four-month siege. James Edward Stuart arrives in Scotland in an unsuccessful attempt to wrest the throne from the Stuarts. The New and Old East India companies amalgamate as the United East India Company; it is the most influential power on the coast of India.

1709   Iron-worker Abraham Darby invents a production method that leads to the mass-production of iron. Postage rates begin to be regulated by mileage. Richard Steele publishes the first issue of *The Tatler*.

1710   The Tories come to power; they reduce Britain's involvement in the European War.

1711   *The Spectator* is first published by Steele and Addison. The first horse-racing meeting takes place at Royal Ascot, attended by Queen Anne.

1712   Robert Walpole is expelled from the Commons and imprisoned in the Tower for for six months, for corruption. Thomas Newcomen develops the first piston-operated steam engine. The last execution for witchcraft takes place. In Scotland, Rob Roy MacGregor becomes an outlaw. John Arbuthnot writes *The History of John Bull*.

1713   The Treaty of Utrecht makes peace with France and ends the War of the Spanish Succession; Gibraltar and Minorca are ceded to Britain. The South Sea Company takes over the entire National Debt at 8 per cent interest. Britain obtains the right from Spain to supply slaves to the Spanish colonies for 30 years. John Gay writes *The Wife of Bath*.

1714   Queen Anne dies; her cousin, the German Prince George Louis of Hanover, who speaks no English, becomes King George I; his son is created Prince of Wales. Lord Townsend, Lord Stanhope and Robert Walpole form a Whig Ministry. The Board of Longitude, a government body formed in 1714 to solve the problem of finding longitude at sea, offers a prize of £20,000 for the discovery of a northwest passage to the Far East. Alexander Pope writes *The Rape of the Lock*.

1715   The Earl of Mar leads the Jacobite rising, known as the '15', to install the 'Old Pretender', James Edward Stuart, on the throne; he takes Perth but the Battle of Sherrifmuir is indecisive; Mar marches into England, but planned uprisings in other parts of the country fail to materialize and he surrenders at Preston; James Edward Stuart arrives in Scotland but fails to inspire his followers. A new parliament meets with a large Whig majority. The brokers of the Treaty of Utrecht: Robert Harley, Earl of Oxford and Mortimer, Ormond and Lord Bolingbroke are impeached for surrendering British honour and interests; Oxford is sent to the Tower and the others flee to France. George Frideric Handel composes his *Water Music*.

1716   The Jacobite army disperses and James Edward Stuart spends the remainder of his life in Rome. The duration of a parliament is increased from three to seven years. Cheltenham becomes a popular spa when mineral waters are discovered. Architect Nicholas Hawksmoor begins work on St Mary Woolnoth, his finest church.

1717   Britain, France and the Netherlands form an alliance to uphold the terms of the Treaty of Utrecht. Walpole resigns, Lord Stanhope becomes First Lord of the Treasury. The maypole that has stood in the Strand since 1661 is used by Sir Isaac Newton to support his new telescope. The value of the golden guinea is fixed at 21 shillings. The first Freemasons' Grand Lodge, the Grand Lodge of England, is inaugurated in London.

1718   Lord Stanhope becomes Secretary of State. Thomas Lombe patents a machine to make thrown silk; it is the first powered, continuous-production unit in the world. Lady Mary Wortley Montagu introduces inoculation against smallpox. Britain, France, the Netherlands and Austria form an alliance against Spain after Spain captures Sicily; Admiral Byng destroys the Spanish fleet off Cape Passarro.

1719   In the Battle of Glenshiel, a Spanish and Jacobite alliance is defeated by a government force; it is the last close engagement of British and foreign troops on mainland British soil. Daniel Defoe writes *Robinson Crusoe*.

Bonnie Prince Charlie
1720

Charles Edward Stuart, or Bonnie Prince Charlie, as he is most affectionately known, was born in December 1720 to James Francis Edward Stuart. As a young man he resolved to overthrow King George II in favour of his father, James. On 5 July 1745, Charles set sail for France in order to gather support for his campaign, but one of his ships – *The Elspeth* – which was carrying his weapons and his gold, collided with a Royal Naval ship and the convoy was forced to return to Scotland. On 23 July 1745, Charlie landed in Eriskay in the Western Isles, where he began building an army. In the following September they took Perth and Edinburgh. In October they moved south, reaching Derby in early December. By this time Charles had realized that support from the English Jacobites was not growing as he had hoped. He wanted to continue to London, but his appointed council feared defeat and voted for a retreat. Retreat they did, but the Duke of Cumberland pursued them. The two sides met at the battle of Culloden on 16 April 1746. The Jacobeans were defeated, and Charles fled. He remained a fugitive for five months, but Bonnie Prince Charlie was never betrayed by the loyal highlanders, and he managed to escape to safety in France.

1720 The South Sea Bubble – an economic bubble that has occurred through speculation in the company shares – bursts; thousands of investors are ruined. The Quadruple Alliance makes peace with Spain. Walpole and Stanhope are recalled to office. Ralph Allen establishes a postal system of post-boys on horseback. Sir John Vanbrugh's Blenheim Palace is completed and his Seaton Delaval in Northumberland is begun.

1721 Sir Robert Walpole becomes the first British prime minister; his policy of maintaining a permanent National Debt brings prosperity. The directors of the South Sea Company are prosecuted. The woodcarver Grinling Gibbons the finest woodcarver of all time, dies. Daniel Defoe writes *Moll Flanders*.

1722 The Atterbury Plot, a plan to restore the Old Pretender, is uncovered; Francis Atterbury, Bishop of Rochester, is arrested and banished for life. The Habeas Corpus Act is suspended. The Duke of Marlborough dies. Daniel Defoe writes *Journal of the Plague Year*.

1723 The Workhouse Test Act gives help to the poor if they enter a workhouse. Sir Christopher Wren dies, aged 91. Adam Smith, the economist and philosopher and the painter, Sir Joshua Reynolds are born.

1724 The king's favourite, John Carteret, becomes Lord Lieutenant of Ireland. Longman's, the publishing house, is founded.

1725 Britain, France and Prussia sign the Treaty of Hanover. Guy's Hospital in London is founded. Lord Burlington and William Kent build Chiswick House in London.

1726 The future George II's son, William Augustus, becomes Duke of Cumberland. General George Wade builds 250 miles (400 km) of roads in Scotland. Blood pressure is measured for the first time by Stephen Hales, clergyman and physicist. *Lloyd's List*, a journal of shipping news, is published for the first time in London. Jonathan Swift writes *Gulliver's Travels*.

1727 George I dies of apoplexy at Osnabruck; he is succeeded by his son, 44-year-old George II. Britain and Spain go to war over Gibraltar. Walpole replaces the incompetent Sir Spencer Compton as prime minister. The first railway bridge is built by Ralph Wood over a colliery railway at Causey Dell in County Durham. Handel writes *Zadok the Priest*. Sir Isaac Newton dies.

1728 Spain lifts the siege of Gibraltar after 14 months; the Convention of Prado ends the war between Spain and Britain. It is decided that the publication of parliamentary debates is a breach of privilege. John Gay's *The Beggar's Opera* is first performed. Ephraim Chambers publishes *Cyclopaedia, or Universal Dictionary of Arts and Sciences*. Explorer Captain James Cook, architect and designer Robert Adam and poet, novelist and dramatist Oliver Goldsmith are born.

1729 Spain and Britain sign the Treaty of Seville; Britain retains Gibraltar. The Methodist movement begins in Oxford. Lack of money forces Samuel Johnson to leave Pembroke College, Oxford, after 13 months. Statesman and philosopher Edmund Burke is born in Dublin. Dramatist William Congreve dies.

1730 Townsend resigns from the government and becomes an agricultural pioneer. English inventor John Hadley invents the sextant.

1731 The Treaty of Vienna is signed by Britain, Austria and the Netherlands. Number 10, Downing Street becomes the prime minister's official residence. Captain Robert Jenkins of the English ship, *Rebecca*, loses an ear in a skirmish with Spanish coastguards;

in 1739, this would become the pretext for the War of Jenkins' Ear with Spain. George Lillo writes *The London Merchant*, the first serious play in which the main characters are not from the upper classes. Robert Hamblin patents the first lightship in the world, the *Nore*. Novelist Daniel Defoe dies.

1732 In America, Georgia is founded, the last of the 13 colonies making up the English East Coast of America. Covent Garden Opera House is opened.

1733 The Molasses Act bans trade between Britain's American and West Indian colonies. Walpole's attempt to introduce excise duty on wine and tobacco leads to unrest; the Excise Bill is withdrawn. John Kay invents the flying shuttle. Jethro Tull publishes *The New Horse-Hoeing Husbandry*.

1735 William Pitt enters parliament. Consorting with evil spirits is no longer a hanging offence. Clockmaker John Harrison invents the ship's chronometer, enabling ships to determine longitude at sea. William Hogarth publishes *The Rake's Progress* engravings.

1736 Brothers John and Charles Wesley begin their evangelical mission. Scottish engineer and inventor James Watt is born. Architect Nicholas Hawksmoor dies.

1737 Queen Caroline dies; Walpole's authority is weakened; Frederick, Prince of Wales, quarrels with his father and takes the side of the anti-Walpole faction which calls itself 'The Patriots'. The Licensing Act subjects all plays to censorship by the Lord Chamberlain. Sculptor Joseph Nollekens, historian Edward Gibbon and political thinker Thomas Paine are born.

1738 The first spinning-machines are patented in England by Swiss physicist, Lewis Paul. The future George III, and astronomer Sir William Herschel are born.

1739 The War of Jenkins' Ear between Britain and Spain begins, despite Walpole's opposition. Highwayman Dick Turpin is hanged at York.

1740 Inventor and steel manufacturer Benjamin Huntsman invents the crucible method of making steel from scrap iron. Samuel Richardson writes the bestselling *Pamela*. Playwright, actor and poet laureate Colley Cibber writes the first personal, anecdotal autobiography, *An Apology for the Life of Mr Colley Cibber*. Philosopher David Hume writes *A Treatise on Human Nature*.

1741 Walpole wins, but performs poorly in the general election. David Garrick makes his first appearance on a London stage in Shakespeare's *Richard III*. The Royal Military Academy at Woolwich, is founded.

1742 Walpole's support for Austria in the War of Austrian Succession and his opposition to war with Spain, lead to his downfall; he is succeeded by Lord Carteret as prime minister. Britain forms an alliance with Russia. Cotton factories are opened in Birmingham and Northampton. The first performance of Handel's greatest work, *Messiah*, takes place in Dublin. Henry Fielding writes *Joseph Andrews*.

1743 George II is the last British monarch to command an army on the field of battle at Dettingen in Bavaria; he defeats the French. Henry Pelham, a Whig, becomes prime minister.

1744 Britain and France will be at war continuously in Europe, India, North America and the West Indies until 1815. Robert Clive arrives in Madras as an employee of the East India Company. William Hogarth paints the six pictures of *Marriage à la Mode*. The poet Alexander Pope dies.

1745   The British army, commanded by the Duke of Cumberland, is defeated by the French at the Battle of Fontenoy. Charles Edward Stuart lands in Scotland to claim the throne; he raises his father's standard at Glenfinnan; 2,000 Jacobites enter Edinburgh; Bonnie Prince Charlie wins at Prestonpans against an English army led by Sir John Cope; Charles leads his army into England, hoping to gain popular support; he reaches Derby and there is panic in London, but the support is non-existent and he is forced to return to Scotland. The first-known performance of the National Anthem, written by Thomas Arne, takes place at Drury Lane Theatre. Satirist, Jonathan Swift, and former Prime minister, Sir Robert Walpole die.

1746   The Jacobites win the Battle of Falkirk; the Duke of Cumberland routs Charles's troops at Culloden; this defeat finally ends Stuart attempts to regain the throne; the Highlanders are disarmed and forbidden to wear their tartans; the hereditary authority of the Highland Chieftains is abolished; Charles sails to France.

1747   The Duke of Cumberland is defeated by the French at Lauffeld in the Netherlands. Britain, the Netherlands and Russia sign the Convention of St. Petersburg. David Garrick changes the layout of the theatre; audiences are removed from the stage and the orchestra is brought down from the gallery. Politician and writer, Horace Walpole acquires Strawberry Hill at Twickenham; with his alterations, it will become the stimulus for the Gothic revival in English architecture.

1748   The treaty of Aix-la-Chapelle ends the Austrian War of Succession. John Palmer starts a Mail-Coach service; it has armed guards to protect against highwaymen. Tobias Smollett writes *Roderick Random*.

1749   Rioting breaks out at Bedminster in Bristol against turnpike tolls. Handel's *Music for the Royal Fireworks* is first performed in Green Park in London. John Cleland writes *Fanny Hill*. Henry Fielding writes *Tom Jones*.

1750   From now on, interest on the National Debt is reduced to 3% and the Bank of England assumes responsibility for it. The Iron Act prevents American colonies from manufacturing their own iron. In India, Robert Clive captures Arcot from the French. Jonas Hanway is the first person to use an umbrella; he is ridiculed.

1751   With a force of only 500 men, Robert Clive holds Arcot against the French; British control over southern India is established. The Prince of Wales dies. William Hogarth paints *Gin Lane*. Thomas Gray writes *An Elegy Written in a Country Churchyard*.

1752   Britain adopts government by a cabinet of the heads of the main administrative departments. The Gregorian calendar is adopted; an adjustment has to be made and 11 days between September 3 – 13 are lost; people protest in the belief that their lives have been shortened. 1 January becomes New Year's Day.

1753   A Land Tax of two shillings in the pound is introduced in England and Wales. The Marriage Act states that banns of marriage must be published in the parish church where the couple lives for three successive Sundays. The Broad Wheels Act aims to reduce damage to road surfaces by fixing a minimum width for wheels.

1754   Henry Pelham dies; he is succeeded as prime minister by his brother, the Duke of Newcastle.

1755

Samuel Johnson (left) publishes *A Dictionary of the English Language*; it has taken 10 years to compile.

1756 The Seven Years' War; Britain, competing with France for colonial possessions in India and America, declares war; the French take Minorca; there is an outcry which brings down the Duke of Newcastle; he is succeeded by the Duke of Devonshire with William Pitt as Secretary of State. In India, 122 Britains die in the Black Hole of Calcutta.

1757 The Duke of Newcastle becomes prime minister again. The Duke of Cumberland is defeated in the Battles of Hastenbeck and Klosterseven. Admiral John Byng is court-martialled and executed by firing squad on the quarter-deck of the *Monarque* after losing Minorca. Robert Clive takes Bengal at the Battle of Plassey. Road engineer Thomas Telford and poet, artist and visionary William Blake are born.

1758 Generals George Washington and John Forbes capture Fort Duquesne from the French and rename it Pittsburgh. The Duke of Cumberland is replaced as commander-in-chief of the British-Hanoverian forces by Duke Ferdinand of Brunswick. As predicted by Edmund Halley in 1682, Halley's Comet returns. Scottish philosopher David Hume writes *An Enquiry Concerning Human Understanding*. Horatio Nelson is born.

1759 General James Wolfe is given command of British forces in Canada; Wolfe defeats the French on the Plains of Abraham and captures Quebec, but is killed; British supremacy in Canada is established. It is a 'Year of Victories' for Britain with wins at Quebec, Minden, Lagos and Quiberon Bay. English engineer James Brindley begins the construction of the Bridgewater canal, the first British canal of the modern era. The British Museum is opened to the public. Samuel Johnson writes *Rasselas*. The poet Robert Burns, anti-slavery campaigner William Wilberforce and future prime minister William Pitt the Younger are born. Composer George Frideric Handel dies.

INDUSTRIAL
REVOLUTION

1760 – 1899

1760 George II dies, aged 76; he is succeeded by his grandson, George III. Colonel Eyre Coote takes Madras, ending French ambitions in India. The first school for the deaf, Braidwood's Academy, is founded by Thomas Braidwood in Edinburgh. Kew Botanical Gardens are opened.

1761 William Pitt receives no support for the war on Spain and resigns; the Duke of Newcastle becomes prime minister for the second time. In India, Pondicherry is captured from the French; in the Caribbean, Belle Isle and Dominica are captured.

1762 Britain declares war on Spain and takes Havana, Manila, Martinique, St Lucia, St Vincent and Grenada; the Spanish are driven out of Portugal. The Tory Earl of Bute succeeds the Duke of Newcastle as prime minister.

1763 The treaty of Paris, signed by Britain, France and Spain, cedes Canada, Cape Breton, Nova Scotia, Minorca, Tobago, St Vincent, Grenada and Florida to Britain. The Earl of Bute resigns and is followed as prime minister by the Whig, Charles Grenville. Radical MP John Wilkes is expelled from parliament and outlawed for attacking the king and the government; he is released when he claims parliamentary privilege, but is outlawed.

1764 There is opposition in America to the Sugar Act, with which Britain aims to recover revenue from the colonies. Inventor, James Hargreaves invents the Spinning-Jenny (left); it allows several threads to be spun at once. The first numbers begin to appear on houses in London. The painter William Hogarth dies.

1765 The Regency Bill is drawn up as a result of the king's worsening mental condition; Grenville deliberately omits the queen's name from the list of possible regents and is forced to resign; he is succeeded by another Whig, the Marquis of Rockingham. Colonists are angered by the American Stamp Act, another attempt to raise revenue from them; they convene the Stamp Act Congress in response, petitioning the king and the prime minister. In India, the British now rule Bengal and Bihar, governing 30 million people through a puppet Mogul emperor and bringing in a revenue of £4 million. James Watt invents the steam engine. Nelson's flagship, HMS *Victory*, is launched. Horace Walpole writes *The Castle of Otranto*, the first Gothic novel. The Duke of Cumberland, son of George II, dies.

1766 The Vatican recognizes the Hanoverian dynasty as lawful rulers of England, Scotland and Ireland. Rockingham repeals the American Stamp Act. The king dismisses Rockingham; William Pitt becomes prime minister again. James Christie founds auction house

Christie's. Henry Cavendish's discovery of the gas hydrogen, makes the development of the hot air balloon possible. James Stuart, son of James II, dies in Rome.

1767   The Chancellor of the exchequer, Charles Townsend, imposes import taxes on tea, glass, paper and lead to pay for the defence and government of the colonies. Robert Clive leaves India for the last time. John Wood the Younger builds Royal Crescent, Bath. Robert Adam remodels Kenwood House in London. Lawrence Sterne writes *Tristram Shandy*. Joseph Priestley publishes *The History and Present State of Electricity*.

1768   George III's Second Parliament; the Duke of Grafton becomes prime minister again. Outlawed MP John Wilkes is elected member for Middlesex; he waives his parliamentary privilege and is sentenced to two years' imprisonment and fined £1,000 for his offences in 1763. Seven die in the St George's Fields riots when a mob tries to free him. Captain James Cook begins his first voyage of exploration. The Royal Academy of Arts is founded; Sir Joshua Reynolds is its first president. Richard Arkwright invents the water frame, a water-powered machine for spinning cotton into strong thread. The first edition of the *Encyclopaedia Britannica* is published. Laurence Sterne's *Sentimental Journey* is published.

1769   Captain Cook arrives in New Zealand. James Watt patents his steam engine. Soldier and statesman, the Duke of Wellington, Anglo-Irish politician, Lord Castlereagh and English portrait painter, Thomas Lawrence are born. Josiah Wedgwood sets up his pottery works at Etruria in Staffordshire.

The Life and Works of Josiah Wedgwood
1769

Josiah Wedgwood was born into a family of potters at Burslem, Staffordshire in 1730. As a nine-year-old boy he was employed as a thrower in the family business, becoming an apprentice to his brother Thomas. In 1768, an attack of smallpox meant that he had to have a leg amputated, which cut short his career as a thrower. However, as a result of his disability he began to explore more creative options and gain an insight into the craft of pottery. Josiah emerged as a talented craftsman and a very able businessman, inventing new techniques and glazes as well as radical new working practices for his employees which provided British manufacturing with a working template for centuries to come. He was also quick to realise the importance of canal transport, and in 1766 he joined with the Duke of Bridgewater and James Brindley to start building the Trent and Mersey canal. It was finally completed in 1777, and Josiah Wedgwood used the canal system to transport Cornish clay to his factories and to transport finished goods to major cities such as Liverpool and Hull.

1770   The Duke of Grafton is dismissed by George III and replaced by Tory Lord North; North attempts to placate the colonists by abolishing all the import duties apart from the one on tea. Captain Cook discovers the east coast of Australia, landing at Botany Bay. Scottish traveller and writer James Bruce discovers the source of the Blue Nile. Thomas Gainsborough paints *The Blue Boy*. Oliver Goldsmith writes *The Deserted Village*. George Stubbs paints *White Horse Frightened by a Lion*. William Wordsworth the poet and George Canning, future Tory prime minister are born. The poet Thomas Chatterton commits suicide.

1771 Spain cedes the uninhabited Falkland Islands to Britain. Richard Arkwright builds a spinning mill, using his water-powered spinning machine. Engineer Richard Trevithick industrialist and social reformer Robert Owen, novelist Sir Walter Scott and surgeon and explorer Mungo Park are born. Poet Thomas Gray and novelist Tobias Smollett die.

1772 Warren Hastings is appointed Governor General of India. Cook sets sail on his second voyage of discovery.

1773 The Boston Tea Party; a group of radical colonists disguise themselves as Native Americans, board British ships and pour their cargoes of tea into the sea; the British government closes the port of Boston and withdraws the colony's charter. The crown takes direct control of the East India Company. Samuel Johnson and James Boswell embark on their tour of Scotland. Oliver Goldsmith writes the comedy *She Stoops to Conquer*.

1774 Angry American colonists convene a congress at Philadelphia; the import of goods is prohibited. Joseph Priestley discovers oxygen. John Wilkes is elected Lord Mayor of London. Poet laureate Robert Southey is born. Playwright Oliver Goldsmith dies. Robert Clive commits suicide.

1775 The American War of Independence begins; George Washington leads American settlers to victory at Lexington and Concord; the Philadelphia Congress sets up an army under Washington's command. In India, the British take control of Ghazipur in the Ganges Valley. Sheridan's *The Rivals* is first performed at Covent Garden. John Wood the Younger completes the Royal Crescent in Bath. Samuel Johnson writes *A Journey to the Western Isles*. Essayist Charles Lamb, painter J M W Turner, Irish nationalist leader Daniel O'Connell and novelist Jane Austen are born.

1776 Britain recruits 29,000 Hessian mercenaries to fight the American war; a submarine attacks British ships in New York harbour, the first time a submarine is used in warfare; British troops are forced out of Boston; on 4 July, the American Congress draws up and passes the Declaration of Independence. Captain Cook sets out on his third voyage of exploration. Edward Gibbon begins *The Decline and Fall of the Roman Empire*. Economist Adam Smith writes his great work, *The Wealth of Nations*. The artist John Constable is born. John Harrison, clockmaker and inventor of the chronometer, dies.

1777 The British General Burgoyne surrenders at Saratoga; Washington defeats a British force at Princeton; British troops win the Battle of Brandywine Creek, but fail to follow up, allowing the colonial army to escape. The Habeas Corpus Act is suspended. Richard Sheridan writes *The School for Scandal*.

1778 France and the Netherlands form an alliance with the Americans against Britain; Britain declares war on France; France captures Dominica; in India, Warren Hastings captures Chandernagore from the French. Sir Humphry Davy, scientist and inventor, is born. William Pitt the Elder, the composer Thomas Arne and Spinning Jenny inventor James Hargreaves die.

1779 Spain declares war on Britain; France and Spain begin the siege of Gibraltar; the British capture Senegal from France; France takes St. Vincent and Grenada; an Irish Protestant Volunteer Movement raises a force 40,000 strong to defend Ireland in the event of a French invasion. Samuel Compton invents the spinning mule, making mass production possible in the textile industry. Abraham Darby builds The Iron Bridge at Coalbrookdale, in Shropshire the first iron bridge. Captain James Cook is murdered by Hawaiian natives. Actor and theatre manager David Garrick dies.

1780 Petitions are organized across the country against high taxes. Britain declares war on the Netherlands because of its support for the American colonists; Admiral Rodney destroys the Spanish fleet at Cape St Vincent and lifts the siege of Gibraltar. Henry Grattan, a member of the Irish House of Commons, demands Home Rule for Ireland; Lord North allows Ireland to trade freely with the colonies. The *British Gazette and Sunday Monitor* is the first Sunday newspaper. The Derby is run for the first time; it is won by Diomed. The Gordon Riots take place in opposition to the Catholic Relief Act of 1778.

1781 The French fleet wins the Battle of Chesapeake Bay; Lord Cornwallis and an army of 7,000 troops surrender at Yorktown, Virginia; this defeat ends fighting in the American War of Independence. William Pitt the Younger enters parliament. English mechanical engineer George Stephenson is born.

1782 Lord North resigns; the Marquis of Rockingham becomes prime minister again, but dies, and he is succeeded by Lord Shelbourne; in Paris, Grenville negotiates a peace settlement with Benjamin Franklin and the Comte de Vergennes; Britain, France, Spain and the Netherlands agree to recognize the 13 United States. In Ireland, Henry Grattan demands legislative freedom for the Irish and sets out his Irish Declaration of Rights; the Repeal of Ireland Bill grants the Irish parliament legislative rights, bringing an end to British control of Irish parliaments.

1783 Shelbourne is censured over the peace negotiations with America and resigns; he is succeeded as prime minister by the Duke of Portland; he is followed in December by the Tory, William Pitt the Younger, who becomes Britain's youngest prime minister at the age of 24. The Treaty of Versailles formally recognizes American independence; Britain cedes Tobago, St Lucia, Senegal, Pondicherry and Chandernagore to France in exchange for Grenada, Dominica, St Vincent, Nevis, Montserrat, St Kitts and the Gambia; Britain gives Spain, Florida and Minorca in exchange for Providence, the Bahamas and Gibraltar. The landscape gardener Lancelot 'Capability' Brown dies.

1784 Warren Hastings makes peace with the Mahrathas in India; the East India Company is placed under a Board of Control. The first Royal Mail coach operates from Bristol to London. Writer and lexicographer Samuel Johnson dies.

1785 Warren Hastings resigns in protest at the control imposed by Pitt on the East India Company; he is replaced by Charles Cornwallis. Edmund Cartwright's invention of the power loom mechanizes weaving. Jean-Pierre Blanchard and John Jeffries make the first crossing of the English Channel by balloon. James Hutton's *Theory of the Earth* paves the way for modern geology.

1786 Britain enters a period of economic boom, based on the expansion of the cotton and coal mining industries; industrial towns are expanding in the Midlands, North of England and in the Scottish Lowlands. In the Anglo-French trade treaty, duty is reduced on English clothes, cotton and iron goods and, in return, duty is lowered on imports into Britain of French olive oil, soap and wine. Robert Burns publishes his *Poems*. William Beckford writes the Gothic novel *Vathek*. William Herschel publishes his *Catalogue of Nebulae*.

1787 The Committee for the Abolition of the Slave Trade is formed. Warren Hastings is impeached for irregularities during his administration in India.

1788 George III's mental condition worsens, but he recovers. Warren Hastings' trial begins; it lasts seven years and he is acquitted. The first shipload of transported English convicts arrives in Australia. Sierra Leone becomes a British refuge settlement for freed slaves. Mechanical engineer, Andrew Meikle, patents a threshing machine. The first edition of *The Times* is published on 1 January. The poet George Gordon Lord Byron and Sir Robert Peel, future prime minister are born. The Young Pretender, Charles Edward Stuart, the composer Joseph Gibbs and the evangelist, Charles Wesley, die.

The Madness of King George III
1738–1820

King George III is largely remembered for suffering from periods of mental instability. He was born on 4 June 1738 to the Prince of Wales and Princess Augusta of Saxe Gotha, but he did not begin to suffer from bouts of madness until his 50s. Until the 1970s, scientist and historians believed that King George III was simply insane, but it is very likely that King George's illness was actually due to a hereditary physical condition called Porphyria. The symptoms of the condition include abdominal pain, constipation, rashes, confusion and severe weakness of the limbs. The royal physicians of the day were not permitted to conduct in-depth physical examinations on the king – so they had to depend on whatever information he chose to disclose about his condition. After his death, an unknown attendant took some hair from the king's head and stored it away in a handmade paper envelope marked 'Hair of his late Majesty King George the third'. The hair was eventually discovered and tested by the Harwell International Business Centre for Science and Technology in Didcot, Oxfordshire, where it was found to contain over 300 times the toxic level of arsenic. It is true that arsenic was an ingredient in many skin and wig creams of the day and the effect of applying large amounts of the stuff, quite apart from doing damage in it's own right, could act as a trigger for attacks of acute porphyria. King George was also taking a medicine called antimony, which contained large amounts of arsenic. Ironically, doctors were prescribing King George regular doses of antimony in order to control his madness, but they were inadvertently making his condition much, much worse. King George III eventually died, blind, deaf and mad on 29 January 1820. His ill-health meant that he had become deeply unpopular with the British public, and for the last ten years of his life he was judged unfit to reign England.

1789 The French Revolution sends Britain into a state of shock. George III's son, William, is created Duke of Clarence. William Blake publishes his *Songs of Innocence*.

1790 Pitt wins the general election with an increased majority. The first purpose-built lifeboat comes into use at South Shields. The economist Adam Smith dies.

1791 The Society of United Irishmen is formed in Ireland; it tries to persuade France to invade Ireland, drive out the English and found a republic. A parliamentary motion by William Wilberforce for the abolition of slavery is carried. *The Observer* is first published. James Boswell writes *The Life of Samuel Johnson*. Thomas Paine writes *The*

Rights of Man. Michael Faraday, chemist and physicist, is born. The founder of the Methodist movement, John Wesley, dies.

1792 Coal gas is used for the first time in lighting. Mary Wollstoncraft writes *Vindication of the Rights of Women*. Astronomer John Herschel is born. Artist Sir Joshua Reynolds, architect and designer Robert Adam, and inventor Sir Richard Arkwright die.

1793 The French Republic declares war on Britain; the British economy goes into depression.

1794 Lord Howe defeats the French fleet at Brest. The Habeas Corpus Act is suspended. Poet, Samuel Taylor Coleridge, leaves Cambridge without a degree. Anne Radcliffe writes the Gothic novel, *The Mysteries of Udolpho*. William Blake writes *Songs of Experience*. Historian Edward Gibbon dies.

1795 Britain declares war on the Netherlands which has allied with France; Britain takes Ceylon (Sri Lanka) and the Cape of Good Hope from the Dutch. Mungo Park explores the Gambia and the Niger rivers in Africa. James Bramah invents the hydraulic press, a machine for printing banknotes with sequential serial numbers. Josiah Wedgwood, potter and James Boswell, biographer, die.

1796 A French invasion of Ireland is aborted when the French fleet is scattered by a storm. Edward Jenner proves the vaccination theory; it leads to the eradication of smallpox in Britain.

1797 Britain is invaded by 1,400 French troops who land in Dyfed; they surrender to British troops; it is the last invasion of Britain; in the Battle of Camperdown, off the Dutch coast, the British fleet defeats the Dutch fleet. James Hetherington is charged with a breach of the peace when he wears a top hat in public for the first time. One pound notes and copper pennies are introduced. Samuel Taylor Coleridge meets the Wordsworths, William and Dorothy; the beginning of an important creative relationship. Ornithologist Thomas Bewick, writes his *History of British Birds*. Writer Mary Shelley is born. The political writer Edmund Burke and political radical John Wilkes die.

1798 Britain and Russia form a Second Coalition against France; in the Battle of the Nile, Nelson destroys 11 of 13 French battleships, trapping the French army in the Middle East. A rebellion begins in Ireland; rebels are defeated at Vinegar Hill. The Duke of Wellington's older brother, Richard Wellesley, is appointed Governor General of India. Scientist, Henry Cavendish works out the mean density of the Earth. The Romantic movement begins when Wordsworth and Coleridge publish *Lyrical Ballads*. Political economist, Robert Malthus writes *An Essay on the Principle of Population as it Effects the Improvement of Society*.

1799 Britain and Austria reject a French peace offer; the Duke of York surrenders to French troops at Alkmaar. Britain takes southern India after the last ruler of Mysore, Tipu Sahib, dies in battle. Pitt introduces income tax to raise money for the war; two shillings in the pound on earnings of more than £200. The Combination Laws make trade unions illegal. The rebellion of the United Irishmen is quashed.

1800 Britain captures Malta. Russia, Denmark, Sweden and Prussia form the Armed Neutrality of the North against British naval power. Sir William Herschel discovers infra-red rays in sunlight. The Royal College of Surgeons is founded in London. The lathe is invented by Henry Maudslay. *Castle Rackrent*, by Mary Edgeworth, is the first historical novel, as well as the first regional novel in English; it is also the first novel in English to use an unreliable narrator.

1801 **January** The Act of Union; the United Kingdom of Great Britain and Ireland is created; Ireland sends 100 MPs and 32 peers to Westminster. **February** The United Kingdom parliament meets for the first time; William Pitt the Younger is not allowed to include concessions to Catholics in the plan for Union and resigns as prime minister. **March** In the Second Battle of Abukir, a British force defeats the French. The first British census shows the population of England and Wales to be 8.9 million. Henry Addington, 1st Viscount Sidmouth, becomes prime minister. Britain wins the Battle of Alexandria. **April** Horatio Nelson defeats a Danish-Norwegian fleet at Copenhagen; Nelson puts his telescope to his blind eye in order not to see the signal to break off engagement. **June** Britain takes Cairo. **July** At Algeciras, the French fleet defeats the British. **December** Richard Trevithick demonstrates the first steam-powered passenger-carrying vehicle.

1802 **March** The War of the Second Coalition is ended by the Treaty of Amiens between France and the UK; Britain returns most of the gains made in the Revolutionary Wars. **August** Addington's Tories win the general election. **December** The Factory Act regulates conditions of child workers. Marie Tussaud opens her wax museum in London. Thomas Telford begins building roads in the Highlands. The first proposal for a Channel Tunnel is made. Ceylon becomes a crown colony.

1803 **January** William Symington demonstrates the first practical steamboat, the Charlotte Dundas. **May** France refuses to withdraw from Dutch territory; the UK declares war; Napoleon assembles a huge fleet and army for an invasion of Britain. **July** Robert Emmet leads an uprising in Ireland. **August** The Second Anglo-Maratha War begins. **September** Irish rebel, Robert Emmet, is executed. In the Battle of Assaye in India, British-led troops defeat Maratha forces.
Books & Literature: Thomas Chatterton *Collected Poems*.
Died: Arthur Guinness, Irish brewer.

1804 **February** Richard Trevithick builds the first steam locomotive to haul a load successfully. **March** Henry Addington resigns; he is succeeded by William Pitt the Younger. The Royal Horticultural Society is founded. **December** Spain declares war on Britain.
Books & Literature: William Wordsworth *Intimations of Immortality*; William Blake *Jerusalem*.
Born: Benjamin Disraeli, future prime minister.
Died: Joseph Priestley, chemist.

1805 **June** The first Trooping the Colour ceremony takes place. **October** The Napoleonic Wars: in the Battle of Trafalgar, Admiral Horatio Nelson's British fleet defeats a Franco-Spanish fleet; Nelson is killed. **December** Napoleon wins the Battle of Austerlitz.
Books & Literature: William Wordsworth *The Prelude*.
Died: William Petty, 2nd Earl of Shelburne, prime minister; Charles Cornwallis, 1st Marquess Cornwallis, general; Horatio Nelson, admiral.

1806 Rear-Admiral Sir Francis Beaufort devises the Beaufort Scale. **January** Cape Colony becomes British. **February** The Royal Navy defeats a French fleet off Santo Domingo. William Pitt the Younger dies; a Whig coalition government is formed by Lord Grenville. **July** Britain defeats France at Maida in Calabria. **November** Napoleon declares a blockade of Britain; food prices rise and the textile industry declines. **December** A general election sees

Grenville continue as prime minister

Born: Elizabeth Barrett Browning, poet; Isambard Kingdom Brunel, engineer; John Stuart Mill, philosopher.

Died: William Pitt the Younger, prime minister; George Stubbs, painter; Mungo Park, explorer.

1807 **January** Pall Mall in London becomes the first street with gas lighting. **March** Grenville's coalition collapses when he rejects Catholic Emancipation; the Tory Duke of Portland is asked to form a government. The slave trade is abolished in the British Empire. The Oystermouth Railway, between Mumbles and Swansea, is the first passenger-carrying railway in the world. **June** The Duke of Portland wins the general election. **July** Napoleon forms an alliance with Russia against Britain. Henry Benedict Stuart, the last Stuart claimant to the throne, dies; Jacobitism comes to an end. **September** The British navy bombards Copenhagen to prevent Denmark from surrendering its fleet to Napoleon; 2,000 citizens are killed.

Books & Literature: Charles and Mary Lamb *Tales From Shakespeare*; William Wordsworth *Poems in Two Volumes*.

Died: Henry Benedict Stuart, claimant to the throne of the UK.

1808 **February** The French occupy Spain; the Peninsular war begins. **August** British troops under Sir Arthur Wellesley defeat the French at Vimiero, near Lisbon. **December** The original Covent Garden Theatre in London is destroyed by a fire.

Architecture: The Bank of England, designed by Sir John Soane, is completed.

Born: Thomas Cook, travel entrepreneur.

1809 **January** In the Peninsular War, the British defeat the French at the Battle of Corunna. **April** The Two Thousand Guineas horse race is run for the first time. **May** Dartmoor Prison opens; it houses French prisoners of war. **July** A British invasion army lands in Walcheren in the Netherlands, led by Lord Chatham, William Pitt's older brother; it fails to take Antwerp; Wellesley defeats the French in the Battle of Talavera in Catalonia, Spain. **September** A new Royal Opera House opens in Covent Garden. **October** The Duke of Portland resigns due to ill health; Tory, Spencer Percival becomes prime minister.

Born: Charles Darwin, naturalist; Alfred Lord Tennyson, poet; William Ewart Gladstone, prime minister; Edward Fitzgerald, poet and scholar.

Died: Anna Seward, writer; William Cavendish-Bentinck, 3rd Duke of Portland, prime minister; Thomas Paine, political activist.

1810 King George III is recognized as insane. Sir Arthur Wellesley builds the line of forts known as the Lines of Torres Vedras, to defend Lisbon.

Born: Elizabeth Gaskell, novelist.

Died: Henry Cavendish, scientist.

1811 **February** George, Prince of Wales, becomes regent because of his father's insanity; he is known as the Prince Regent; the period known as the English Regency begins. **March** The British fleet defeats the French in the Battle of Lissa, in the Adriatic. The poet Percy Bysshe Shelley is sent down from Oxford for publishing *The Necessity of Atheism*. **November** Luddite uprisings and machine-breaking erupt in Nottinghamshire and Yorkshire; unemployed weavers fear the impact of mechanization.

Books & Literature: Jane Austen *Sense and Sensibility*.

Born: William Makepeace Thackeray, novelist.

Died: Nevil Maskelyne, Astronomer Royal; Augustus FitzRoy, 3rd Duke of Grafton, prime minister.

1812 The Elgin Marbles are brought to Britain from Athens. The waltz craze arrives in Britain. **February** Lord Byron makes his first speech as a member of the House of Lords; he defends Luddite action against Industrialism in Nottinghamshire; Byron becomes a celebrity this year through the unprecedented popularity of his poetic work, *Childe Harold's Progress*. **March** Luddites attack a wool-processing factory in Yorkshire. **May** Insane bankrupt banker, Francis Bellingham, assassinates prime minister Spencer Perceval in the House of Commons; the Earl of Liverpool becomes prime minister. **June** The War of 1812 between the US and the UK begins. **July** At Salamanca, in Spain, British forces, led by Sir Arthur Wellesley, defeat the French. **August** The British enter Madrid. In the War of 1812, American General William Hull surrenders Fort Detroit without a fight; *USS Constitution* defeats HMS *Guerriere* off the coast of Nova Scotia. **October** American forces capture two British ships in a naval engagement on Lake Erie; at Queenston Heights, in Ontario, American forces are stopped from invading Canada by British and native troops, led by Sir Isaac Brock. **November** The Earl of Liverpool's Tory Party wins the general election.
Books & Literature: Lord Byron *Childe Harold's Progress*; Thomas Rowlandson *The Tour of Dr Syntax*.
Born: Augustus Pugin, architect; Robert Browning, poet; Edward Lear, poet and artist.
Died: Spencer Perceval, prime minister (assassinated); Isaac Brock, general (killed in battle).

1812
Born: Charles Dickens, writer.

1813 The Monopoly of the British East India Company is abolished. The last gold guineas are minted. **June** British troops defeat a larger American force in the Battle of Stoney Creek. In the Peninsular War, at the Battle of Victoria, an allied force defeats the French under Joseph Bonaparte. **September** Oliver Hazard Perry defeats a British fleet in the Battle of Lake Erie. **October** Sir Arthur Wellesley is defeated by the Fourth Coalition at the Battle of the Nations, at Leipzig. In America, the British are defeated at the Battle of the Thames. **December** British soldiers burn Buffalo, New York.
Books & Literature: Jane Austen *Pride and Prejudice*; Robert Owen *A New View of Society*.
Born: David Livingstone, missionary and explorer.

1814 George Stephenson designs his first locomotive, *Blücher*. Guyana is transferred from the Netherlands to Britain; it is renamed 'British Guiana'. **January** Britain makes peace with Denmark. The last River Thames frost fair takes place in London. **March** Allied forces defeat Napoleon at the Battle of Laon; Wellesley takes Bordeaux; the allies enter Paris; Napoleon is declared deposed by the French Senate. **April** Napoleon surrenders; Wellesley wins the Battle of Toulouse and is created Duke of Wellington; hundreds die pointlessly as news of Napoleon's surrender has not reached France; Napoleon abdicates. **May** The First Peace of Paris stipulates that France must return to her 1792 borders. **June** Lord's, in London, hosts its first cricket match. **July** In the Battle of Chippewa, Ontario, an American force beats the British; a British-Canadian force puts the Americans to flight Lundy's Lane. **August** British troops burn Washington DC. **September** The Congress of Vienna aims to negotiate the Resettlement of Europe.
Art: John Constable *Old Sarum*.
Books & Literature: Walter Scott *Waverley*; Jane Austen *Mansfield Park*.

1815 Sir Humphrey Davy invents the miners' safety lamp. John Loudon McAdam improves roads with crushed stone and tarmac. The use of the pillory is limited to punishment for perjury. **January** Austria, Britain and France form a secret defensive alliance against Prussia and Russia. **February** Napoleon escapes from Elba. **March** The Corn Law is passed; imports of foreign grain are banned; bread prices go up. **June** The Battle of Waterloo ends in victory for Blücher and Wellington; Napoleon abdicates for a second time. **November** The Second Peace of Paris restricts France to its 1790 borders.
Born: Anthony Trollope, author.

1816 Lord Elgin sells the Elgin Marbles to the British Museum. Britain enters economic depression following the Napoleonic Wars; thousands lose their jobs. **March** The 10 per cent income tax is abolished in an attempt to alleviate Britain's economic problems. **December** The Spa Fields riot: a mass meeting of protestors against the Government is dispersed by the police.
Books & Literature: Jane Austen *Emma*.
Born: Charlotte Brontë, novelist.
Died: Samuel Hood, 1st Viscount Hood, admiral; Richard Brinsley Sheridan, Irish playwright; Charles Stanhope, 3rd Earl Stanhope, statesman and scientist.

1817 The Elgin Marbles are put on show in the British Museum. Workers riot against low pay and unemployment in Derbyshire. A rebellion in India against British rule leads to the Third Mahratha War. **March** The Blanketeers march from Manchester to London to protest; the Habeas Corpus Act is suspended after a secret report about an imminent rebellion. **July** The sovereign is first minted; it is worth one pound.
Books & Literature: John Keats *Poems*; Sir Walter Scott *Old Mortality*; David Ricardo *On the Principles of Political Economy and Taxation*.
Died: Jane Austen, novelist.

1818 The first iron ship is built on the Clyde. **August** The Earl of Liverpool's Tories win the general election. **October** The US and UK agree the US northern boundary as the forty-ninth parallel.
Books & Literature: Jane Austen *Northanger Abbey* and *Persuasion* (published posthumously); John Keats *Endymion*; Mary Shelley

Frankenstein; Sir Walter Scott *The Heart of Midlothian* and *Rob Roy*.
Born: Emily Brontë, novelist.
Died: Warren Hastings, Governor General of India.

1819　The Factory Act is passed following a campaign by social reformer, Robert Owen. The size of political meetings is limited to stop rioting; a tax is imposed on newspapers and libel penalties are increased. **February** Britain acquires Singapore; Sir Thomas Stamford Raffles establishes a trading settlement. **June** The SS *Savannah*, the first steamship to cross the Atlantic Ocean, arrives at Liverpool. **August** 11 people die and more than 400 are injured in the Peterloo Massacre in St Peter's Field, Manchester; cavalry charge into a crowd of people holding a radical parliamentary reform meeting.
Architecture: Thomas Telford builds the Menai Straits Suspension Bridge.
Books & Literature: Sir Walter Scott *Ivanhoe*; Lord Byron *Don Juan* (first cantos).
Born: John Ruskin, writer, artist and social critic; Henry Tate, sugar magnate; Queen Victoria; Charles Kingsley, novelist; Richard Dadd, painter; Prince Albert of Saxe-Coburg-Gotha, prince consort to Queen Victoria; George Eliot, novelist.
Died: James Watt, inventor.

1820　**January** George III dies; George IV becomes king, ending the Regency; his long-separated queen, Caroline of Brunswick, returns from the continent. **February** A plot to murder the Cabinet, the Cato Street conspiracy, is exposed. **April** The Radical War in Scotland; a week of strikes, unrest and demands for reform. The first British settlers arrive in South Africa. **May** The Cato Street conspirators are executed for treason. **June** The Pains and Penalties Bill, designed to deprive Caroline, George IV's wife, of the title of queen consort, is heavily defeated in the Commons.
Books & Literature: Percy Bysshe Shelley *Prometheus Unbound*.
Born: Anne Brontë, author; John Tenniel, illustrator; Anna Sewell, writer; Florence Nightingale, nurse.
Died: King George III of the UK; Sir Joseph Banks, naturalist and botanist.

1821　Sir Charles Wheatstone demonstrates that sound reproduction is possible. **January** The Tories, under the Earl of Liverpool, win the general election. **July** George IV's wife, Caroline, is excluded from his coronation.
Art: William Blake, illustrations for *Jerusalem*; John Constable *The Hay Wain*.
Books & Literature: Sir Walter Scott *Kenilworth*; Michael Faraday *Principles of the Electric Motor*; Thomas de *Quincey Confessions of an English Opium Eater*.
Died: John Keats, poet, aged 25; Caroline of Brunswick, queen consort of King George IV.

1822　Hieroglyphs are deciphered by Thomas Young and Jean-François Champollion using the Rosetta Stone, discovered by the French in 1799. Britain removes the death penalty from over 100 crimes. The Royal Academy of Music is founded in London. The first fossil recognized as that of a dinosaur is discovered by Gideon Mantell in West Sussex. **June** Charles Babbage proposes a difference engine, a rudimentary calculator. **July** Chippewas turn over a huge tract of land in Ontario to the UK. The last public whipping takes place in Edinburgh. The poet Shelley drowns off Leghorn in Italy. **August**

King George IV visits Scotland. The English ship *Orion* lands at Yerba Buena, present-day San Francisco, under the command of William A Richardson.

Architecture: John Nash completes the Royal Pavilion in Brighton.

Born: Sir Francis Galton, explorer and biologist; Matthew Arnold, poet.

Died: Thomas Coutts, banker; Percy Bysshe Shelley, poet.

1823 The Gaols Act, based on the prison reform campaign of Elizabeth Fry, becomes law. Chemist and inventor Charles Mackintosh invents waterproof fabric. **September** In the First Burmese War, the Burmese attack the British on Shapura, an island close to Chittagong. **November** Brighton's Chain Pier is opened.

Architecture: WH Playfair designs the Royal Scottish Academy, in Edinburgh. Thomas Cubitt builds Polesden Lacey, in Surrey.

Books & Literature: Charles Lamb *Essays of Elia*.

Died: Edward Jenner, physician and medical researcher; David Ricardo, economist.

1824 The Combination Acts, banning trade unions, are repealed. **January** The Ashanti crush British forces in the Gold Coast. **March** Sir William Hillary founds the National Institution for the Preservation of Life from Shipwreck, now known as the Royal National Lifeboat Institution. **April** The National Gallery is established when the House of Commons purchases the collection of the late London merchant, John Julius Angerstein. The poet Byron dies of marsh fever at Missolonghi in Greece, during the Greek struggle for independence. **May** The British take Rangoon in Burma. **October** Edinburgh Town Council establishes the Edinburgh Municipal Fire Brigade, the first fire brigade in Britain.

Books & Literature: Lord Byron *Don Juan*; Percy Bysshe Shelley *Posthumous Poems*; James Hogg *Private Memoirs and Confessions of a Justified Sinner*.

Born: Wilkie Collins, novelist; Lord Kelvin, physicist and engineer.

Died: Lord Byron, poet.

1825 The first horse-drawn buses begin operating in London. London becomes the largest city in the world. John Nash begins the reconstruction of Buckingham Palace. Trade unions become legal. An act is passed to regulate cotton mills and factories; children are not permitted to work more than 12 hours a day. **April** A Royal Charter is granted to the Geological Society of London. **September** A Royal Charter is granted to the Royal Society of Literature. The world's first modern railway, the Stockton and Darlington Railway, opens; the steam locomotive *Active* pulls the first train 27 miles (43km) ; it is the first railway to carry goods and passengers.

Books & Literature: Lord Braybrooke (ed) *Samuel Pepys' Diary*.

1826 The first railway tunnel is built on the line between Liverpool and Manchester. The Royal Zoological Society is founded in London by Sir Stamford Raffles. When his publisher collapses, novelist, Sir Walter Scott, is financially ruined. **January** Thomas Telford's Menai Suspension Bridge is opened between Anglesey and the Welsh mainland. **February** The Treaty of Yandaboo ends the First Burmese War; Britain is victorious. **June** Tories under the Earl of Liverpool win an increased majority over the Whigs in the general election.

Art: John Constable *The Cornfield*.

Books & Literature: Sir Walter Scott *Woodstock*.

Died: Sir Stamford Raffles, colonial governor and founder of Singapore.

1827 **January** The Duke of Wellington becomes Commander-in-Chief of the British Forces. **April** George Canning succeeds the Earl of Liverpool as British prime minister. **May** Launch of the *Standard* newspaper of London. **July** The Treaty of London, signed by France, Britain and Russia, demands that Turkey agrees to an armistice in Greece. **August** Viscount Goderich becomes prime minister following the death of Canning. **October** British, French and Russian ships destroy the Turko-Egyptian fleet at Navarino in Greece; the last naval battle to be fought entirely by sailing ships.

Architecture: John Nash builds Cumberland Terrace, Regent's Park in London.

Born: Joseph Lister, 1st Baron Lister, surgeon; Frederick Augustus Abel, chemist; Holman Hunt, painter.

Died: George Canning, prime minister; William Blake, poet, painter and printmaker.

1828 Britain, France and Russia recognize Greek independence. **January** The Duke of Wellington succeeds Goderich as prime minister; he repeals the Test Act, emancipating all Catholics, and introduces the Roman Catholic Relief Act. **April** Regent's Park in London opens. **July** A new Corn Law allows imports of foreign grain with duties on a sliding scale. **December** The trial of the body snatchers, William Burke and William Hare, begins.

Born: Dante Gabriel Rossetti, poet and painter.

Died: Robert Jenkinson, 2nd Earl of Liverpool, prime minister.

1828
September Sir Robert Peel's police force starts in London.

1829 Irish MP, Daniel O'Connell, agitates for the repeal of the Act of Union. The Earl of Surrey becomes the first Catholic MP. **January** Murderer and body-snatcher, William Burke, is hanged; his associate, William Hare testifies against him and is released. **June** The Metropolitan Police Force is created. The first university Boat Race is won by Oxford. **July** The first scheduled bus service is introduced in London by George Shillibeer. **October** George Stephenson's steam locomotive, the *Rocket*, defeats John Ericsson's the *Novelty* to win the Rainhill Trials held near Liverpool. **December** Suttee, the practice of sacrificing a widow on her husband's funeral pyre, is made illegal in India. Thomas Maynard is the last person to be hanged for forgery.

Architecture: Thomas Hamilton builds the Royal High School in Edinburgh: John Nash designs St James's Park in London; Decimus Barton begins the Athenaeum Club in London.

Born: Catherine and William Booth, founders of the Salvation Army.

Died: Sir Humphry Davy, chemist; James Smithson, founder of the Smithsonian Institute.

1830 The British East India Company takes Mysore. **June** William IV succeeds George IV as king. Peter Bossey is the last person to be put in the pillory in England. **August** In the Swing Riots, named after nominal leader, 'Captain Swing', across southern and eastern England, rural workers protest about mechanisation and reductions in wages. Edwin Beard Budding patents the lawnmower. **September** The Liverpool and Manchester Railway is the world's first intercity passenger railway operated solely by steam locomotives. **November** The Whig, Earl Grey, succeeds the Duke of Wellington as prime minister.

Architecture: Covent Garden Market, London.

Books & Literature: Charles Lyell *Principles of Geology*; Alfred, Lord Tennyson *Poems*; William Cobbett *Rural Rides*.

Died: King George IV of the UK; Thomas Lawrence, painter; William Hazlitt, essayist.

1831 The Tithe War in Ireland; a series of periodic skirmishes and violent incidents resisting to the obligation of Catholics to pay tithes for the upkeep of the Church of Ireland. Rioting over wage reductions and ruthless debt-collection breaks out in Merthyr Tydfil. Britain and France guarantee the independence of Belgium. Michael Faraday discovers electro-magnetic induction. **February** Captain John Briscoe discovers Antarctica. **March** The Commons passes the Reform Bill, but it is defeated in the House of Lords. **April** Lord Grey dissolves parliament and calls an election with the Reform Bill as the main issue; his Whig party wins. **June** James Clark Ross leads the first expedition to reach the Magnetic North Pole. **September** The coronation of William IV. The Second Reform Bill is passed, but again rejected by the Lords; there is great unrest. **October** Britain's first cholera epidemic begins in Sunderland. Rioters protesting about electoral reform burn down 100 houses in Bristol; Dragoons charge the crowd with drawn swords; hundreds die. **December** Charles Darwin embarks on his historic journey aboard the HMS *Beagle*.

Born: James Clerk Maxwell, physicist.

1832 The Irish Reform Act is passed. **February** A cholera epidemic kills 3,000. **June** The Great Reform Bill becomes law in the UK, but not before the Lords demand amendments and more unrest spreads across the country.

Architecture: William Wilkins designs the National Gallery in London.

Born: Lewis Carroll, author.

Died: Thomas Lord, founder of Lord's Cricket Ground; Jeremy Bentham, philosopher; Walter Scott, historical novelist and poet.

1833 The East India Company's charter is renewed on condition that its monopoly on trade with India and China ends. The Oxford Movement in the Anglican church begins. **April** The Coercion Bill gives the Lord Lieutenant of Ireland powers to suppress public meetings. **August** The Slavery Abolition Act frees all slaves in the

British Empire; £20 million compensation is paid to slave owners. It becomes illegal to employ children younger than nine-years-old in the textile industry and for children aged nine to thirteen to work more than nine hours' a day. The Irish Church Temporalities Bill attempts to reduce the burden of tithes; Daniel O'Connell and his followers are outraged.

Born: Charles George Gordon, British army officer and administrator.

Died: Richard Trevithick, inventor, engineer and builder of the first working railway steam locomotive; Edmund Kean, actor; William Wilberforce, abolitionist.

1834 Murderer, James Cook is the last man to be hanged in chains upon a gibbet in England. The exchequer is abolished as a revenue-collecting department of the British government. Michael Faraday discovers electrical self-induction. **January** Robert Owen sets up the Grand National Consolidated Trades Union; he plans to organize a general strike in favour of an eight-hour working day. **March** The Tolpuddle Martyrs, six Dorset farm labourers, are sentenced to transportation for forming a branch of the Grand National Union. **April** Britain, France, Spain and Portugal form the Quadruple Alliance to protect Spain and Portugal. **July** Viscount Melbourne succeeds Earl Grey as prime minister. **August** The New Poor Law Amendment Act provides workhouses for the destitute; no able-bodied man can receive assistance unless he enters a workhouse. **October** The Palace of Westminster is destroyed by fire. **November** Opposing reform, William IV dismisses Melbourne's government; Wellington forms a caretaker government. **December** Conservative Sir Robert Peel becomes prime minister. The Hansom cab is patented by Joseph Hansom.

Born: William Morris, artist, writer, socialist and activist; John Venn, mathematician.

Died: William Wyndham Grenville, 1st Baron Grenville, prime minister; Samuel Taylor Coleridge, poet, critic and philosopher; Thomas Telford, engineer; Thomas Malthus, demographer and economist; Charles Lamb, essayist.

1835 The end of the East India Company's monopoly increases British trade with China. 4,000 Boers begin the Great Trek in South Africa to find territory free from British rule. The Municipal Corporations Act requires town councillors to be elected. The British Geological Survey is founded. **April** Peel, unable to form a majority, is replaced by the Whig Viscount Melbourne. **September** Charles Darwin arrives at the Galapagos Islands.

Architecture: Sir Charles Barry and Augustus Pugin – the Houses of Parliament (begun).

Died: John Nash, architect; William Cobbett, journalist and author.

1836 Sir Francis Smith invents the screw propeller. **October** Naturalist Charles Darwin completes his five-year journey collecting biological data he will later use to develop his theory of evolution.

Architecture: Isambard Kingdom Brunel – the Clifton Suspension Bridge (begun); the Scott Monument in Edinburgh.

Books & Literature: Charles Dickens *Pickwick Papers (begun)*; Frederick Marryat *Mr Midshipman Easy.*

Born: Robert Halpin, mariner and cable layer; Isabella Beeton, cook; Joseph Rowntree, Quaker and philanthropist; Joseph Chamberlain, politician; Henry Campbell-Bannerman, prime minister.

Died: John Loudon McAdam, engineer and road builder.

1837 Isaac Pitman invents his shorthand system. Registration of births, marriages and deaths begins. **February** Postal reformer, Rowland Hill, invents envelopes and stamps to prove that postage had been paid; previously, postage has been paid by the recipient. **May** William Fothergill Cooke and Charles Wheatstone patent the electrical telegraph. **June** King William IV dies; his niece, Princess Victoria of Kent, ascends the throne as Queen Victoria. **July** Queen Victoria is the first monarch to live in Buckingham Palace. Euston Station, London's first railway station, is opened.
Books & Literature: Thomas Carlyle *The French Revolution, A History*.
Born: James Murray, lexicographer; Charles Swinburne, poet.
Died: King William IV; John Soane, British architect; John Constable, painter.

1838 The First Afghan War breaks out as Britain tries to curtail Russian influence. **January** A fire destroys Lloyd's Coffee House and the Royal Exchange in London. **April** Regular steamship services start between Britain and America; Brunel's *Great Western* leaves for New York; the *Sirius* becomes the first ship to cross the Atlantic entirely under steam power. **May** The Chartist Movement sets out a programme for reform in the People's Charter; it demands universal male suffrage, vote by ballot, the abolition of property qualifications for MPs, equal electoral districts and annual parliaments. The National Gallery opens. **June** The coronation of Queen Victoria takes place at Westminster Abbey. **September** Grace Darling rescues nine survivors from the wreck of the *Forfarshire* off the Farne Islands.
Art: JMW Turner *The Fighting Temeraire*.
Books & Literature: Charles Dickens *Oliver Twist*.
Born: Henry Irving, actor; William Perkin, chemist; Octavia Hill, social reformer.

1839 Michael Faraday publishes *Experimental Researches in Electricity*, clarifying the true nature of electricity. William Fox Talbot invents photography. Edward John Eyre explores the interior of South Australia. A regular steamship service begins between Britain and Egypt. **January** The British East India Company takes Aden. **February** The first National Convention of Chartists is held. The first Grand National steeplechase is run at Aintree. **March** The first Henley Royal Regatta is held. **April** The world's first commercial electric telegraph line comes into operation alongside the Great Western Railway line from Paddington station to West Drayton. The Treaty of London establishes Belgium as a kingdom. **May** The Bedchamber Crisis; Robert Peel asks that Queen Victoria dismiss her Whig-appointed Ladies of the Bedchamber as a condition for his forming a government; when Victoria refuses, Peel resigns. The People's Charter is rejected by parliament. **July** British forces capture the fortress city of Ghazni, in Afghanistan. Chartist rioting breaks out in Birmingham. **August** British forces seize Hong Kong; the First Opium War begins. **November** At Newport, several thousand miners try to liberate Chartist prisoners; 20 are shot dead.
Books & Literature: Charles Dickens *Nicholas Nickleby*.
Born: John Butler Yeats, artist.

1840 David Livingstone leaves for Africa. *Punch* magazine begins publication. Sir William Grove invents the incandescent electric light. The Afghans surrender, ending the First Afghan War. The vote is given to all men paying rent of at least £10 a year. **January** Penny postage is introduced. British colonists reach New Zealand. **May** The Penny Black, the world's first postage stamp, is issued. **July** Samuel Cunard founds the Cunard Steamship Company; the Cunard Line's 700-tonne wooden paddlewheel steamer *RMS Britannia* departs from Liverpool to Halifax, Nova Scotia, on the first transatlantic passenger cruise. Austria, Britain, Prussia and Russia sign the London Treaty with the Ottoman Empire. The Province of Canada is created by the Act of Union. **September** Ottoman and British troops bombard Beirut and land troops to pressure the Egyptian Muhammad Ali to withdraw from Lebanon. Philanthropist Joseph Strutt creates the Arboretum, England's first public park. **October** Lebanese emir Bashir Shihab II surrenders to British troops and goes into exile.

Art: JMW Turner *The Slave Ship*.

Born: John Boyd Dunlop, inventor; John Philip Holland, submarine inventor; Thomas Hardy, writer.

Died: Fanny Burney, novelist; Sidney Smith, admiral.

1840
February The Treaty of Waitangi grants Britain sovereignty in New Zealand. Queen Victoria marries Prince Albert of Saxe Coburg-Gotha (left).

1841 Britain, Russia, France and Austria agree to close the Dardanelles and the Bosphorus to foreign shipping. The British Pharmaceutical Society is founded. The 1841 Census is the first to record the names of everyone in a household or institution. **January** Charles Elliot and Qishan of Qing sign the Convention of Chuenpeh; the UK occupies Hong Kong. **August** Robert Peel resigns as prime minister, again. **September** The UK annexes Sarawak from Brunei; James Brooke is appointed Rajah. **November** Physician James Braid first sees a demonstration of *animal magnetism*, which leads to his study of the subject he eventually calls 'hypnosis'. **December** At a meeting with the Afghan general Akbar Khan, diplomat Sir William Hay Macnaghten, is torn to pieces.

Books & Literature: Charles Dickens *The Old Curiosity Shop* and *Barnaby Rudge*.

Born: Henry Morton Stanley, explorer and journalist.

1842 The Treaty of Nanking ends the Opium Wars; Chinese ports are open to British trade. The Mines Act prevents the employment of children or women underground. Elphinstone's army is massacred on the road from Kabul to Jalalabad, Afghanistan, by Akbar Khan.

The British Empire annexes Hong Kong. The Income Tax Act levies 7 pence in the pound for incomes over 150 pounds. **April** The Second National Convention of Chartists is held; its second petition to parliament is rejected.

Books & Literature: Lord Macaulay Lays of Ancient Rome; Alfred Tennyson The Lady of Shalott; Illustrated London News.

Born: Arthur Sullivan, composer; Edward VII.

Died: Henry Shrapnel, soldier and inventor of shrapnel.

1843 Irish political leader, Daniel O'Connell, demands the repeal of the Union; he and his supporters are arrested. The Maoris revolt in New Zealand. The world's first commercial Christmas cards are printed by Sir Henry Cole. *The Economist* is first published. **March** The Thames Tunnel, between Rotherhithe and Wapping, is the first tunnel under the Thames. **April** William Wordsworth is appointed poet laureate. The royal yacht, *Victoria and Albert* is launched. **May** Natal becomes a British colony. The Disruption of the Church of Scotland takes place; 450 ministers form the Free Church of Scotland. **June** The Royal College of Surgeons is founded. **July** The SS *Great Britain*, the world's first all-metal liner, is launched from Bristol. **October** The *News of the World* is published for the first time. **November** Nelson's Column is erected in Trafalgar Square.

Architecture: Edward Bulwer-Lytton refashions Knebworth House in Hertfordshire, in the High Gothic style.

Art: Edward Bailey *Statue of Nelson* (Nelson's Column).

Books & Literature: Edward Fox Talbot *The Pencil of Nature* (the first photographic book); John Stuart Mill *A System of Logic*; Charles Dickens *A Christmas Carol*.

Died: Robert Southey, poet; Prince Augustus Frederick, Duke of Sussex.

> *With fingers weary and worn,*
> *With eyelids heavy and red,*
> *A woman sat in unwomanly rags,*
> *Plying her needle and thread –*
> *Stitch! stitch! stitch!*
> *In poverty, hunger and dirt,*
> *And still with a voice of dorolous pitch*
> *She sang the 'Song of the Shirt.'*

Thomas Hood, The Song of the Shirt, 1843

1844 Sir Henry Hardinge is appointed Governor General of India. Railway mania grips Britain; 5,000 miles of track will be built by 1846. The Bank of England is given a monopoly on printing money in England and Wales. The first workers' Co-operative Society is opened, the Pioneers of Rochdale. **June** George Williams founds the Young Men's Christian Association (YMCA) in London. **October** The Royal Exchange in London is opened by Queen Victoria.

Architecture: Sir William Tite – the Royal Exchange in London.

Art: JMW Turner *Rain, Steam, Speed*.

Books & Literature: Charles Dickens *Martin Chuzzlewit*; William Thackeray *Barry Lyndon*.

Born: Gerard Manley Hopkins, poet; Robert Bridges, poet; Alexandra of Denmark, queen consort of Edward VII.

Died: Henry Addington, 1st Viscount Sidmouth, prime minister; John Dalton, chemist and physicist.

1845 The Irish Potato Famine begins; more than a million people die by 1849. The Earl of Rosse builds the world's largest telescope; it allows viewers to see galaxies beyond our own for the first time. **March** Henry Jones patents self-raising flour. In the Flagstaff War in New Zealand, Māoris burn the British colonial settlement of Kororareka. Stephen Perry patents the rubber band. **October** The eminent and controversial Anglican John Henry Newman is received into the Roman Catholic church. **December** At the Battle of Ferozeshah, in the Punjab, British forces defeat the Sikhs. Scottish engineer Robert Thompson patents pneumatic tyres.
Died: Charles Grey, 2nd Earl Grey, prime minister; Elizabeth Fry, humanitarian.

1845
July SS Great Britain embarks on her maiden voyage to New York.

1846 The potato famine continues in Ireland; there is mass emigration to the US; English landlords evict thousands who cannot pay their rent. The Electric Telegraph Company is founded; the world's first public telegraph company. Railway Mania peaks; 272 Acts of Parliament are passed, setting up new railway companies. **January** The United States House of Representatives votes to stop sharing the Oregon Territory with the UK. **March** The Treaty of Lahore ends the Sikh War in India; Kashmir is ceded to the British East India Company and the Koh-i-Noor diamond is surrendered to Queen Victoria. Parliament repeals the Corn Laws, replacing the old Colonial mercantile trade system with free trade. **May** The Customs Law abolishes duty on all live animals and almost every type of meat and reduces duty on other foods. **June** Peel resigns following a revolt led by Disraeli, blocking a new Coercion Bill to control Ireland; he is succeeded by Lord John Russell.
Architecture: Sir Charles Barry – the Treasury, Whitehall.
Books & Literature: Edward Lear *Book of Nonsense*.
Born: Kate Greenaway, children's book illustrator and writer; Charles Stuart Parnell, Irish political leader; Anna Kingsford, physician, advocate of women's rights, anti-vivisection and vegetarianism.

1847 Famine continues in Ireland. The United Presbyterian Church of Scotland is constituted. A Factory Act prohibits women and young people aged thirteen to eighteen from working more than 10 hours a day. Chloroform is first used as an anaesthetic by Dr James Simpson. **April** The world's first civic public park, Birkenhead Park, opens in Merseyside. **August** Lord Russell's Whigs win the general election. **September** The Vegetarian Society is formed.

Architecture: Sir Robert Smirke – British Museum (completed).

Books & Literature: Emily Brontë *Wuthering Heights* (under the pen name of Ellis Bell); Charlotte Brontë *Jane Eyre* (under the pen name of Currer Bell); Frederick Marryatt *Children of the New Forest*.

Born: Alexander Graham Bell, inventor.

Died: Archibald Primrose, 5th Earl of Rosebery, prime minister; George Grossmith, actor and comic writer.

1848 The Pre-Raphaelite Brotherhood is founded. The Public Health Act stipulates that every house must have a toilet. **April** A Chartist rally is held in Kennington Park, London; a petition is presented to parliament. Sir John Franklin and his crew perish attempting to chart and navigate the Northwest Passage. **November** WH Smith's first railway bookstall is opened at Euston station.

Architecture: Sir Charles Cockerell – St George's Hall in Liverpool. Richard Turner and Decimus Burton – the Palm House at Kew.

Art: George Cruikshank *The Drunkard's Children*.

Books & Literature: John Stuart Mill *Principles of Political Economy*; Anne Brontë *The Tenant of Wildfell Hall*; William Thackeray *Vanity Fair*; Charles Dickens *Dombey and Son*.

Born: William Waldorf Astor, 1st Viscount Astor, financier and statesman; Arthur James Balfour, prime minister.

Died: George Stephenson, locomotive pioneer; William Lamb, 2nd Viscount Melbourne, prime minister; Emily Brontë, author.

1849 **January** In the Second Anglo-Sikh War, British forces retreat from the Battle of Chillianwala; the city of Multan falls to the British East India Company following a siege; Britain wins the Battle of Gujarat. **March** The UK annexes the Punjab. **April** In Ireland, 96 inmates of the overcrowded Ballinrobe Union Workhouse die over the course of one week from hunger and famine-related conditions.

Born: Lord Randolph Churchill, statesman; John Ambrose Fleming, electrical engineer and inventor.

Died: Anne Brontë, author; Adelaide of Saxe-Meiningen, queen consort of William IV.

1850 The railway line from London to Edinburgh is completed. The Public Libraries Act, the basis of the modern public library system in Britain is passed. Southwark Cathedral is the first Catholic cathedral to be built in England since the Reformation. **March** The opening of the Britannia Bridge across the Menai Strait between the island of Anglesey and the mainland of Wales. **April** The Clayton-Bulwer Treaty is signed between the UK and the US; both nations agree not to colonize or to control any Central American republic; the main purpose is to prevent one country from building a canal across Central America that the other would not be able to use. **December** Alfred, Lord Tennyson is appointed poet laureate.

Architecture: Robert Stephenson and William Fairbairn – the Britannia Railway Bridge, Menai Straits; James Bunning – Billingsgate Market; Sir Joseph Paxton – the Crystal palace, Hyde Park, London.

Art: Sir Edwin Landeer *The Monarch of the Glen*; John Everett Millais *Christ in the House of his Parents*.

Books & Literature: Charles Dickens *David Copperfield*.

Born: Thomas Lipton, merchant and yachtsman; Jesse Boot, 1st

Baron Trent, businessman; Horatio Kitchener, 1st Earl Kitchener, field marshal and statesman; Robert Louis Stevenson, writer; Ernest Albert Waterlow, painter.

Died: William Wordsworth, poet; Robert Peel, prime minister.

1851 **March** The 1851 census is the first to record the full details of birth location. Marble Arch is moved from Buckingham Palace to its present site. **May** The Great Exhibition of the Works of Industry of All Nations in the Crystal Palace, Hyde Park, London, is opened by Queen Victoria; the first world fair. **November** A telegraph service is started between London and Paris.

Books & Literature: John Ruskin *Pre-Raphaelitism*.

Died: Mary Shelley, author; JMW Turner, artist.

> ❝ *I made my way into the building;
> a most gorgeous sight; vast;
> graceful; beyond the dreams of the
> Arabian romances. I cannot think
> that the Ceasars ever exhibited
> a more splendid spectacle. I was
> quite dazzled, and I felt as I did
> on entering St Peter's.* ❞

Thomas Babington Macaulay, writing about the Crystal Palace, 1 May 1851

1852 Lord Kelvin and William Rankine invent refrigeration. **January** The UK recognizes the independence of the Transvaal. **February** Great Ormond Street Hospital in London admits its first patient. **March** Lord Eglinton is appointed Lord Lieutenant of Ireland. **April** Britain blockades the port of Rangoon; the Second Burmese War begins. **November** The general election is won by the Earl of Derby's Conservatives. The New Palace of Westminster opens in London. **December** Derby resigns as prime minister when his budget is defeated; Lord Aberdeen leads a coalition government.

Architecture: Lewis Cubitt – King's Cross Station; Sir Charles Barry and Augustus Pugin – the Houses of Parliament; Philip Hardwick – Paddington Hotel, London; Sir Joseph Paxton begins Mentmore in Buckinghamshire.

Books & Literature: Peter Roget *Thesaurus*.

Born: Alice Liddell, schoolgirl inspiration for *Alice's Adventures in Wonderland*; Herbert Henry Asquith, prime minister; John French, 1st Earl of Ypres, World War I field marshal; William Ramsay, chemist and Nobel Prize laureate.

Died: William MacGillivray, naturalist and ornithologist; Augustus Pugin, architect; Arthur Wellesley, 1st Duke of Wellington, general and prime minister; Ada Lovelace, early computer pioneer.

1853 **April** Chloroform becomes Britian's favourite anaesthetic after the Queen uses it to help her through the birth of her seventh child. **December** A protocol is signed with France, Austria and Prussia for restoring peace between Russia and Turkey.

Architecture: Cuthbert Broderick – Leeds Town Hall; Edward Walters – Free Trade Hall, Manchester.

Books & Literature: Charles Dickens *Bleak House*.

Born: Cecil Rhodes, businessman and politician.

1854 An epidemic of cholera kills 10,000 in London; Dr John Snow traces the source of one outbreak to a single water pump, validating his theory that cholera is waterborne, and founding the science of epidemiology. The Chartist Movement comes to an end. **February** Britain recognizes the independence of the Orange Free State. Britain sends Russia an ultimatum to withdraw from the Ottoman provinces, Moldavia and Wallachia. **March** Britain declares war on Russia; the Crimean War begins. **June** On the island of Bomarsund in Åland, in the Baltic, Royal Navy mate Charles D Lucas throws a live Russian artillery shell overboard by hand before it explodes; he is awarded the first Victoria Cross in 1857. **August** Russia rejects peace terms; Russian troops on Bomarsund surrender to French-British troops. **September** The Franco-British alliance wins the Battle of the Alma, the first battle of the Crimean War. **October** The allies bomb Sebastopol; a lengthy siege ensues. The great fire of Newcastle and Gateshead is preceded by a warehouse explosion; 53 die. Florence Nightingale leaves for the Crimea; the allies win the Battle of Balaclava, but it includes the disastrous cavalry Charge of the Light Brigade, led by Lord Cardigan; only 200 out of 700 men survive. **November** The Russians lose the Battle of Inkerman.
Architecture: Sidney Smirke – the Reading Room, British Museum, London.
Art: John Everett Millais *Ophelia*; Holman Hunt *Light of the World*.
Books & Literature: Charles Dickens *Hard Times*; Lord Tennyson *The Charge of the Light Brigade*.
Born: Oscar Wilde, writer.

1855 David Livingstone discovers the Victoria Falls. Stamp duty is removed from newspapers creating mass-market media. Alexander Parkes patents celluloid. Florence Nightingale reforms nursing practice during the Crimean War. Robert Bunsen invents the Bunsen Burner. **January** Lord Aberdeen resigns as prime minister over the management of the Crimean War. **February** Whig/Liberal Viscount Palmerston, becomes prime minister. **June** The first issue of the *Daily Telegraph* is published. **September** The last Bartholomew Fair is held in London. Sevastapol falls to the British troops.
Books & Literature: Charles Kingsley *Westward Ho!*
Died: Dorothy Wordsworth, poet and diarist; Charlotte Brontë, author.

1856 Lord Dalhousie annexes Oudh in India. Big Ben, the clock-tower bell of the Houses of Parliament, is cast at Whitechapel. **January** Queen Victoria institutes the Victoria Cross. The Welsh national anthem, *Hen Wlad Fy Nhadau*, is composed by James James with lyrics by his father, Evan James. **February** Russia agrees to preliminary peace conditions at Vienna. **March** The Treaty of Paris is signed, ending the Crimean War. Fire destroys the second Covent Garden Theatre in London. **November** War breaks out between Britain and Persia. **December** The city of Bushehr, in the Persian Gulf, surrenders to the British.
Born: Bramwell Booth, Salvation Army General; Henry Rider Haggard, writer.

1857 Divorce without parliamentary approval becomes legal; divorce courts are established in England and Wales. **January** The London General Omnibus Company starts to run services. **March** France and the UK declare war on China in the Second Opium War; the French and British take Canton. Prince Albert is created prince consort. **April** The Anglo-Persian War ends. **May** The Indian

Mutiny begins; elements of the Bengal army revolt against the British East India Company; the Indians capture Delhi; the Siege of Delhi leads to the banishment of Bahadur Shah and the end of the Mughal Empire. **September** Lucknow in India is relieved. **October** Sheffield FC, the world's first football team, is founded in Sheffield.

Books & Literature: Thomas Hughes *Tom Brown's Schooldays*; Charles Dickens *Little Dorrit*.

Born: Robert Baden-Powell, founder of the Scouting movement; Edward Elgar, composer.

1858   The British Empire takes over the powers and properties of the British East India Company; Queen Victoria is proclaimed Sovereign of India. The property qualification for MPs is abolished. The British stop using prison hulks. **January** *The Wedding March* by Felix Mendelssohn becomes popular after it is played at the marriage of Victoria, Queen Victoria's daughter. **February** The Earl of Derby becomes prime minister again. Richard Burton and John Hanning Speke discover Lake Tanganyika. **May** The present Royal Opera House is opened. **July** Papers by Darwin and Wallace propounding a theory of evolution by natural selection are read at London's Linnaean Society. The Lutine Bell is salvaged and hung at Lloyd's of London. **August** US President James Buchanan inaugurates the new transatlantic telegraph cable, exchanging greetings with Queen Victoria.

Books & Literature: RM Ballantyne *The Coral Island*.

Born: E Nesbit, author; Andrew Bonar Law, prime minister.

1859
November Charles Darwin publishes *The Origin of Species*; its initial print run immediately sells out; Trinity College, Cambridge, bans it.

SOCIETY FOR THE PREVENTION OF CRUELTY TO ANIMALS. PRES. BERGH

MR. BERGH TO THE RESCUE.
THE DEFRAUDED GORILLA. "That Man wants to claim my Pedigree. He says he is one of my Descendants."
Mr. BERGH. "Now, Mr. DARWIN, how could you insult him so?"

1859   Solar flares are first observed on the Sun by the astronomer Richard Carrington. **May** Lord Derby resigns when his government is defeated on Disraeli's Reform Bill. Palmerston's Whigs win the general election. **October** The steamship *Royal Charter* is wrecked on the coast of Anglesey with 454 dead.

Books: Charles Darwin *The Origin of Species*; Charles Dickens *A Tale of Two Cities*; John Stuart Mill *On Liberty*; George Eliot *Adam Bede*; Edward Fitzgerald *Omar Khayyam*.

Born: George Nathaniel Curzon, statesman and Viceroy of India;

Kenneth Grahame, author; Alfred Edward Housman, poet; Arthur Conan Doyle, writer.

Died: Isambard Kingdom Brunel, engineer; Thomas de Quincey, writer; Thomas Babington Macaulay, 1st Baron Macaulay, poet, historian and politician.

1860 In New Zealand, the Second Maori War begins. Robert Burke and William Wills cross Australia from south to north. Joseph Lister introduces antiseptic surgery. **August** The first tramway in Britain comes into operation in Birkenhead. **October** In the Second Opium War, Lord Elgin's forces burn Beijing's Old Summer Palace; the first Convention of Peking ends the Second Opium War. The first Open Golf Championship is played at Prestwick in Scotland. **December** HMS *Warrior*, the world's first iron-hulled, armoured battleship is launched.

Books & Literature: George Eliot *The Mill on the Floss*; Wilkie Collins *The Woman in White*; Florence Nightingale *Notes on Nursing*.

Born: JM Barrie, author.

Died: Sir Charles Barry, architect; George Hamilton-Gordon, 4th Earl of Aberdeen, prime minister.

1861 The death penalty is restricted to murder, embezzlement, piracy and arson on docks or ammunition depots. Daily weather forecasts begin. The Post Office Savings Bank is established. **February** Storms damage the Crystal Palace in London and cause the collapse of the steeple of Chichester Cathedral. **November** A tenement collapses in Edinburgh, killing 35.

Books & Literature: Mrs Beeton *Book of Household Management*; George Eliot *Silas Marner*; Charles Dickens *Great Expectations*; Francis Palgrave *The Golden Treasury of English Songs and Lyrics*.

Born: Douglas Haig, 1st Earl Haig, soldier.

Died: Elizabeth Barrett Browning, poet; Prince Albert of Saxe-Coburg-Gotha, husband of Queen Victoria (of typhoid).

1862 The Companies Act introduces limited liability companies. There is a shortage of cotton; Lancashire mill-workers starve. **January** French and British forces arrive in Mexico, beginning the French intervention in Mexico. A total of 204 miners die in a disaster at the Hartley Colliery in Northumberland. **March** James Bruce, 8th Earl of Elgin, is appointed Governor General of India. **September** The Namamugi Incident; four British nationals are killed at Namamugi in Japan, for not showing respect to the Daimyo (warlord) of Satsuma.

Art: James McNeill Whistler *Symphony in White, No. 1*: The White Girl.

Born: Frederick Delius, composer; Joseph Merrick, 'The Elephant Man'.

Died: James Clark Ross, naval officer and explorer.

1863 A scarlet fever epidemic causes over 30,000 deaths. **January** The first section of the London Underground opens the Metropolitan Line from Paddington to Farringdon Street. **February** HMS *Orpheus* sinks attempting to enter Manukau Harbour in New Zealand; 189 drown. A new Post Office mailbag service begins using pneumatic conveyors beneath London's streets. **May** Broadmoor Asylum for the Criminally Insane is founded at Crowthorne in Berkshire. **August** The Royal Navy bombards the town of Kagoshima in Japan in retribution for the Namamugi Incident of 1862. **October** The Football Association is founded.

Architecture: Sir George Gilbert Scott – the Albert Memorial (begun); John Hawkshaw and EH Barry – Charing Cross Station and Hotel.

Books & Literature: Charles Kingsley *The Water Babies*; Thomas Huxley *Evidence as to Man's Place in Nature*.

Born: David Lloyd George, prime minister; Henry Royce, automobile pioneer.

Died: William Makepeace Thackeray, novelist.

1864 Social reformer, Octavia Hill, begins her reforming work in London slums. James Clerk Maxwell discovers microwaves. John Alexander Reina Newlands produces the first periodic table of the elements. John Wisden publishes the first edition of *Wisden Cricketers' Almanack*. **March** The Great Sheffield Flood: the Dale Dike Dam bursts, killing 270 and destroying 800 houses. Britain hands the Ionian Islands over to Greece. **June** Charles Dickens is involved in a train crash at Staplehurst in Kent; he has to return to his wrecked carriage to retrieve the manuscript of *Our Mutual Friend*. **September** Bombardment of Shimonoseki; an American, British, Dutch and French alliance engages the powerful Japanese warlord Lord Mori Takachika of the Chōshū clan; he has expelled foreigners and fired on foreign shipping.

Died: John Hanning Speke, explorer; George Boole, mathematician and philosopher.

1865 Francis Galton formulates eugenics. The Hong Kong and Shanghai Banking Corporation (HSBC) is founded in Hong Kong by Thomas Sutherland. The Second Maori War ends. **July** The general election is won by Palmerston's Liberals. William and Catherine Booth found the Salvation Army, in Whitechapel, London. The 'Red Flag Act' introduces Britain's first speed limit of 2mph in town and 4mph in the country. Edward Whymper makes the first ascent of the Matterhorn. The *Great Eastern* departs on a voyage to lay a transatlantic telegraph cable. **October** Earl Russell becomes prime minister again, following the death of Lord Palmerston. **November** The five-month Duar War with Bhutan ends with the Treaty of Sinchula, in which Bhutan cedes control of its southern passes to Britain for an annual payment.

Books & Literature: Lewis Carroll *Alice's Adventures in Wonderland*; Charles Dickens *Our Mutual Friend*.

Born: King George V; Rudyard Kipling, writer.

Died: Isabella Beeton, cook and expert on household management; Henry John Temple, 3rd Viscount Palmerston, prime minister; Elizabeth Gaskell, novelist and biographer.

1866 A cholera epidemic in London kills more than 5,000. Thomas Barnardo opens his first home for destitute children. John Langdon Down describes Down's syndrome. Elizabeth Garrett Anderson opens the St Mary's Dispensary, where women can seek medical advice from female practitioners. Colman's mustard receives a Royal Warrant. **May** The London bank Overend, Gurney and Company collapses owing £11 million, precipitating a financial crisis; more than 200 companies fail. **June** Earl Russell is succeeded by the Conservative Earl of Derby. **July** The Transatlantic telegraph cable is completed; transatlantic telegraph communication is possible for the first time.

Books & Literature: Algernon Swinburne *Poems and Ballads*.

Born: George Herbert, 5th Earl of Carnarvon, financier of Egyptian excavations; Beatrix Potter, children's author; HG Wells, writer; Ramsay MacDonald, prime minister.

Died: Thomas Love Peacock, satirist; George Everest, geographer.

1867 The Second Reform Bill adds 938,000 to the electorate. There is a Fenian rising in Ireland. **April** Singapore becomes a crown colony. **May** The foundation stone of the Royal Albert Hall is laid. **June** Joseph Lister performs the first operation under antiseptic conditions, at Glasgow Infirmary. **July** The Dominion of Canada, the first independent dominion in the British Empire, is created by the British North America Act. Swedish chemist Alfred Nobel demonstrates dynamite for the first time at Merstham quarry in Redhill, Surrey.

Architecture: Captain Francis Fowke and Colonel HY Darracott Scott of the Royal Engineers – the Royal Albert Hall in London.

Books & Literature: Walter Bagehot *The English Constitution*.

Born: Stanley Baldwin, prime minister; John Galsworthy, writer and Nobel Prize laureate.

Died: Michael Faraday, chemist and physicist.

1867
January Nelson's Column, with its statue and four lions, is unveiled in Trafalgar Square in London.

1868 The Third Maori War begins in New Zealand. **January** Robert Napier leads an expedition to Abyssinia to free captive British officials and missionaries. **February** The War Office establishes the Army Post Office Corps. The Earl of Derby resigns as prime minister on health grounds; the Conservative, Benjamin Disraeli succeeds him. Robert Napier defeats Tewodros II of Abyssinia in the Battle of Magdala. **May** The last public hanging is of Fenian bomber Michael Barrett at Newgate Prison. **June** The first Trades Union Congress is held in Manchester. **December** The Liberals win the general election; William Ewart Gladstone becomes prime minister.

Books & Literature: Wilkie Collins *The Moonstone*; Robert Browning *The Ring and the Book*.

Born: Robert Falcon Scott, explorer; Charles Rennie Mackintosh, architect; Gertrude Bell, archaeologist, writer and spy.

1869 **March** The first international cycle race is held at Crystal Palace, London. **October** England's first residential college for women, Girton College, is founded. **November** The first issue of scientific journal *Nature* is published. The clipper ship *Cutty Sark* is launched In Dumbarton, Scotland. The opening of the Suez Canal revolutionizes trade between Britain and India.

Books & Literature: R D Blackmore *Lorna Doone*.

Born: Henry Wood, conductor; Neville Chamberlain, prime minister; Lawrence Binyon, poet and scholar

Died: Peter Roget, lexicographer; Edward Smith-Stanley, 14th Earl of Derby, prime minister.

1870 The Married Women's Property Act; women gain more right to property in marriage. **August** The Education Act provides for compulsory primary education. **October** The postcard is introduced.

Architecture: Sir Gilbert Scott – Glasgow University; AJ Humbert – Sandringham, Norfolk.

Born: Marie Lloyd, music hall singer; Hilaire Belloc, writer.

Died: Charles Dickens, writer.

1871 Britain annexes the diamond mines at Kimberley in South Africa. Catering services are provided on British trains for the first time. **January** The Irish Episcopal church is disestablished. The Rugby Union is founded in London. **March** The Albert Hall is opened by Queen Victoria. Scotland beats England in the first rugby international. **May** Whit Monday is Britain's first Bank Holiday. **June** Trade unions are legalized in Britain. **July** CW Alcock suggests that *'a Challenge Cup should be established in connection with the Association'*; the FA Cup is born. **November** Henry Morton Stanley greets missing explorer and missionary David Livingstone with the words *'Dr Livingstone, I presume?'*.

Art: Lewis Carroll *Through the Looking Glass*.

Born: Lottie Dod, athlete.

Died: John Herschel, astronomer; Charles Babbage, mathematician and inventor; George Hudson, railway financier.

1871
Art: James McNeill Whistler *The Artist's Mother*.

1872 The London Metropolitan Police go on strike. Lord Kelvin invents a machine for taking depth soundings at sea. Third Class passengers are now carried on trains. The Ballot Act introduces the secret ballot. **March** In the first ever FA Cup final, Wanderers defeat Royal Engineers 1 – 0 at The Oval in Kennington, London. **September** A band of Icaiche Maya attack Orange Walk Town in British Honduras; Britain sends troops. **November** England and Scotland draw the first ever international football at Hamilton Crescent cricket ground in Glasgow; it ends 0 – 0. **December** HMS *Challenger* undertakes a four-year scientific expedition that will lay the foundation for the science of oceanography.

Books & Literature: Samuel Butler *Erewhon*.

Born: Bertrand Russell, philosopher and mathematician, recipient of the Nobel Prize in Literature; Heath Robinson, cartoonist and illustrator; Aubrey Beardsley, artist; Lord Birkenhead, politician; Max Beerbohm, writer and caricaturist; Ralph Vaughan Williams, composer.

1873   The UK declares war against Ghana's King Kofi Kari-Kari, who is involved in slave-trading, beginning the Second Anglo-Ashanti War. Britain persuades Sultan Barghash Sayyid to close slave markets in Zanzibar. Sleeping cars are provided on trains. **February** Gladstone resigns as prime minister when the Irish Universities Bill is defeated; Disraeli refuses to take office with a minority government; Gladstone returns. The High Court of Justice and the Court of Appeal are instituted by the Judicature Act. **March** The Scottish Football Association is founded. **April** The British steamer RMS *Atlantic* sinks off Nova Scotia; 547 drown. **June** Alexandra Palace in London is destroyed by fire only 16 days after its opening.

Born: Ford Maddox Ford, writer.

Died: Edward George Bulwer-Lytton, writer; Sheridan Le Fanu, writer; David Livingstone, explorer; John Stuart Mill, philosopher; Henry Landseer, painter.

1874   The Second Anglo-Ashanti war ends; the Gold Coast (Ghana) becomes a British colony. Fiji is annexed by Britain. Agricultural workers strike in eastern England. **February** Major Walter Wingfield patents a game called 'sphairistike', which became lawn tennis. **March** Benjamin Disraeli's Conservative Party wins the general election despite polling fewer votes than Gladstone's Liberal Party.

Books & Literature: Thomas Hardy *Far from the Madding Crowd*.

Born: William Somerset Maugham, author; Ernest Shackleton, explorer; Howard Carter, archaeologist; GK Chesterton, author; Gustav Holst, composer; Winston Churchill, prime minister.

1875   Peaceful picketing is permitted by legislation. **January** *The Times* is the first newspaper to publish daily weather forecasts. **May** SS *Schiller* is wrecked on rocks off the Isles of Scilly; 335 die. **August** Captain Matthew Webb becomes the first person to swim the English Channel. **November** Disraeli buys a large portion of Suez Canal shares, gaining a controlling interest for Britain. **December** Passenger steamship, *Deutschland*, runs aground at Kentish Knock; 157 die.

Born: Edgar Wallace, writer; Samuel Coleridge-Taylor, composer; Aleister Crowley, occultist; John Buchan, writer and politician.

Died: Charles Kingsley, writer; Sir Charles Lyell, geologist.

1876   Alexander Graham Bell invents the telephone. Charles Wells opens his brewery in Bedford. Henry Wickham smuggles rubber seeds out of Brazil to Malaysia; it brings about the eventual collapse of the Amazon rubber boom. **April** The Settle-Carlisle Railway is opened to passenger traffic. Queen Victoria becomes Empress of India. Robert Bulwer-Lytton, 1st Earl of Lytton, becomes Viceroy of India. **August** Benjamin Disraeli is made Earl of Beaconsfield by Queen Victoria. **September** Gladstone's *Bulgarian Horrors* pamphlet is published; it talks about massacres of Christians in Turkish-occupied Bulgaria.

Books & Literature: Anthony Trollope *The Prime Minister*; George Eliot *Daniel Deronda*.

Born: Havergal Brian, composer; GM Trevelyan, historian.

1877   Six Scotch whisky distilleries combine to form Distillers Company Limited. The first shipment of Argentinian meat arrives in Britain; a milestone in international trade. Stanley traces the course of the River Congo. **March** The first Test cricket match between England and Australia takes place; the Australians win. For the only time in history, the Boat Race is a dead heat. **April** Britain annexes the South African Republic, violating the Sand River Convention of 1852 and starting a war. **June** The Ambulance Association, later the St John Ambulance Brigade, is founded. **July** The Cabinet decides to declare war on Russia if it occupies Constantinople in the Russo-Turkish War.

Art: James McNeill Whistler *Nocturne in Black and Gold*.

Books & Literature: Anna Sewell *Black Beauty*.

Died: Walter Bagehot, businessman, essayist and journalist; William Fox Talbot, photographer.

1877
July The All England Lawn Tennis and Croquet Club stages its first tennis tournament at Wimbledon; Spencer Gore (left) wins.

1878   HJ Lawson invents the chain-driven safety bicycle. Joseph Swan demonstrates the first reliable filament electric lamp. David Edward Hughes invents the microphone. William Crookes invents the Crookes tube, which produces cathode rays. The Criminal Investigation Department (CID) is established. **January** Cleopatra's Needle arrives in London. Disraeli orders the British fleet to the Dardanelles. **February** The British fleet anchors off Constantinople – Russia does not carry out its threat to occupy Constantinople. **March** The frigate *Eurydice* sinks; 300 die. Russia rejects the British proposal to put the San Stefano Treaty between Russia and the

Ottoman Empire before a European congress; in anticipation of war with Russia, Disraeli mobilizes reserves and calls up Indian troops. **June** In the Cyprus Convention, the Ottoman Empire cedes Cyprus to the UK. **September** Over 640 die when the crowded pleasure boat *Princess Alice* collides with the *Bywell Castle* on the River Thames. **October** The first floodlit football match is played in Sheffield. **November** The Second Afghan War begins when the British attack Ali Masjid fort in the Khyber Pass.

Architecture: Thomas Bouch – Tay Bridge.

Books & Literature: Thomas Hardy *Return of the Native*.

Music: Gilbert & Sullivan *HMS Pinafore*.

Born: Herbert Chapman, football manager; John Masefield, poet and novelist; Augustus John, painter.

Died: Anna Sewell, author.

1879 **January** The Anglo-Zulu War begins; Zulu troops massacre British troops at the Battle of Isandlwana. In Ireland, Charles Parnell mobilizes Irish nationalists. **January** At Rorke's Drift, outnumbered British soldiers resist a huge Zulu force. **March** At Intombe, a British force is ambushed and destroyed by Zulu forces; British forces lose the Battle of Hlobane; British forces defeat 20,000 Zulus in the Battle of Kambula. **April** British troops lift the two-month Siege of Eshowe. **May** Russia and the UK sign the Treaty of Gandamak, establishing an Afghan state. **July** The British win at Ulundi and capture Zulu leader Cetewayo; Zulu military power is broken. **September** Blackpool's illuminations are switched on for the first time. **December** The Tay Bridge Disaster: The central part of the Tay Rail Bridge, in Dundee, collapses as a train passes over it, killing 75.

Architecture: Alfred Waterhouse – the Natural History Museum in London.

Books & Literature: Robert Louis Stevenson *Travels with a Donkey*.

Music: Gilbert & Sullivan *Pirates of Penzance*.

Born: EM Forster, writer; Frank Bridge, composer; William Beveridge, economist and social reformer; Thomas Beecham, conductor; Viscount Waldorf Astor, businessman and politician.

Died: James Clerk Maxwell, physicist.

1880 The Second Afghan War ends. The Transvaal becomes a republic. All of Britain begins to observe Greenwich Mean Time. **January** The first telephone directory contains 255 entries. **April** Disraeli is succeeded by Gladstone as prime minister. **December** In the Transvaal, the Boers revolt against British rule; the First Boer War begins.

Born: Christabel Pankhurst, suffragette; Jacob Epstein, sculptor.

Died: George Eliot, writer.

1881 Work begins on the Channel Tunnel; it stops after only 879 yards (804m). The Land Act is designed to satisfy Irish demands for fair rents and fixed tenure; it proves unpopular with both landlords and tenants. Flogging is abolished in the navy and the army. **January** The first postal orders are issued. **March** The Boers in the Transvaal achieve self-government. **October** In Ireland, Charles Parnell and other nationalists are imprisoned for inciting Irishmen to intimidate tenants trying to take legitimate advantage of the Land Act. A total of 189 haddock fishermen from Eyemouth die in a storm.

Born: Ernest Bevin, Labour politician; PG Wodehouse, writer.

Died: Thomas Carlyle, historian; Benjamin Disraeli, prime minister.

1881
February The Boers beat British troops at Schuinshoogte and Majuba Hill; a truce is signed.

1882 The Married Women's Property Act permits women to buy, own and sell property and to keep their own earnings. The St Andrew's Ambulance Association is founded in Glasgow. **April** Charles Parnell is released when he agrees the Kilmainham Treaty with Britain; it is seen as a triumph for the Nationalists as they achieve reform. **March** The first electric trams begin to operate in London. **May** 'Invincibles', militant Irish republicans, assassinate Lord Frederick Cavendish, chief secretary for Ireland, and permanent undersecretary Thomas Henry Burke in Phoenix Park, Dublin; Parnell distances himself from the killings. **July** In the Anglo-Egyptian War, British troops occupy Alexandria and the Suez Canal. Irish extremists resort to a terrorism campaign. The Treaty of Pretoria acknowledges the independence of the Transvaal. **September** British troops occupy Cairo; Egypt becomes a British protectorate.
Born: A A Milne, author; Virginia Woolf, writer; Eric Gill, sculptor and writer; Leopold Stokowski, conductor; Wyndham Lewis, painter; Eamon de Valera, Irish prime minister and president.
Died: Dante Gabriel Rossetti, poet and painter; Charles Darwin, naturalist; Anthony Trollope, writer.

1883 Britain occupies Egypt. **August** The parcel post is introduced. The eruption of Krakatoa, between Sumatra and Jakarta, causes spectacular red sunsets in Britain. **October** Sir William Smith founds the Boys' Brigade.
Books & Literature: Robert Louis Stevenson *Treasure Island*.
Born: Clement Atlee, prime minister; Compton Mackenzie, writer; Edward Fitzgerald, poet; Arnold Bax, composer.
Died: Karl Marx, social and political philosopher.

1884 British police officers go on armed patrol in London because of the Irish threat. Inventor, William Friese-Green invents the cine camera. The Mahdi leads an uprising against the British in Sudan; Major-General Charles George Gordon is sent to Khartoum to relieve the garrison; he is himself besieged; an expedition is sent to rescue him. **January** The Fabian Society is founded in London. Dr William Price attempts to cremate the body of his infant son, setting a legal precedent for cremation. **February** The first portion of the *Oxford*

English Dictionary is published. **April** An earthquake in Colchester is the UK's most destructive; four die. **October** At the International Meridian Conference in Washington DC, the Greenwich meridian is fixed as the world's prime meridian. **December** All males are given the vote by the Franchise Act; it adds two million voters.

Born: Arthur Ransome, author and journalist; Sir Hugh Walpole, novelist; Sean O'Casey, playwright; John McCormick, singer.

Died: John Wisden, compiler of the annual *Wisden* cricket books.

1885 The office of secretary of state for Scotland is created. Sir James Dewar invents the vacuum flask. The first modern bicycle, the Rover, is created by John K Starley. **January** The Mahdi takes Khartoum; General Gordon is killed by a spear. **March** The UK establishes a protectorate over Bechuanaland. **June** Gladstone resigns; Robert Cecil, Lord Salisbury becomes prime minister. Randolph Churchill becomes secretary of state for India. **July** Professional football (soccer) is legalised. **September** A British force abolishes the Boer republic of Stellaland and adds it to British Bechuanaland. **December** Gladstone begins to favour the idea of Home Rule for Ireland. John Boyd Dunlop patents the pneumatic tyre.

Books & Literature: Rider Haggard *King Solomon's Mines*.

Music: Gilbert & Sullivan *The Mikado*.

Born: Malcolm Campbell, land and water racer; D H Lawrence, author.

Died: Charles Gordon 'of Khartoum', general (killed in battle).

1886 Kenya becomes a British colony. Gold is found in the Transvaal. **January** Following the Third Burmese War, Burma is formally annexed by Britain. The Mersey Railway Tunnel opens. **February** Gladstone becomes prime minister for the third time. **March** The first Crufts dog show is held in London. **June** Gladstone's Irish Home Rule Bill is defeated. **July** The general election is won by the Conservative Party under Lord Salisbury.

Art: John Everett Millais *Bubbles*; George Frederick Watts *Hope*.

Books & Literature: Thomas Hardy *The Mayor of Casterbridge*; Robert Louis Stevenson *Kidnapped* and *Dr Jekyll and Mr Hyde*; Henry James *The Bostonians*.

Born: George Mallory, climber.

Died: Samuel Ferguson, poet and artist; Fred Archer, jockey (suicide).

1887 Zululand becomes a British colony. **January** Queen Victoria is proclaimed Empress of India in Delhi. **May** Buffalo Bill's Wild West Show opens in London. **June** Britain celebrates Queen Victoria's Golden Jubilee; she has ruled for 50 years. **September** The Theatre Royal in Exeter burns down; 186 people die. **October** The British Empire takes over Baluchistan and unites it with India. **November** Bloody Sunday; in London, police clash with Irish protestors; three die and hundreds are injured.

Architecture: The second Tay Bridge; W H Lever and William Owen – Port Sunlight.

Books & Literature: Sir Arthur Conan Doyle *A Study in Scarlet*.

Born: Julian Huxley, biologist; Rupert Brooke, war poet; Barnes Wallis, scientist, engineer and inventor; L S Lowry, painter; Bernard Montgomery, World War II commander; Boris Karloff, actor.

1888 Sarawak and Borneo become British protectorates. The first recorded film, Roundhay Garden Scene, is made by French inventor, Louis Le Prince, in Leeds; it is 2 seconds and 18 frames in length.

The Miners' Federation of Great Britain is founded. county councils are established by the Local Government Act. **March** The Football League is formed. **June** Annie Besant organizes the London match-girls strike. **August** Mary Ann Nichols is murdered, the first of Jack the Ripper's victims. **September** The body of Annie Chapman is found, the Ripper's second victim. In England, the first six Football League matches are played. The bodies of Elizabeth Stride and Catherine Eddowes are found; the third and fourth victims of the Ripper. **November** The body of Mary Jane Kelly is found; the fifth, and last, of Jack the Ripper's victims.

Books & Literature: Rudyard Kipling *Plain Tales from the Hills*.

Music: Gilbert & Sullivan *The Yeomen of the Guard*.

Born: Thomas Sopwith, aviation pioneer and yachtsman; John Logie Baird, inventor; TE Lawrence ('Lawrence of Arabia') soldier, writer and academic; TS Eliot, poet; J Arthur Rank, film magnate.

Died: Edward Lear, artist and writer; Matthew Arnold, poet.

1889   Sir Frederick Abel invents cordite. The Socialist anthem *The Red Flag* is written by Irishman, Jim Connell. **June** 88 are killed in the Armagh rail disaster in Northern Ireland. **July** Several aristocrats are implicated in the Cleveland Street scandal, after police raid a male brothel in London. **August** London dockers go on strike and gain 6d in wages.

Books & Literature: Jerome K Jerome *Three Men in a Boat*; H G Wells *The War of the Worlds*; Robert Louis Stevenson *The Master of Ballantrae*.

Music: Gilbert & Sullivan *The Gondoliers*; Jim Connell *The Red Flag*.

Born: Adrian Boult, conductor; Charlie Chaplin, actor and film director; Paul Nash, painter.

Died: Gerard Manley Hopkins, poet; Wilkie Collins, novelist; Robert Browning, poet.

1890   Charles Parnell is cited in a divorce case; he is forced to resign as leader of the Irish Parliamentary Party. **March** The Forth Bridge in Scotland is opened; it is the longest bridge in Britain. **May** The first official County Championship cricket match is played in Bristol; Yorkshire beats Gloucestershire. The first comic paper, *Comic Cuts*, is published. **July** The Heligoland-Zanzibar Treaty gives Germany Heligoland and Britain the small Sultanate of Wituland in East Africa. Battersea Bridge opens. **September** The Southampton Dockers go on strike.

Architecture: Sir Benjamin Baker and Sir John Fowler – the Forth Railway Bridge.

Books & Literature: Sir James Frazer *The Golden Bough*.

Born: Stan Laurel, actor; Agatha Christie, writer; Richmal Crompton, writer; AP Herbert, writer.

Died: Joseph Merrick, 'Elephant Man'; John Henry Newman, Roman Catholic cardinal; Richard Francis Burton, explorer.

1891   Joseph Chamberlain becomes leader of the Liberal Unionist party; they advocate Irish Home Rule, the disestablishment of the Welsh church, three-year parliaments and reform of the Lords. The Public Health Act (London) tries to control smoke pollution in the capital. **March** In a powerful storm off England's south coast, 14 ships sink. The London-Paris telephone system comes into operation. **March** The British steamship SS *Utopia* sinks off the coast of Gibraltar; 574 drown. **October** A collection in Manchester for Lifeboat Day is the first street collection for charity.

Books & Literature: Thomas Hardy *Tess of the d'Urbevilles*; Rudyard

Kipling *Barrack Room Ballads*; Oscar Wilde *The Picture of Dorian Gray*; George Gissing *New Grub Street*.

Born: Ronald Colman, actor; Stanley Spencer, painter.

Died: Sir Joseph Bazalgette, civil engineer; Charles Stuart Parnell, Irish nationalist leader; WH Smith, newsagent.

1892 Abu Dhabi becomes a British protectorate. **January** Prince Albert Victor, Duke of Clarence, second in line to the throne, dies; next in line is Prince George. **May** British troops defeat Ljebu infantry at the battle of Yemoja river, in modern-day Nigeria; the beginning of a major extension of colonial power into the Nigerian interior. Oscar Wilde falls in love with Lord Alfred Douglas. **July** In the general election, the Unionist government loses its majority. **August** Gladstone becomes prime minister for the fourth time; his Liberal government enjoys Irish Nationalist Party support.

Architecture: Sir Alfred Gilbert – Eros, Piccadilly Circus.

Books & Literature: Arthur Conan Doyle *The Adventures of Sherlock Holmes*; George and Weedon Grossmith *Diary of a Nobody*.

Born: J R R Tolkien, professor and author; Hugh MacDiarmid, poet; Osbert Sitwell, writer.

Died: Prince Albert Victor, Duke of Clarence; Thomas Cook, travel agent; Alfred Lord Tennyson.

1892
August Keir Hardie becomes the first Labour MP.

1893 Natal, in South Africa, is granted self-government. **January** The Independent Labour Party has its first meeting under the chairmanship of Keir Hardie. **February** The Second Home Rule Bill is introduced. The first stretch of the Liverpool Overhead railway is opened. **June** Prince George, Duke of York, marries Mary of Teck. HMS *Victoria*, flagship of the Mediterranean Fleet, collides with HMS *Camperdown* due to confusion over an order and sinks in 10 minutes – 358 sailors die, including vice-admiral Sir George Tryon. **September** The Second Home Rule Bill is rejected by the Lords.

Art: Aubrey Beardsley *Siegfried* and *Morte d'Arthur*.

Books & Literature: Oscar Wilde *Salome* and *Lady Windermere's Fan*; W B Yeats *The Celtic Twilight*.

Born: Ivor Novello, actor and musician; W E Johns, writer; Wilfred Owen, soldier and poet; Leslie Howard, actor; Victor Gollancz, publisher; Leslie Hore-Belisha, 1st Baron Hore-Belisha, statesman after whom Belisha beacons are named; Dorothy Sayers, writer; Alexander Korda, film producer.

1894 Patrick Manson, a British physician, develops the theory that malaria is spread by mosquitoes. **February** A French anarchist attempts to blow up the Royal Greenwich Observatory in London. **March** Gladstone resigns over Irish Home Rule; Lord Rosebery becomes prime minister and forms a minority Liberal government. **May** The Manchester Ship Canal is opened to traffic, linking Manchester to the Irish Sea. **June** The future Edward VIII is born. Tower Bridge in London is opened for traffic. **September** The first branch of Marks and Spencer opens.

Architecture: Sir Horace Jones – Tower Bridge, London.

Born: Harold Macmillan, prime minister; Edward VIII; Aldous Huxley, writer; J B Priestley, novelist and playwright.

Died: Robert Louis Stevenson, author.

1894
May Blackpool Tower opens.

1895 Uganda becomes a British colony. Work begins on Westminster Roman Catholic Cathedral, the last major building in Britain to be constructed in brick without steel reinforcement. The Glasgow Subway underground railway opens. **January** The National Trust is founded. **February** The lowest UK temperature of -27.2°C (-17°F) is recorded at Braemar in Aberdeenshire. **February** Oscar Wilde's last play *The Importance of Being Earnest* is first performed at the St James' Theatre in London). **May** After the loss of his libel case against the Marquess of Queensbury, Oscar Wilde is arrested and convicted of 'sodomy and gross indecency' and sentenced to two years' hard labour. **August** The general election is won by the Conservative Party under Lord Salisbury. Rugby league is created at a meeting in the George Hotel, Huddersfield. **October** The Promenade Concerts are founded by Sir Henry Wood. The first motor show takes place in Tunbridge Wells. **December** The Jameson Raid into the Boer colony of Transvaal in support of the European settlers fails.

Architecture: John Francis Bentley – Westminster Roman Catholic Cathedral; Charles Rennie Mackintosh – Glasgow Herald Building.

Books & Literature: Oscar Wilde *The Importance of Being Earnest*; H G Wells *The Time Machine*.

Born: Malcolm Sargent, conductor; Robert Graves, writer; Sir Brian Horrocks, general; King George VI; Henry Williamson, writer.

Died: Lord Randolph Churchill, statesman.

1896 Cecil Rhodes gives up the premiership of Cape Colony. General Kichener begins the reconquest of the Sudan. **January** There is an outburst of anti-German sentiment in Britain when Kaiser Wilhelm sends a telegram to President Kruger of the Transvaal, congratulating him on defeating the Jameson Raid. Walter Arnold of Kent receives the first speeding conviction. **May** Lord Northcliffe founds the *Daily Mail*. **August** The Anglo-Zanzibar War is the shortest war in history; it lasts 45 minutes. **September** Queen Victoria becomes the longest-reigning monarch in British history – 59 years.

Architecture: Charles Rennie Mackintosh – Glasgow School of Art (begun); Sir Edwin Lutyens – Munstead Wood, Surrey.

Books & Literature: A E Houseman *A Shropshire Lad*; Thomas Hardy *Jude the Obscure*; H G Wells *The Island of Dr Moreau*; the *Savoy Magazine*.

Music: Sir Edward Elgar *Enigma Variations*.

Born: Wallis, The Duchess of Windsor, American wife of Edward VIII; Oswald Mosley, leader of the British Union of Fascists; Sir Michael Balcon, film producer.

Died: Sir John Everett Millais, painter; William Morris, designer and craftsman.

1897 Sir J J Thomson discovers the electron. A British military force is ambushed in Benin; in retaliation, Benin City is torched by British forces. **March** Bob Fitzimmons is the first British boxer to win the heavyweight championship of the world. **May** The Blackwall Tunnel, at the time the longest underwater tunnel in the world, is opened. **June** Queen Victoria celebrates her Diamond Jubilee. **August** The Automobile Club of Great Britain, later named the RAC, is founded. **September** George Smith is the first motorist to be convicted of drink-driving.

Architecture: Tate Gallery, London.

Books & Literature: Bram Stoker *Dracula*; H G Wells *The Invisible Man*.

Born: Anthony Eden, prime minister; Sir Sacheverell Sitwell, 6th Baronet, writer; Dennis Wheatley, writer; Enid Blyton, writer; Aneurin Bevan, politician.

Died: Isaac Pitman, inventor of Pitman Shorthand.

1898 **February** Henry Lindfield is the first person in the world to die in a car crash. **September** In the Battle of Omdurman, British and Egyptian troops led by Lord Kitchener defeat Sudanese tribesmen led by Khalifa Abdullah al-Taashi, establishing British dominance in the Sudan. The Fashoda incident; Britain wins a diplomatic dispute with France over African territorial ambitions. **June** Britain leases Hong Kong's New Territories from China for 99 years.

Books & Literature: Henry James *The Turn of the Screw*; Oscar Wilde *The Ballad of Reading Gaol*.

Born: Ninette de Valois, Irish dancer and founder of The Royal Ballet; Henry Moore, sculptor; C S Lewis, author; Alfred Hitchcock, film director.

Died: Lewis Carroll, writer and mathematician; Aubrey Beardsley, artist; William Ewart Gladstone, prime minister; Samuel Plimsoll, politician and social reformer; Sir Edward Burne-Jones, painter.

1899 Ernest Rutherford identifies alpha and beta rays. **January** Lord Curzon becomes Viceroy of India. **March** Guglielmo Marconi successfully transmits a radio signal across the English Channel. **October** The Second Boer War between the UK and the Boers of the Transvaal and Orange Free State breaks out in South Africa. **October** In South Africa, the Siege of Mafeking begins. **November** British forces are surrounded by Transvaal forces in Ladysmith. In the Sudan, British forces kill the Khalifa.

Architecture: Palace Pier, Brighton.

Born: John Barbirolli, conductor; Noel Coward, actor, playwright and composer; Charles Laughton, actor; C S Forester, writer.

Died: Prince Alfred of Edinburgh and Saxe-Coburg-Gotha; Sir Henry Tate, sugar magnate.

THE 20TH CENTURY –
PRESENT DAY

1900 – 2008

1900 **January** General White repels a Boer attack on Ladysmith; Britain suffers heavy losses at Spion Kop. An influenza epidemic in London kills 50 people a day. **February** Britain and the US sign a treaty to build a canal through Nicaragua. The Labour Party is formed; Ramsay MacDonald is secretary. In South Africa, British troops are defeated at Ladysmith; 20,000 British troops invade the Orange Free State; the 118-day Siege of Ladysmith is lifted. **May** The Siege of Mafeking ends; it has lasted 217 days. **June** British troops take Pretoria, South Africa. **August** An international contingent of troops, under British command, invades Peking, freeing a number of Europeans held hostage. British troops defeat Boer commandos at Bergendal. **September** General Frederick Roberts annexes the Transvaal. **December** The Conservative Party, under Lord Salisbury, wins the general election.

Architecture: E W Mountford – Central Criminal Courts, Old Bailey.

Books & Literature: Joseph Conrad *Lord Jim*.

Music: Edward Elgar *Dream of Gerontius*.

Born: Prince Henry, Duke of Gloucester; Elizabeth Bowes-Lyon, consort of King George VI; Earl Louis Mountbatten, admiral and statesman.

Died: Oscar Wilde, poet and dramatist; John Ruskin, writer and social critic; John Sholto Douglas, 9th Marquess of Queensberry, nobleman and boxer; Arthur Sullivan, composer.

1901 English engineer Hubert Cecil Booth invents the vacuum cleaner. **January** The British colonies of New South Wales, Queensland, South Australia, Tasmania, Victoria and Western Australia become the Commonwealth of Australia. Nigeria becomes a British protectorate. Queen Victoria dies at Osborne House, aged 81; her son, Prince Albert Edward, Prince of Wales, becomes King Edward VII. **April** The *Daily Express* is first published. **June** Liberal MP David Lloyd George denounces the high death rate amongst women and children in British concentration camps set up in South Africa; 26,000 have died. **August** The Commons vote an extra £12 million for naval and war budgets. **September** A smallpox epidemic spreads. **October** The Royal Navy launches its first submarine, *Holland 1*. **November** Prince George, Duke of Cornwall, becomes Prince of Wales. 200 people die in gales. An official report rejects charges of neglect and brutality in South African concentration camps. **December** The first transatlantic radio signal, the letter 'S', is received by Marconi in Newfoundland.

Architecture: Sir Edwin Lutyens – the Deanery, Sonning; Giles Gilbert Scott – Liverpool Cathedral.

Books & Literature: George Douglas *The House with the Green Shutters*; Rudyard Kipling *Kim*; H G Wells *The First Men in the Moon*.

Music: Edward Elgar *Pomp and Circumstance*.

Born: Princess Alice, Duchess of Gloucester; Barbara Cartland, writer.

Died: Queen Victoria; Kate Greenaway, children's book illustrator and writer; Edward John Eyre, explorer; Richard D'Oyly Carte, theatre impresario.

1902 **January** London's population is 6.5 million. More than 2,000 people have now died of smallpox. **April** The treadmill is abolished in prisons. **May** The Treaty of Vereeniging brings the Boer War to an end; the Transvaal and Orange Free State accept British sovereignty.

July Lord Salisbury retires as prime minister; Arthur Balfour succeeds him. **August** The coronation of Edward VII. **September** The first conviction is secured using fingerprint evidence. **October** The first Borstal opens, at Borstal, near Rochester. **December** Scott, Shackleton and Wilson arrive at the furthest southern point reached by man – 82°17'S.

Books & Literature: Arnold Bennett *Anna of the Five Towns*; Joseph Conrad *The Heart of Darkness*; Beatrix Potter *The Tale of Peter Rabbit*; Sir Arthur Conan Doyle *The Hound of the Baskervilles*.

Born: Hartley Shawcross, prosecutor at the Nuremberg trials; William Walton, composer.

Died: Cecil Rhodes, businessman and politician; Samuel Butler, author.

The Suffragette Movement
1903

The suffragette movement began in 1897, when Millicent Garrett Fawcett founded the National Union of Women's Suffrage. Fawcett created the union in order to fight for women's right to vote. She believed in the power of peaceful protest, and felt that the use of violence would only convince men that women could not be trusted to take part in the electoral process. Many men held the opinion that the majority of women would not be able to understand the complexities of the British political system. The National Union's progress continued to be slow, regardless of the validity of their arguments they were too easily ignored by government. That is until 1903 when the Women's Social and Political Union was founded by Emmeline Pankhurst together with her daughters Christobel and Sylvia. They were prepared to use less peaceful methods in order to achieve their objectives. A campaign of obstruction, criminal damage and loud protest followed, culminating at the Derby of June 1913, when suffragette Emily Wilding Davison threw herself under the king's horse, Anmer. Her death did more harm than good to the Suffragette's cause. Davison was an educated woman, and male politicians argued that her actions showed once more that even educated women could not be trusted to behave in a civilized manner. The outbreak of war in 1914 put a stop to the suffragette's campaign of violence, but it was not until 1918, when World War I ended, that the Representation of the People Act was passed. This Act meant that the millions of women who had worked so hard for the war effort were finally granted access to their own government.

1903 **January** Edward VII is proclaimed Emperor of India. **March** Marconi's wireless is used to broadcast a regular news service between New York and London. **July** Britain takes over the Fulani Empire in Africa. Britain and Japan demand that Russia gets out of Manchuria. The government announces that large numbers of troops are to be sent to India. **October** Emmeline Pankhurst founds the Women's Social and Political Union to campaign for votes for women. **November** The *Daily Mirror* is first published.

Architecture: Letchworth, the first garden city; Charles Rennie

Mackintosh – Hill House, Helensburgh.

Books & Literature: Henry James *The Ambassadors*; George Bernard Shaw *Man and Superman*; Bertrand Russell *Principles of Mathematics*.

Born: Barbara Hepworth, sculptor; Bob Hope, comedian; George Orwell, author; Alec Douglas-Home, prime minister.

Died: Lord Salisbury, prime minister.

1904   **January** Earl Russell has the first car number plate, A1. **March** Britain's first electric trains run from Liverpool to Southport. **April** Britain and France sign the Entente Cordiale. **May** Frederick Henry Royce and Charles Stuart Rolls form Rolls-Royce. **August** A British expedition under Colonel Francis Younghusband takes Lhasa in Tibet. The first Atlantic weather forecast is received by wireless. **September** Britain signs a treaty with Tibet. **October** The Russians sink two Hull trawlers; only French diplomacy stops war. **November** 800,000 are receiving poor relief in England and Wales; 250,000 are living in workhouses.

Books & Literature: J M Barrie *Peter Pan*.

Born: Cary Grant, actor; Sir John Gielgud, actor; Cecil Day-Lewis, poet; Christopher Isherwood, novelist; George Formby, entertainer; Graham Greene, novelist.

Died: Henry Morton Stanley, explorer and journalist.

1905   **May** A Bill to give women the vote fails. The Automobile Association is founded. **October** HMS *Dreadnought* revolutionizes battleship design; the naval arms race starts. **November** Irish republican, Arthur Griffith, founds Sinn Féin ('Ourselves') to promote Home Rule for Ireland.

Books & Literature: Oscar Wilde *De Profundis*; Baroness Orczy *The Scarlet Pimpernel*; Sir Arthur Conan Doyle *The Return of Sherlock Holmes*.

1906   **February** Henry Campbell-Bannerman's Liberal Party wins the general election. **March** Parliament approves old age pensions in principle. The Bakerloo Line of the London Underground opens. **April** The Labour Party calls for votes for women. **May** British troops kill 60 Zulus at Durban. **June** The world's largest and fastest passenger liner, the *Lusitania*, is launched. **October** 11 suffragettes are sent to prison for causing a disturbance in parliament. **December** The Piccadilly Line on the London Underground is opened.

Books & Architecture: John Galsworthy *The Man of Property*.

Born: Hugh Gaitskell, British Labour politician; John Betjeman, poet; Samuel Beckett, playwright.

1907   Rudyard Kipling wins the Nobel Prize for Literature. **February** The Central Criminal Court opens at the Old Bailey in London, on the site of Newgate Prison. **March** Keir Hardie's Women's Enfranchisement Bill is defeated. The Channel Tunnel Bill is defeated. **May** The first TT motorcycle race is held on the Isle of Man. **July** The dreadnought, HMS *Bellerophon* is launched. Brooklands motor-racing circuit is opened near Weybridge. **August** Robert Baden-Powell leads the first Boy Scout camp on Brownsea Island. Britain and Russia sign the Anglo-Russian Entente. **September** Britain's first military airship flies at Farnborough.

Books & Literature: Edmund Gosse *Father and Son*; J M Synge *The Playboy of the Western World*.

Born: W H Auden, poet; Daphne du Maurier, author; Sir Laurence Olivier, actor and director; Viscount William Waldorf Astor,

politician; Louis MacNeice, poet; Sir Basil Spence, architect.
Died: Lord Kelvin, physicist and engineer.

1908 British suffragettes begin their campaign. **April** Sir Henry Campbell-Bannerman resigns due to ill health; Herbert Asquith becomes prime minister. **June** The Invalid and Old Age Pensions Act is passed; non-contributory pensions for all over 70. 200,000 demonstrate in Hyde Park for votes for women. **August** W.G. Grace retires from cricket. **October** A penny post to the USA is launched. The first British aeroplane flight takes place at Farnborough. **November** Elizabeth Garrett Anderson is the first woman mayor.
Architecture: Selfridges, London.
Books & Literature: *The Children's Encyclopedia*; W H Davies *The Autobiography of a Super-Tramp*; Kenneth Grahame *The Wind in the Willows*; E M Forster *A Room with a View.*
Music: Frederick Delius *In a Summer Garden*; Sir Edward Elgar *First Symphony.*
Born: Ian Fleming, writer.
Died: Henry Campbell-Bannerman, prime minister.

1908
The summer Olympics are held in London.

1909 The first Rolls-Royce, Silver Ghost, is tested. **January** The Old Age Pension becomes available. Ernest Shackleton's expedition to the South Pole is forced to turn back 11 miles from the Pole. **February** The government announces the building of six new dreadnoughts. Colour films are shown for the first time in Brighton. Selfridges is London's first department store. **June** The Imperial Cricket Conference is formed. The Victoria and Albert Museum opens in London. **July** The South African Union Bill denies blacks the vote. **September** It is admitted in the Commons that some imprisoned suffragettes are being force-fed. **October** Twickenham hosts its first rugby football match. **November** The House of Lords' rejection of Lloyd George's 'People's Budget' provokes a constitutional crisis. **December** Edward VIII dissolves parliament.
Architecture: Charles Rennie Mackintosh – Glasgow School of Art (completed).
Music: Vaughan Williams *The Wasps.*
Born: Francis Bacon, painter; Stephen Spender, poet.
Died: Algernon Swinburne, poet.

1910 The Girl Guides' Association is founded. The tango becomes popular.
January The Liberals win the general election with a reduced majority. Halley's Comet is sighted. **February** The first labour exchanges open. **April** The Commons passes David Lloyd George's 1909 'People's Budget'. **May** George V becomes king upon the death of his father, Edward VII, of pneumonia. The Lords' power of veto is limited. **June** Captain Robert Falcon Scott sets out for the South Pole. **November** On 'Black Friday' 300 suffragettes clash with police outside parliament. **December** The year's second general election to resolve the battle of wills between the Commons and the Lords results in a dead heat; Asquith continues as prime minister. 350 die in the Hulton Colliery disaster.
Books & Literature: H G Wells *The History of Mr Polly*; E M Forster *Howard's End*; George Bernard Shaw *Pygmalion*.
Music: Vaughan Williams *A Sea Symphony, Fantasia Concertante on a Theme of Thomas Tallis*.
Died: Thomas Crapper, inventor; King Edward VII; Charles Stuart Rolls, aviator and automobile manufacturer; Florence Nightingale, nurse; William Holman Hunt, painter.

1911 Ernest Rutherford demonstrates that the atom has a nuclear structure. **January** In the Siege of Sidney Street, in London, four Latvian anarchists shoot three policemen in a botched raid on a jewellers; three are arrested, other members of the gang escape but are cornered by 1,000 soldiers and police in Sidney Street. **March** Five more battleships are to be built. **May** The first British airship crashes at Aldershot. The Festival of Empire opens at Crystal Palace. The White Star liner, *Titanic*, is launched. **June** A Liverpool transport strike begins. **July** The future Edward VIII is invested as Prince of Wales at Caernarfon Castle. The Lords Veto Bill is passed by the Lords with amendments; George V guarantees that he will create the requisite number of peers to get the Bill through the Lords unamended. **August** There is a national strike of railwaymen, dockers and carters; cities are brought close to famine. The Lords Veto Bill is at last passed unamended. The Official Secrets Act is introduced. There are anti-semitic riots in Wales. 36.7°C (98°F) is recorded, the highest UK temperature until 1990. MPs vote to receive salaries for the first time. **October** The navy's biggest battleship, HMS *King George V*, is launched. **December** The National Insurance Act provides sickness and unemployment benefits for all with incomes below £150.
Born: W V Awdry, writer; Mervyn Peake, writer and illustrator; William Golding, writer Nobel Prize laureate; Chad Varah, priest and humanitarian; Terence Rattigan, playwright.
Died: Sir Francis Galton, explorer and biologist.

1912 The Post Office takes over the National Telephone Company. **January** Amundsen beats Scott to the South Pole by 35 days. **March** Suffragettes smash shop windows in London's West End; 96 are arrested when they attack the House of Commons; the Women's Enfranchisement Act is defeated. **April** Scott's expedition perishes in Antarctica. RMS *Titanic* sinks on her maiden voyage; 1,500 die. There is a total eclipse of the sun. **May** The Royal Flying Corps (later the Royal Air Force) is established. 100,000 dockers strike in London. **September** Ulster demonstrates against Home Rule. **October** HMS *Iron Duke*, the world's largest battleship, is launched. **November** A Censor of Films is appointed.

Architecture: County Hall, London.

Died: Joseph Lister, 1st Baron Lister, surgeon; George Grossmith, actor and comic writer; Robert Falcon Scott, explorer; Bram Stoker, writer; William Booth, founder of the Salvation Army.

1913　**January** The first sickness, unemployment and maternity benefits are introduced. **February** Suffragette, Sylvia Pankhurst, goes to prison; a suffragette bomb destroys Lloyd George's house; Emmeline Pankhurst is sentenced to three years in connection with it. **May** A suffragette bomb is found in St Paul's; public meetings of suffragettes are banned. The first Chelsea Flower Show is held. 150,000 Ulstermen pledge to resist Home Rule; the House of Lords rejects the Home Rule Bill for the second time. **July** 50,000 suffragettes march in Hyde Park, London. **August** Harry Brearley invents stainless steel. **October** 439 die in a mining disaster in Glamorgan.

Art: Walter Sickert *Ennui*; Jacob Epstein *Rock Drill*.

Books & Literature: D H Lawrence *Sons and Lovers*.

1913
June Emily Wilding Davison, a suffragette, is killed when she runs out in front of the king's horse, at the Derby.

1914　The Welsh church is disestablished. Sir Ernest Swinton invents the tank. **January** Doctors at the Middlesex Hospital treat cancer with radium. **May** The House of Commons passes the Irish Home Rule Bill. **June** Two million British workers are on strike. Sylvia Pankhurst is arrested for the eighth time. **August** German troops invade neutral Belgium; Britain declares war on Germany; British vessels sink three German cruisers at Heligoland; a British Expeditionary Force of 70,000 men lands in France; the British are defeated at Mons. **September** In the First Battle of the Marne, the British Expeditionary Force and the French 6th army, under General Maunoury, attack German forces nearing Paris; 500,000 are killed or wounded in the Allied victory; the First Battle of the Aisne ends indecisively; British planes bomb Zeppelin sheds at Düsseldorf. The Third Irish Home Rule Bill gives Home Rule to Ireland, but it is suspended until the end of the War. **October** The first German bomb falls on London; the First Battle of Ypres begins. **November** Britain annexes Cyprus and declares war on the Ottoman Empire; Lloyd George announces the doubling of income tax to pay for the war.

Architecture: A D Smith and Cecil Brewer – Heal's, London.

Books & Literature: Robert Tressall *The Ragged-Trousered*

Philanthropist; James Joyce *The Dubliners*.

Music: Vaughan Williams *The Lark Ascending*; Ivor Novello and Lena Ford *Keep the Home Fires Burning*.

Died: Joseph Chamberlain, politician.

1915 **January** The battleship HMS *Formidable* is sunk off Lyme Regis by a German U-Boat; German Zeppelins bomb Great Yarmouth and King's Lynn for the first time; more than 20 die; Britain wins the naval Battle of Dogger Bank. **February** 104,000 British have died in the war so far. **March** Prime minister Asquith forms an all-party coalition. **April** Britain launches an offensive at Ypres with heavy casualties; the Germans use chlorine gas; a landing on the Gallipoli Peninsula of British, Australian and New Zealand troops is bitterly resisted by the Turks. **May** 200 are killed in the Quintinshill rail crash in Scotland; The RMS *Lusitania* is sunk by a German U-boat, killing 1,198; There is resentment at new anti-alcohol measures aimed at increasing workers' productivity. **June** The Women's Institute is founded. **July** 200,000 Welsh miners strike for more money. **September** Sir Cecil Chubb buys Stonehenge at auction for £6,600 as a present for his wife. **October** British nurse Edith Cavell is executed by a German firing squad for helping allied soldiers to escape from Belgium. **November** British war casualties total 510,000. Ernest Shackleton's *Endurance* is crushed by pack-ice and sunk; Shackleton and his men drift on the ice for four months. **December** In the Battle of the Falklands, a British squadron sinks four out of the five German ships; Sir Douglas Haig takes command of British forces on the Western Front; allied troops withdraw from Gallipoli; 25,000 have died.

Books and Literature: Rupert Brooke *1914 and Other Poems*; D H Lawrence *The Rainbow*; W Somerset Maugham *Of Human Bondage*; John Buchan *The Thirty-Nine Steps*.

Died: Rupert Brooke, poet.

1916 **January** The Royal Army Medical Corps performs the first successful blood transfusion. Single men are conscripted. **February** National Savings Certificates go on sale. The Germans begin a massive offensive at Verdun; it lasts until **December** with enormous casualties on each side. **April** The Easter Rising in Ireland; Irish Nationalists seize the Post Office in Dublin, proclaiming a provisional government; 14 rebel leaders are executed; nationalist leader, Roger Casement, is arrested after landing in Ireland from a German submarine. Shackleton reaches South Georgia. **May** Daylight saving time is introduced in Britain. **June** The naval Battle of Jutland is indecisive; Lord Kitchener dies when HMS *Hampshire* hits a mine off the Orkney Islands. **July** The Battle of the Somme begins. **August** Roger Casement is hanged for treason. Shackleton and his crew are rescued. **September** Tanks are used in battle, at the Somme, for the first time. **November** The First Battle of the Somme ends; 10 miles have been gained; more than a million men have died. **December** A coalition government is formed with Liberal Lloyd George as prime minister.

Books & Literature: James Joyce *Portrait of the Artist as a Young Man*; D H Lawrence *Women in Love*; John Buchan *Greenmantle*.

Music: Gustav Holst *The Planets*.

Died: Herbert Kitchener, 1st Earl Kitchener, field marshal and statesman; Henry James, novelist.

1917 **February** Unrestricted submarine warfare begins. Bread rationing is introduced. **March** Britain occupies Baghdad. The Women's

Army Auxiliary Corps founded. **April** A British offensive near Arras achieves little. **June** Haig launches a new Flanders offensive. **July** King George V announces that the Royal Family will take the surname Windsor; the Battenbergs become Mountbatten. The Third Battle of Ypres begins. **August** Captain Noel Chavasse, one of only three people to be awarded the Victoria Cross twice, dies of his wounds. **October** The British win at Passchendale Ridge. **November** The Balfour Declaration proclaims British support for Jewish settlement of Palestine. In the Third Battle of Gaza, British forces capture Gaza from the Ottoman Empire; British troops occupy Tel Aviv and Jaffa in Palestine; the Battle of Cambrai begins. **December** British troops take Jerusalem from the Ottoman Empire. Britain refuses to recognize the Bolshevik regime in Russia.

Books & Literature: W Somerset Maugham *The Moon and Sixpence*; T S Eliot *Prufrock and Other Observations*.

1918 The flu pandemic hits Britain; 3,000 a week die in London alone. The school leaving age is fixed at 14. The British occupy Palestine. **February** The Representation of the People Act gives the vote to men over 21 and women over the age of 30. **March** The Germans launch an offensive on the Somme. **April** The Royal Air Force is founded; the maximum conscription age is raised to 50. **June** The allies launch a counter-attack on the Western Front; rationing begins at home; **August** The Germans retreat from Amiens; British anti-Bolshevik forces occupy Archangel, Russia, in support of the White Russians. **September** A general offensive on the Western Front accelerates the German retreat. Sir Cecil Chubb gives Stonehenge to the nation. **October** The Commons votes to allow women to become MPs.

1918
November World War I ends on 11 November; the German army surrenders to Marshal Foch; Germany signs the armistice in a railway carriage at Compiègne in France.

December Women vote for the first time in the general election; Lloyd George wins.

Books & Literature: Lytton Strachey *Eminent Victorians*; Gerard Manley Hopkins *Poems*; Marie Stopes *Married Love*.

Died: Wilfred Owen, poet (killed in action).

1919 Michael Collins founds the Irish Republican Army to fight for a Republic of Ireland; a long guerrilla campaign begins. The Paris Peace Conference discusses the terms for the Treaty of Versailles. **January** The Battle of George Square: the army is called in to deal with riots about high rents in Glasgow. **April** Eamon de Valera is elected president of Sinn Féin. In India, British and Gurkha troops kill 400 in a massacre in Amritsar. **June** The Treaty of Versailles is signed. The government recommends nationalizing the coal industry. **July** The British dirigible R34 completes the first crossing of the Atlantic by an airship. 2,000 striking policemen in London and Liverpool are dismissed. **August** A daily air service begins between London and Paris. Afghanistan gains independence from the UK. **September** British troops withdraw from Archangel, Russia. **December** Nancy Astor becomes the first woman MP. The Sex Discrimination Act allows women to be employed in the professions.

Architecture: Sir Edwin Lutyens – the Cenotaph in London; Louis de Soissons – Welwyn Garden City.

Died: William Waldorf Astor, 1st Viscount Astor, financier and statesman.

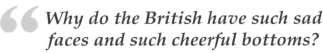

> **“** *Why do the British have such sad faces and such cheerful bottoms?* **”**

Marshal Ferdinand Foch, after seeing the dancing in the ballroom of the Hotel Majestic, headquarters of the British Empire delegation, 1920

1920 **February** The Council of the League of Nations meets for the first time in London. **March** Parliament passes the Government of Ireland Act; Unionist leader Sir Edward Carson opposes the division of Ireland; in the first three months of the year there are 29 political murders. **May** Sinn Féin and Unionists engage in street battles in Londonderry. The government proposes a car tax. **June** Five die in rioting in Ulster; troops are sent to Londonderry. **July** 14 die in riots in Belfast. **August** The government introduces a new bill to 'restore order' in Ireland; it allows for suspension of jury trials. 11 die in street battles in Belfast. **October** Miners go on strike. The first women are admitted to study for full degrees at Oxford University. Sylvia Pankhurst is jailed for six months after urging people to loot the docks. **November** The miners' strike ends. 14 are massacred at a Gaelic football match at Croke Park in Dublin by the Royal Ulster Constabulary.

Books & Literature: Wilfred Owen *Poems*.

Born: Roy Jenkins, politician

1921 The Railways Act gives control of the railways to LMS, LNER, GWR and SR. **February** Eight Sinn Féin supporters are shot dead by British troops. Unemployment stands at over 1 million; the government announces an increase in unemployment benefit. **March** Dr Marie Stopes opens the UK's first birth control clinic in London. A state of emergency is declared after another miners' strike is called. **April** Coal rationing begins. **May** In general elections for the new Northern Ireland parliament, Ulster Unionists win 40 out of 52 seats. **June** Unemployment reaches 2.2 million; two million workers are currently involved in pay disputes. The miners' strike ends. **July** Sinn Féin representatives arrive in London for talks; Ulster Unionist negotiators walk out. **October** The Irish

Treaty Conference opens in London. **November** Troops are sent to restore order after rioting breaks out in East Belfast. The British Legion holds its first Poppy Day. **December** British and Irish negotiators sign an agreement giving independence to the Irish Free State; Parliament ratifies the Anglo-Irish Treaty; six of the nine counties of Ulster are given limited self-government as Northern Ireland.

Music: Vaughan Williams *Third Symphony*.

Born: Prince Philip, Queen Elizabeth II's consort.

1922 **May** The first British radio station, 2LO, is launched. **August** Irish revolutionary, Michael Collins, is assassinated by republican extremists. **October** Lloyd George's Coalition Ministry resigns; Andrew Bonar Law's Conservatives take office. The British Broadcasting Company (BBC) is formed. **November** The broadcasting licence fee of 10 shillings is introduced. The BBC launches a radio service. The general election is won by the Conservatives under Bonar Law.

1922

November In Egypt, Howard Carter and his men open King Tutankhamun's tomb in the Valley of the Kings.

December The Irish Free State comes into existence; George V becomes the Free State's monarch.

Architecture: E T and E S Hall – Liberty's, London.

Books & Literature: Richmal Crompton *Just William*; James Joyce *Ulysses*; T S Eliot *The Waste Land*; Ludwig Wittgenstein *Tractatus Logicus*.

Died: Sir Ernest Shackleton, explorer; Alexander Graham Bell, inventor.

1923 **January** The BBC makes the first outside broadcast. **April** Prince Albert (later George VI) marries Lady Elizabeth Bowes-Lyon in Westminster Abbey. Wembley Stadium is opened for the FA Cup Final between Bolton Wanderers and West Ham United. **May** Bonar Law resigns due to ill health; Stanley Baldwin becomes prime minister. **July** Women are allowed to divorce on grounds of adultery. **October** Britain agrees to the creation of Southern Rhodesia (now Zimbabwe). **December** Big Ben's chimes are broadcast for the first time.

Books & Literature: Aldous Huxley *Antic Hay*; George Bernard Shaw *Saint Joan*; P.G. Wodehouse *The Inimitable Jeeves*.
Died: Katherine Mansfield, novelist; George Herbert, 5th Earl of Carnarvon, financier of Egyptian excavations; Andrew Bonar Law, prime minister.

1924 Work begins on a trunk road system. **January** Ramsay MacDonald becomes the first Labour prime minister. **February** The UK recognizes the Soviet Union. The BBC broadcasts hourly time signals ('pips') for the first time. **April** King George V broadcasts for the first time, opening the British Empire Exhibition at Wembley. **June** George Mallory and Andrew Irvine disappear near the summit of Mount Everest. **October** The Foreign Office publishes the Zinoviev Letter; it has been concocted by British security to create anxiety about Communism in Britain and to help the Conservatives defeat Labour in the general election; Baldwin becomes prime minister for the second time.
Books & Literature: E M Forster *A Passage to India*
Died: E Nesbit, author; Joseph Conrad, author.

1925 The first double-decker buses appear in London. George Bernard Shaw is awarded the Nobel Prize for Literature. **May** Cyprus becomes a British colony. **August** The Summer Time Act makes changing clocks in summer a permanent institution. **October** John Logie Baird creates Britain's first TV transmitter. **December** The Irish boundary agreement fixes the border between Northern Ireland and the Irish Free State.
Books & Literature: Virginia Woolf *Mrs Dalloway*; Noel Coward *The Vortex*; Ezra Pound *A Draft of XVI Cantos*.
Born: Margaret Thatcher, prime minister
Died: Joseph Rowntree, Quaker and philanthropist; George Nathaniel Curzon, 1st Marquess Curzon of Kedleston, Viceroy of India; H Rider Haggard, writer; John French, 1st Earl of Ypres, World War I field marshal.

1926 **January** The first widows' pensions are paid. John Logie Baird demonstrates a mechanical television system in London. British and Belgian troops end their occupation of the Rhineland. **May** The miners go on strike; a General Strike begins in support; martial law is declared in Britain; when the general strike ends, the miners remain on strike. **October** The miners' strike ends. **November** The British Empire is renamed the British Commonwealth.
Architecture: Sir Giles Gilbert Scott – telephone booth Model No 2.
Books & Literature: T E Lawrence *Seven Pillars of Wisdom*; Agatha Christie *The Murder of Roger Ackroyd*; D H Lawrence *The Plumed Serpent*; A A Milne *Winnie-the-Pooh*.
Born: Ian Paisley, politician; Queen Elizabeth II; Geoffrey Howe, politician.
Died: Gertrude Bell, archaeologist, writer, spy and administrator.

1927 **January** The BBC is granted a Royal Charter; Sir John Reith is the first director-general. The first transatlantic telephone call is made. A rugby international is the first live sports broadcast on the BBC. **February** Sir Malcolm Campbell sets a new world land speed record of 174.88mph (286.26 kph). **March** 1,000 people a week are dying from an influenza epidemic. **April** Strikes of support are banned. The UK of Great Britain and Ireland is renamed the UK of Great Britain and Northern Ireland. **May** British police raid the office of Soviet trade delegation; Britain severs diplomatic relations with the Soviet Union because of revelations of espionage. Saudi

Arabia becomes independent. **June** The Soviet Union executes 20 British subjects for espionage. **July** Christopher Stone presents a radio record programme, becoming the first British disc jockey. **November** The first automatic traffic lights begin working in Wolverhampton.

Art: Stanley Spencer *The Resurrection.*

Books & Literature: Henry Williamson *Tarka the Otter.*

Died: Jerome K Jerome, writer.

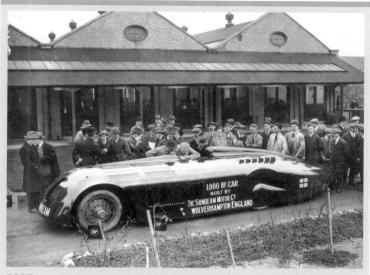

1927
March Henry Segrave breaks the world land-speed record at 203mph (326.69 kph).

1928 The right to vote is extended to all women in the UK. **March** Malta becomes a British dominion. *The Revised Book of Common Prayer* is published. **July** John Logie Bairde transmits the first colour television pictures. **August** The Morris Minor first appears. **September** Alexander Fleming discovers penicillin.

Books & Literature: Evelyn Waugh *Decline and Fall*; D H Lawrence *Lady Chatterley's Lover*; A A Milne *The House at Pooh Corner.*

Died: Thomas Hardy, writer; Douglas Haig, 1st Earl Haig, soldier; Herbert Henry Asquith, prime minister; Charles Rennie Mackintosh, architect; Emmeline Pankhurst, suffragette.

1929 **May** The general election returns a hung parliament. **June** Ramsay MacDonald leads a new Labour government. **August** Britain agrees to evacuate troops from Egypt apart from the Suez Canal Zone. The first transmissions of John Logie Baird's experimental 30-line television system are made by the BBC. **October** The union between the Church of Scotland and the United Free Church of Scotland takes place. Shares fall sharply and there is economic crisis after the Wall Street Crash. **December** The first telephone boxes appear in London.

Architecture: Sir Giles Gilbert Scott – Battersea Power Station (begun).

Art: Ben Nicholson *Still Life*; Henry Moore *Reclining Figure.*

Died: Lord Rosebery, prime minister.

1930 Frank Whittle invents the jet engine. **April** The UK, Japan and the US sign the London Treaty treaty regulating submarine warfare and limiting shipbuilding. **May** Amy Johnson is the first woman to fly solo from England to Australia. **June** Britain recognizes Iraq as an independent state. **July** The BBC transmits the first TV drama. **October** The British Airship R101 crashes in France, en-route to India on its maiden voyage; 48 die.

Books & Literature: Arthur Ransome *Swallows and Amazons*; J B Priestley *Angel Pavement*; Evelyn Waugh *Vile Bodies*; Noel Coward *Private Lives*.

Born: Ted Hughes, poet; Harold Pinter, playwright and Nobel Prize laureate.

Died: D H Lawrence, writer; Arthur Balfour, prime minister; Robert Bridges, poet laureate; Arthur Conan Doyle, author; Sir Henry Segrave, world land-speed record-breaker.

1931 **January** The Road Traffic Act introduces traffic police and compulsory insurance for motorists. **February** Malcolm Campbell breaks the world land-speed record with 245mph. Sir Oswald Mosley forms his New Party. **July** The population of the UK is 44.8 million. **August** Ramsay MacDonald's Labour government resigns and is replaced by a National government, a coalition under MacDonald; MacDonald is expelled from the Labour Party. **September** The value of the pound falls dramatically from 4.86 to 3.49 dollars. **October** Another election produces a National government landslide; Macdonald remains prime minister. **December** Britain formally recognizes the independence of the Commonwealth nations.

Books & Literature: Virginia Woolf *The Waves*.

Music: Sir William Walton *Belshazzar's Feast*.

Died: Arnold Bennett, author.

1932 Unemployment reaches 2.75 million; the trade unions organize the largest-ever hunger march on London. **January** The Archbishop of Canterbury forbids church remarriage of divorcees. **May** James Chadwick discovers the neutron. Ireland abolishes the Loyal Oath to the king.

1932
December George V makes the first Royal Christmas Day broadcast to the Commonwealth.

Architecture: Sir Owen Williams – Daily Express Building, Fleet Street, London; G Val Myer and M T Tudsbery – Broadcasting House, London.

Books & Literature: Aldous Huxley *Brave New World*; Stella Gibbons *Cold Comfort Farm*; Graham Greene *Stamboul Train*.

Died: Giles Lytton Strachey writer and biographer; Kenneth Grahame, author; Ronald Ross, Nobel Prize-winning physician.

TIMELINE OF BRITAIN

124   *1930–1932*

1933 **May** The TUC calls for a boycott of Germany as a protest about Hitler's regime. **September** There are forest fires after a long drought. **October** Mosley and Fascist sympathizers are stoned in Manchester.

Books & Literature: George Orwell *Down and Out in Paris and London*; Vera Brittain *Testament of Youth*.

Died: John Galsworthy, writer, Nobel Prize laureate; Henry Royce, car manufacturer.

1934 Schoolchildren are to be given 0.284 ltr, (0.5 pint) of milk a day to improve nutrition. A speed limit of 30mph (48kph) is introduced in built-up areas. **January** The British Union of Fascists holds a large rally in Birmingham. **February** Lord Privy Seal, Anthony Eden, meets Hitler. **March** Driving tests are introduced. **April** Britain and France warn Germany about defaulting on war reparations. **August** The British Empire Games are held in London. **September** 266 miners die in an explosion at Gresford Colliery in Wrexham. The liner *Queen Mary* is launched.

1934
November The locomotive, the *Flying Scotsman* achieves a record speed of 97mph (156kph).

Architecture: Berthold Lubetkin – Penguin Pool, London Zoo.
Art: Henry Moore *Two Forms*.
Books & Literature: Robert Graves *I, Claudius*; James Hilton *Goodbye, Mr Chips*.
Died: Edward Elgar, composer; Gustav Holst, composer; Frederick Delius, composer; Alice Liddell, inspiration for *Alice's Adventures in Wonderland*.

1935 A prototype of the Spitfire fighter plane is built. **February** Robert Watson-Watt first demonstrates radar. **March** Malcolm Campbell sets a new world land-speed record of 276mph. **May** George V celebrates his Silver Jubilee. The RAF is to be trebled in size to match the German air force. **June** Ramsay Macdonald resigns for health reasons; Conservative Stanley Baldwin returns as prime minister at the head of a national government. The Anglo-German Naval Agreement: Britain agrees to a German navy equal to 35% of her own naval tonnage. **July** Allen lane publishes the first Penguin paperback books. **August** The government of India Act is a step towards self-government.

Books & Literature: Christopher Isherwood *Mr Norris Changes Trains*; T S Eliot *Murder in the Cathedral*.
Died: T E Lawrence 'of Arabia' soldier and writer.

1936 **January** King George V dies; Edward, Prince of Wales, becomes Edward VIII. **April** The government announces the building of 38 new warships. **June** Gatwick Airport opens. **July** The Education Act raises the school-leaving age to 15. Britain starts mass-producing gas masks. **August** The first television broadcast is made from Alexandra Palace. **September** Pinewod film studios open. **November** The BBC launches world's first regular television service. The Crystal Palace is destroyed in a fire. The Post Office introduces the 'Speaking Clock'. **October** The Jarrow Hunger march begins; Baldwin refuses to meet leaders. Mosley's Black Shirts clash with opponents in London's East End. **December** The king abdicates because of his relationship with the divorced Mrs Wallis Simpson; Prince Albert, Duke of York, becomes King George VI;
Architecture: Erno Goldfinger – Hill pasture, Essex.
Books & Literature: Daphne du Maurier *Jamaica Inn*.
Died: Rudyard Kipling, writer and Nobel Prize laureate; King George V; A E Housman, poet; G K Chesterton, author.

1937 **January** The Public Order Act is brought in to end the British Union of Fascists' marches. **March** Edward VIII, is created Duke of Windsor. The first British aircraft carrier, the *Ark Royal* is launched. **May** Neville Chamberlain becomes prime minister, leading a coalition government. **July** The 999 emergency telephone service is inaugurated. **October** The Duke and Duchess of Windsor meet Hitler in Berlin. Lord Halifax holds talks with Hitler; the first steps in the policy of appeasement. **December** Ireland takes the name Eire. The first issue of *The Dandy* comic is published.
Books & Literature: J R R Tolkien *The Hobbit*.
Died: Austen Chamberlain, English statesman and Nobel Peace Prize-winner; J M Barrie, novelist and dramatist; Ramsay MacDonald, prime minister; Lord Rutherford, founder of atomic theory.

1938 **February** The British naval base at Singapore is opened. **March** £11 million is to be spent building new airfields. Britain and America abandon the London naval treaty and begin building battleships. An Anglo-Italian agreement is signed; Anthony Eden resigns in protest. **May** The Women's Voluntary Service is founded. **June** Britain buys 400 planes from America and orders the building of 1,000 Spitfires. **September** Prime minister Neville Chamberlain signs the Munich Agreement, a guarantee to Czechoslovakia against German aggression; he gives his 'Peace in our time' speech on his return. The British navy is mobilized. The liner *Queen Elizabeth* is launched. **October** Hitler invades the Sudetenland. **November** *Picture Post* magazine is first published. **December** A national register for war service is opened. £200,000 is allocated to building air-raid shelters.
Books & Literature: Daphne du Maurier *Rebecca*; Graham Green *Brighton Rock*.

1939 The IRA launch a bombing campaign in Britain; five are killed in Coventry. **February** IRA bombs explode in London tube stations. Britain recognizes Franco's government in Spain. **April** Britain, France and Poland sign a mutual assistance pact; conscription of men aged 20 – 21 begins; Hitler tears up the 1934 treaty with Britain. **May** Chamberlain warns Hitler that if he uses force in Danzig, there will be war. **August** The Germans sign a pact with the Soviet Union; valuable treasures in British galleries and museums are moved to safety.

September World War II begins; Britain declares war on Germany at 11am on 3 September as a result of the German invasion of Poland; children are evacuated to the country from major UK cities; conscription is introduced for all men aged 18 to 41; the first raid by the Royal Air Force on German shipping takes place at the Kiel Canal; HMS Courageous is sunk in the Atlantic with the loss of 500 men.

October HMS *Royal Oak* is sunk by a German U-boat in Scapa Flow; 810 die.

December The Battle of the River Plate takes place between the Royal Navy and the *Admiral Graf Spee*; the German ship is scuttled by her crew.

Books & Literature: James Joyce *Finnegan's Wake*; Christopher Isherwood *Goodbye to Berlin*; Flann O'Brien *At Swim-Two-Birds*.

Died: Howard Carter, archaeologist; Ford Maddox Ford, novelist, poet, critic and editor; W B Yeats, poet; Sigmund Freud, psychologist.

1940 January Food rationing is introduced. **April** The British campaign in Norway starts. **May** Germany invades Luxemburg, Belgium and the Netherlands; Neville Chamberlain resigns as prime minister; he is replaced by Winston Churchill leading a National government; Churchill, makes his famous '*I have nothing to offer you but blood, toil, tears and sweat*' to the Commons; the Local Defence Volunteers later known as the Home Guard, is created; parliament passes the Emergency Powers Act 1940, giving the government full control over all persons and property; British troops withdraw from Norway. 26 May – 4 June 300,000 troops are evacuated from Dunkirk in France. **June** Italy declares war on France and the UK; Churchill makes his Battle of Britain speech to the House of Commons, '*…the Battle of France is over. The Battle of Britain is about to begin*'; German forces land in Guernsey, the start of the 5-year occupation of the Channel Islands. **July** Hitler makes a peace appeal to the UK in an address to the Reichstag; it is rejected. **September** The Blitz begins; London is bombed for 57 consecutive nights. **October** The Battle of Britain ends; Germany has lost air supremacy and can no longer invade Britain. **November** Coventry is destroyed by 515 German bombers; 568 people are killed. **December** Britain invades Libya.

Died: Neville Chamberlain, prime minister; John Buchan, novelist; Eric Gill, sculptor and engraver.

> **The first thing the rescue squads and the firemen saw, as their torches poked through the gloom and the smoke and the bloody pit which had lately been the most chic cellar in London, was a frieze of other shadowy men, night-creatures who had scuttled within as soon as the echoes ceased, crouching over any dead or wounded woman, any soignée corpse they could find, and ripping off its necklaces, or earrings or brooch: rifling its handbag, scooping up its loose change.**

Nicholas Monsarrat, describing a scene at Café de Paris in London, which took a direct hit on 8 March 1941

1941 **January** Australian and British troops capture Tobruk from the Italians. **February** Swansea is 'blitzed' for three nights. **March** British naval forces sink five Italian warships at Cape Matapan, in the Mediterranean. **April** Income tax is raised to 50 per cent. Greece capitulates; British troops withdraw to Crete. **May** The House of Commons is damaged in an air raid. Rudolf Hess parachutes into Scotland, claiming to be on a peace mission. In the North Atlantic, the German battleship *Bismarck* sinks HMS *Hood*; Fairey Swordfish aircraft from the carrier HMS *Ark Royal* fatally cripple the German battleship *Bismarck* in torpedo attacks. **June** Britain invades Iraq; its pro-Axis government is overthrown. **August** Franklin D Roosevelt and Churchill meet in Newfoundland; the Atlantic Charter is created. **November** The aircraft carrier *Ark Royal* sinks after being hit by a torpedo. **December** Britain declares war on Finland, Romania and Hungary. The US declares war on Japan. HMS *Prince of Wales* and HMS *Repulse* are sunk by Japanese aircraft. Hong Kong surrenders to the Japanese.

Books & Literature: TS Eliot *Burnt Norton*; Noel Coward *Blithe Spirit*.

Died: Amy Johnson, English aviator; Lord Robert Baden-Powell, English soldier and founder of the Boy Scouts; Virginia Woolf, English writer; James Joyce, novelist.

1942 The Beveridge Report recommends state social insurance '*from the cradle to the grave*'. **February** Soap rationing is introduced. Singapore is surrendered to the Japanese. **March** Stafford Cripps offers Gandhi a British plan for Indian independence after the war. **April** Malta is awarded the George Cross for heroism. Lord Mountbatten is given command of allied operations in south-east Asia. The Japanese Navy attacks Colombo in Ceylon (Sri Lanka); Royal Navy Cruisers HMS *Cornwall* and HMS *Dorsetshire* are sunk south-west of the island; Royal Navy Aircraft Carrier HMS *Hermes* and Royal Australian navy destroyer HMAS *Vampire* are sunk off the country's east coast. **June** The Germans take Tobruk. **August** Montgomery becomes commander of the Eighth Army. Prince George, Duke of Kent, George VI's brother, is killed in an air crash in Scotland. **October** British and Commonwealth troops break the German defences at El Alamein. **November** The Second Battle of El Alamein ends when Rommel's German forces are forced to retreat; the allies retake Tobruk.

Books & Literature: T S Eliot *Little Gidding*.

Born: Stephen Hawking, British physicist; Neil Kinnock, British statesman.

Died: Prince George, Duke of Kent, fourth son of King George V; Walter Sickert, painter.

1943 **January** Churchill and Roosevelt meet in Casablanca; they decide on a European offensive. British forces capture Tripoli. **March** The RAF bombs Berlin and Essen. **May** It becomes compulsory for women aged 18 to 45 to do part-time work. The Dambuster Raid takes place; the Royal Air Force uses bouncing bombs to breach German dams in the Rhur Valley. German resistance in Tunisia ends. **July** The allies invade Sicily. **August** The allies bomb Milan, Turin and Rome. **September** Allie troops invade the Italian mainland; Italy surrenders. **November** Roosevelt, Churchill, and Stalin meet in Tehran. **December** The last German battleship, the *Scharnhorst*, is sunk.

Born: John Major, prime minister .

Died: Beatrix Potter, British children's author and illustrator.

1944 **January** The allies land at Anzio, near Rome. **February** The PAYE (pay as you earn) system of tax collection is introduced. **June** allied forces enter Rome. Final preparations for D-Day take place in the South of England. *Operation Overlord* begins with the landing of 155,000 allied troops on the beaches of Normandy in France.

1944
June The first V-1 flying bomb falls on London.

July The evacuation of children from London begins. **August** Paris is liberated by the allies. **September** The first V-2 rocket falls on London. Blackout restrictions are relaxed. Allied paratroops land near Arnhem in Holland. **October** British forces land on the Greek mainland; Athens is captured. Churchill and Stalin hold a conference in Moscow to discuss the future of Europe. **December** The Home Guard is stood down.

Art: Francis Bacon *Three Studies for a Crucifixion*; Henry Moore *Madonna and Child*.

Books & Literature: T S Eliot *Four Quartets*.

Died: Henry Wood, conductor; W Heath Robinson, cartoonist and illustrator; Sir Edwin Lutyens, architect.

1945 **February** Churchill, Stalin and Roosevelt meet at the Yalta. The RAF bombs Dresden; tens of thousands of civilians die. **March** Allied troops cross the Rhine. **April** British forces liberate Belsen concentration camp. Mussolini is shot; Hitler commits suicide. **May** Germany surrenders; VE Day is celebrated throughout Britain. **June** The UK takes over Lebanon and Syria. Family allowances are introduced. **July** The three main allied leaders begin their final summit of the war at Potsdam. Winston Churchill's Conservative Party is defeated by the Labour Party in the general election; Clement Attlee becomes prime minister. **August** Atomic bombs are dropped on Japan; Japan surrenders. **October** The British government signs the United Nations Charter.

1944
November The Nuremberg War Trials begin.

Books & Literature: George Orwell *Animal Farm*; Evelyn Waugh *Brideshead Revisited*.
Music: Benjamin Britten *Peter Grimes*.
Died: David Lloyd George, prime minister; John McCormack, singer.

1946 In the next two years, the Bank of England, the coal industry, railways, road transport, docks and harbours are nationalized. **January** The United Nations Security Council holds its first meeting in London. **February** American dance craze, the Jitterbug, sweeps Britain. **March** Winston Churchill delivers his 'iron curtain' speech; the Cold War begins. **May** Heathrow Airport is opened for civilian use. **June** Television licences are introduced. **July** The US House of Representatives approves a loan to Britain. Bread rationing begins. **August** The Peace Conference begins in Paris. **October** Death sentences on Nazi war criminals are carried out. **November** Eight British servicemen are killed in Jerusalem by Jewish terrorists.
Books & Literature: Bertrand Russell *The History of Western Philosophy*; Mervyn Peake *Titus Groan*.
Music: Benjamin Britten *Young Person's Guide to the Orchestra*.
Died: John Logie Baird, television pioneer; H G Wells, writer.

1947 **January** Britain experiences one of the most severe winters on record. **February** Lord Mountbatten becomes the last governor general of India. **March** Britain experiences the worst floods ever recorded. **April** Fuel shortages force the government to ban the use of coal and gas until September. **June** George VI renounces the title 'Emperor of India'. The Marshall Aid plan to rebuild Europe begins. **August** Pakistan and India gain independence from the UK, remaining Commonwealth Realms under King George VI. The Edinburgh Festival is founded. **September** Cambridge University votes to allow women to become full-time students. **November** The British army begins to withdraw troops from Palestine. Philip Mountbatten is created Duke of Edinburgh, Earl of Merioneth and Baron Greenwich; he marries Princess Elizabeth, at Westminster Abbey. New Zealand becomes independent of legislative control by the UK.

Books & Literature: Malcolm Lowry *Under the Volcano*.

Born: The Duchess of Cornwall (Camilla Parker Bowles), 2nd wife of Charles, Prince of Wales.

Died: Stanley Baldwin, three times prime minister.

1948 T S Eliot wins the Nobel Prize for Literature. **January** British Rail is created. Burma and Ceylon become independent. **March** Britain signs the Treaty of Brussels with Belgium, France, Luxembourg and the Netherlands. **April** Electricity is nationalized. **May** The British mandate for Palestine ends; the state of Israel is proclaimed. **June** The ship *Empire Windrush* arrives in Britain with 492 Jamaican immigrants. **July** The National Health Service (NHS) is founded, giving Britons the right to universal healthcare, free at point of use. **July/August** The Summer Olympics are held in London.

Born: Prince Charles, The Prince of Wales, eldest son of Queen Elizabeth II.

1949 **February** The rationing of clothes ends. **April** The Republic of Ireland leaves the Commonwealth. The Royal Navy frigate HMS *Amethyst* is trapped for 14 weeks on the Yangtse by Communist shelling. **June** There is a dock strike. **July** Women are allowed to sit in the House of Lords. **September** The pound is devalued by 30 per cent against the US dollar.

Books & Literature: George Orwell *Nineteen Eighty-Four*.

1950 Bertrand Russell wins the Nobel Prize for Literature. **January** India becomes a republic. **February** Clement Attlee's Labour Party wins the general election. Britain recognizes Communist China. **March** Physicist, Klaus Fuchs, is convicted of supplying nuclear secrets to the Soviet Union. 80 die in an air crash at Cardiff. **May** Petrol rationing comes to an end. *The Archers* is broadcast for the first time. **August** 4,000 British troops are sent to Korea. The Queen's second child, Princess Anne, is born. **September** Soap rationing ends. **November** King Farouk of Egypt demands the withdrawal of British troops from the Suez Canal. The Stone of Destiny is stolen from Westminster Abbey by Scottish Nationalists.

Born: Princess Anne, daughter of Queen Elizabeth II.

Died: George Orwell, author; George Bernard Shaw, dramatist.

1951 **April** The Stone of Destiny is recovered in Scotland. **May** The Festival of Britain begins. **June** Spies Guy Burgess and Donald Maclean defect to the USSR. **September** The Festival of Britain ends. **October** The Conservative Party, under Churchill, wins the general election. British troops take control of key points on the Suez Canal; four British warships dock at Port Said. Zebra crossings are introduced.

Architecture: Sir Robert Matthew and Sir Leslie Martin – the Royal Festival Hall, London.

Music: Benjamin Britten *Billy Budd*.

Died: Ernest Bevin, politician; Ludwig Wittgenstein, philosopher.

1952 **January** British troops capture the police headquarters at Ismailia; 46 Egyptians are killed. **February** King George VI dies of cancer; Princess Elizabeth becomes Queen Elizabeth II. The government offers farmers £5 an acre to plough up grassland for crops. Identity cards are abolished. **May** The De Havilland Comet is the world's first jet airliner. **October** The government announces an end to tea rationing. Britain tests its first atomic bomb. 108 die when three trains collide at Harrow and Wealdstone in North London. **November** In Kenya, the Mau Mau rebel against British rule. **December** The Great Smog causes chaos and at least 4,000 deaths in London.

Died: King George VI; Sir Stafford Cripps, chancellor of the exchequer; Astor, 2nd Viscount Astor, businessman and politician.

1953 Michael Ventris deciphers the Minoan language Linear B. Winston Churchill wins the Nobel Prize for Literature. **January** A major flood disaster on the east coast from Lincolnshire to Kent kills hundreds. **February** The rationing of sweets ends. James D Watson and Francis Crick discover the structure of the DNA molecule. **March** The Royal Yacht *Britannia* is launched. **May** Edmund Hilary and Sherpa Tensing are the first to climb Mount Everest.

1953
June The coronation of Queen Elizabeth II takes place at Westminster Abbey.

September Sugar rationing ends. **October** The government sends troops to the colony of British Guiana in response to communist unrest. 30,000 new homes are built in this month.

Books & Literature: Ian Fleming *Casino Royale*; Dylan Thomas *Under Milk Wood*; Samuel Beckett *Waiting for Godot*.

Music: Benjamin Britten *Gloriana*; Sir William Walton *Orb and Sceptre*.

Died: Queen Mary, consort of King George V; Dylan Thomas, poet and author; Hilaire Belloc, writer; Sir Arnold Bax, composer.

1954 **March** Parliament approves a plan for commercial television; the Independent Television Authority is created. **April** 40,000 Mau Mau suspects are rounded up in Kenya. **May** Roger Bannister becomes the first athlete to run a mile in under 4-minutes. The Home

Secretary denies that Teddy Boys are a serious problem. **July** Britain pulls its troops out of the Suez Canal zone. All food rationing ends. **August** The United Kingdom Atomic Energy Authority is created. **October** Metal fatigue is identified as the cause of three Comet airliner crashes.

Architecture: Sir Basil Spence – Coventry Cathedral (begun).

Books & Literature: J R R Tolkien *The Lord of the Rings*; Kingsley Amis *Lucky Jim*; William Golding *Lord of the Flies*.

1955 **February** The government announces plans to build 12 nuclear power stations in the next ten years. Britain's largest aircraft carrier, HMS *Ark Royal*, is completed. **March** Train drivers go on strike. **April** Winston Churchill resigns as prime minister due to ill-health. **May** Anthony Eden wins the general election for the Conservative Party. The train drivers remain on strike; a state of emergency is declared. **June** Train drivers return to work. **July** Ruth Ellis is the last woman to be hanged. **August** The first ITV franchises begin broadcasting; the first advert is for Gibbs SR Toothpaste. **October** Princess Margaret calls off her wedding to Peter Townsend; he is a divorcee. **November** British troops fight terrorists in Cyprus. **December** Hugh Gaitskell becomes leader of the Labour Party.

Art: Pietro Annigoni *Portrait of the Queen*.

Books & Literature: *The Guinness Book of Records*.

Born: Tim Berners-Lee, inventor of the World Wide Web.

Died: Sir Alexander Fleming, discoverer of penicillin.

1956 **February** Double yellow no-parking lines first appear, in Slough. **March** There is rioting in Cyprus. Pakistan becomes an Islamic Republic within the Commonwealth. **April** Royal Navy frogman, Lionel 'Buster' Crabb, vanishes near the Soviet cruiser *Ordzhonikidze* during a state visit by Soviet premier, Nikita Khrushchev. **May** The last British troops leave Egypt. **July** Egyptian leader Gamal Abdel Nasser nationalizes the Suez Canal; the Suez Crisis begins. **October** An offensive against Egyptian military targets is launched by Britain and France. The Queen opens the world's first commercial nuclear power station at Calder Hall. **November** Petrol rationing is introduced because of petrol blockades by the Middle East, in response to the Suez Crisis; British and French forces seize control of two Egyptian ports; the Egyptians block the Suez Canal; a ceasefire is declared; a United Nations force takes over from British and French troops. Premium Bonds are introduced. **December** British and French troops withdraw from Suez.

Art: Richard Hamilton *Just What is it that Makes Today's Homes So Different, So Appealing?*

Books & Literature: John Osborne *Look Back in Anger*.

Died: A A Milne, author; Sir Alexander Korda, film producer.

1957 The Rent Act abolishes rent control. **January** Anthony Eden resigns as prime minister due to ill health; Harold Macmillan succeeds him. The Royal Ballet is granted a Royal Charter. **March** The Suez Canal reopens. Ghana gains independence. **April** Singapore becomes independent. **May** Petrol rationing ends. Britain tests its first hydrogen bomb. **July** Harold Macmillan makes his '*never had it so good*' speech. A national bus drivers' strike turns violent. **August** 12,000 dockers are on strike. 2,000 people a week are emigrating. The Federation of Malaya becomes independent. **September** The Wolfenden report recommends the legalization of homosexual acts in private. **October** The Jodrell Bank telescope starts operating. The nuclear reactor at Windscale catches fire; radioactive contamination is spread across the surrounding area. **December** 92 die in the Lewisham train crash. The Queen's Christmas broadcast is televised for the first time.

Art: Peter Blake *On the Balcony*.

Books & Literature: John Braine *Room at the Top*; Alan Sillitoe *Saturday Night and Sunday Morning*.

Died: Wyndham Lewis, painter and author.

1958 **February** 21 people die in the Munich air disaster, including seven Manchester United players. Bertrand Russell launches the Campaign for Nuclear Disarmament (CND). **March** Sir Vivian Fuchs completes the first crossing of the Antarctic. **April** CND's first protest march takes place, from London to Aldermarston, Berkshire. **July** The first parking meters are installed. British paratroopers arrive in Jordan in response to king Hussein's request for help against Iraq. The British Empire and Commonwealth Games take place in Cardiff. The first life peerage is created. The Queen gives her son, Charles the title Prince of Wales. **September** Riots break out between blacks and whites in Notting Hill, London. The First Cod War between UK and Iceland; British trawlers defy Iceland's 12-mile limit. Britain's first ballistic missile, Black Knight, is fired successfully. Work starts on the Forth Road Bridge. **December** Subscriber Trunk Dialling (STD) is inaugurated in the UK. The Preston bypass opens; it is the United Kingdom's first motorway. The drug thalidomide causes an epidemic of deformities in babies.

Books & Literature: Keith Waterhouse *Billy Liar*; Harold Pinter *The Birthday Party*.

Music: Cliff Richard *Move It*.

Died: Christabel Pankhurst, suffragette; Ralph Vaughan Williams, composer; G. E. Moore, philosopher.

1959 **May** Import tariffs are lifted. The first hovercraft flight takes place. **July** The Litter Act becomes law. **August** The Street Offences Act forces prostitution off the streets. **October** Macmillan's Conservatives win the general election. D H Lawrence's novel, *Lady Chatterley's Lover*, is prosecuted for obscenity. Postcodes are used for the first time. Mau Mau leader Dedan Kimathi is arrested and executed in Kenya. **November** The first section of the M1 motorway is opened. The Dounreay Fast Reactor comes on line. Britain becomes a member of the European Free Trade Association (EFTA).

Died: Jacob Epstein, sculptor; Sir Stanley Spencer, painter; the Earl of Halifax, politician and Viceroy of India.

1959
Rock'n'roll music, with performers such as Cliff Richard, begins to dominate youth culture.

1960 **January** The Mau Mau Uprising ends. **February** Harold Macmillan makes the 'Wind of Change' speech to the South African parliament. The government agrees to a US missile early warning system to be built at Fylingdales Moor. Queen Elizabeth's third child, Prince Andrew, is born. **April** Dr Richard Beeching rationalizes the rail network; many branch lines are closed. 60,000 protestors demonstrate in London against nuclear weapons. **May** Princess Margaret marries Antony Armstrong-Jones, 1st Earl of Snowdon, in the first televised Royal marriage. **August** Cyprus gains independence. **September** MOT tests are introduced. The first traffic wardens go to work in London. **October** Nigeria gains independence. The satirical review, *Beyond the Fringe*, opens at the Edinburgh Festival. **November** US Polaris missiles are to be based on the Firth of Clyde. Penguin Books is acquitted in the *Lady Chatterley's Lover* obscenity case and sells 200,000 copies on its first day of publication. **December** Conscription is abolished. The first episode of the television soap, *Coronation Street* is broadcast.
Books & Literature: Harold Pinter *The Caretaker*.
Born: Prince Andrew, Duke of York.
Died: Sylvia Pankhurst, suffragette; Aneurin Bevan, politician.

1961 **January** The farthing coin ceases to be legal tender. **March** Black and white £5 notes cease to be legal tender. The Beatles perform at the legendary Cavern Club for the first time. **May** George Blake is sentenced to 42 years for spying. South Africa becomes a republic and withdraws from the Commonwealth. The first betting shops open as the Betting and Gaming Act becomes law. **June** The British protectorate ends in Kuwait. **August** Britain applies for membership of the EEC. The Geneva Conference fails to ban nuclear weapons testing. The satirical magazine *Private Eye* is first published. **December** Birth control pills become available on the NHS. Tanganyika gains independence.
Books & Literature: Muriel Spark *The Prime of Miss Jean Brodie*.
Born: Diana, Princess of Wales.
Died: Augustus John, painter.

1962 **February** 12 European countries form the European Space Agency. **April** The Commonwealth Immigration Bill; uncontrolled immigration into the UK by citizens of the Commonwealth is ended. **May** The new Coventry Cathedral is consecrated. The Northern Ireland general election again produces a large majority for the Ulster Unionist Party. **July** Smog kills 750 in London. In 'the Night of the Long Knives', Harold Macmillan dismisses a third of his Cabinet. The world's first passenger hovercraft service begins across the River Dee. A crowd assaults a rally by the right-wing Union Movement of Sir Oswald Mosley in London. Jamaica becomes independent. **October** Uganda becomes independent. The Beatles release their first record, *Love Me Do*. **November** Britain and France agree to develop the *Concorde* supersonic airliner. The satirical television programme *That Was the Week That Was* is broadcast for the first time. **December** The 'Big Freeze' in Britain brings the worst snowstorms since 1881.
Architecture: Sir Basil Spence – Coventry Cathedral.
Books & Literature: Anthony Burgess *A Clockwork Orange*.
Died: Stuart Sutcliffe, English artist and musician (The Beatles); Vita Sackville-West, English writer and landscape gardener; G M Trevelyan, English historian.

1963 Double agent Kim Philby defects to the Soviet Union. The National Theatre Company (the Royal National Theatre), is formed under Laurence Olivier. **January** Charles De Gaulle vetoes the UK's entry into the EEC. **March** The Beatles release their first album *Please Please Me*. **April** 70,000 marchers demonstrate against nuclear weapons. **June** The Profumo Affair: John Profumo, Secretary of State for War, resigns over his affair with model Christine Keeler. **August** The US, UK, and Soviet Union sign a nuclear test ban treaty.

1963
August The Great Train Robbery takes place in Buckinghamshire; £2.6 million is stolen.

October Harold Macmillan resigns due to ill health; he is succeeded by Sir Alec Douglas-Home. **November** The first episode of Dr Who is aired. **December** Zanzibar and Kenya become independent.
Architecture: Lord Snowdon, Cedric Price and Frank Newby – Aviary, London Zoo.
Died: Hugh Gaitskell, British Labour politician; William Beveridge, economist and social reformer; John Cowper Powys, British writer; Guy Burgess, British double agent; Louis MacNeice, poet and playwright; Aldous Huxley, novelist; Lord Nuffield, philanthropist; Sir David Low, cartoonist.

1964 **February** The 18th-century novel *Fanny Hill* is declared obscene by a magistrate. **March** Pirate radio station Radio Caroline begins broadcasting from the North Sea. Mods and Rockers clash at several seaside resorts. BBC2 is launched. **April** Seven of the Great Train Robbers are sentenced to 30 years each. **May** Terence Conran opens the first Habitat store on London's Fulham Road. **August** Peter Anthony Allen and Gwynne Owen Evans are the last men to be hanged in Britain. **September** Ian Smith, prime minister of Rhodesia, enters into talks about Rhodesian independence. Malta becomes independent. The Forth Road Bridge opens. **October** Labour narrowly wins the general election; Harold Wilson becomes prime minister. Northern Rhodesia becomes the Republic of Zambia; Harold Wilson warns Prime Minister Smith against a unilateral declaration of independence in Southern Rhodesia. **November** The House of Commons abolishes the death penalty for murder. Britain imposes an arms embargo on South Africa, disapproving of its policy of apartheid. The IMF lends Britain £500 million.

Born: Prince Edward, third son of Queen Elizabeth II.

Died: Brendan Behan, writer; Lady Nancy Astor, politician; Sean O'Casey, playwright; C S Lewis, writer; Dame Edith Sitwell, writer.

1965 A prices and wages freeze is introduced. Mary Quant creates the miniskirt. **January** Winston Churchill dies at the age of ninety. **February** Sir Stanley Matthews plays his final English First Division game, at fifty years of age. Richard Beeching outlines plans for massive railway closures. The Gambia becomes independent. **July** Edward Heath becomes leader of the British Conservative Party. Great Train Robber, Ronald Biggs, escapes from Wandsworth Prison. Cigarette advertising is banned on British television. **September** BP finds oil in the North Sea. **October** The Post Office Tower opens in London. **October** African countries demand that the United Kingdom uses force to prevent Rhodesia from declaring unilateral independence. **November** Martial law is declared in Rhodesia; the white minority regime of Ian Smith unilaterally declares independence; the UN Security Council recommends that all states stop trading with Rhodesia. **December** The British government begins an oil embargo against Rhodesia. A 70 mph speed limit is imposed on roads not restricted to lower speeds.

Died: T. S. Eliot, American-born writer, Nobel Prize laureate; Winston Churchill, Prime Minister, Nobel Prize laureate; W. Somerset Maugham, English writer.

1966 **January** The UK ceases all trade with Rhodesia. **March** Harold Wilson's Labour Party wins the general election with an increased majority. **April** A regular hovercraft service begins across the English Channel. **May** The 'Moors Murderers', Ian Brady and Myra Hindley, are sentenced to life imprisonment. A seamen's strike begins. Guyana achieves independence from the UK. **June** De Valera is re-elected president of the Irish Republic. **July** England beat West Germany 4-2 to win the World Cup. A protest against the Vietnam War outside the US embassy in Grosvenor Square turns violent. Gwynfor Evans becomes the first ever Plaid Cymru MP. **August** The Beatles play their last concert at Candlestick Park in San Francisco. **October** At Aberfan in South Wales, 144 people (including 116 children) are killed by a collapsing coal slag heap. British spy George Blake escapes to Moscow from Wormwood Scrubs prison. Spain closes its Gibraltar border to non-pedestrian traffic. **December** Harold Wilson and Rhodesian prime minister, Ian Smith, negotiate on board HMS *Tiger* in the Mediterranean; Wilson withdraws all his previous offers to the Rhodesian government and announces that he will agree to Rhodesian independence only after the founding of a black majority government; Smith declares that he considers that Rhodesia is already a republic.

Books & Literature: Jean Rhys *Wide Sargasso Sea*.

Died: CS Forester, author; Evelyn Waugh, author.

> *I was determined that no British Government should be brought down by the action of two tarts.*

Harold Macmillan, 1967 (speaking about the Profumo Scandal of 1963)

1967 British troops withdraw from Aden. **January** The UK enters the first round of negotiations for EEC membership, in Rome. Donald Campbell is killed on Coniston Water trying to break the world water-speed record. **February** The British National Front (BNP) is founded. Dominica gains independence from the UK. **March** The first North Sea gas is pumped ashore. **May** The UK and Ireland apply for EEC membership. Celtic is the first British team to win the European Cup. **June** The Beatles release *Sgt. Pepper's Lonely Hearts Club Band*. A British Midland plane crashes at Stockport; 72 die. The world's first automatic cash machine is installed at Barclays Bank in Enfield. **July** The steel industry is nationalized. The first colour TV broadcasts begin. Homosexuality is decriminalized. Pirate radio stations become illegal. **September** The Queen launches the *QE2* at Southampton. Radio 1 is launched. **October** The Abortion Act allows legal termination under certain conditions. Charles De Gaulle vetoes British entry into the EEC again. The breathalyzer is introduced. **November** A train derails at Hither Green, killing 49. The pound is devalued.

Books & Literature: Tom Stoppard *Rosencrantz and Guildenstern are Dead*.

Died: John Masefield, English poet and novelist; Arthur Ransome, author and journalist; Joe Orton, English playwright; Brian Epstein, manager of The Beatles; Malcolm Sargent, English conductor; Clement Attlee, prime minister; Siegfried Sassoon, poet.

1968 **January** C Day Lewis is appointed poet laureate. 20 die in a hurricane in Scotland. **March** A demonstration in London's Grosvenor Square against US involvement in the Vietnam War becomes violent. **April** Enoch Powell makes his controversial '*Rivers of Blood*' Speech.

1968
April The first decimal coins (5p and 10p) are issued

June NHS prescription charges are reintroduced. **August** The French again veto Britain's membership of the EEC. The last steam passenger train service runs in Britain. **September** Swaziland becomes independent. The two-tier postal service is introduced. Censorship in theatres is abolished. **October** The Royal Ulster Constabulary uses batons against a civil rights march in Derry, Northern Ireland.

Died: Mervyn Peake, writer and illustrator; Enid Blyton, author.

1969 The Open University is founded. The Divorce Act makes divorce available for '*irretrievable breakdown*' of a marriage. At Cambridge, Robert Edwards carries out the first fertilization of an egg outside the human body. **January** Australian media baron Rupert Murdoch purchases the largest-selling British Sunday newspaper, *The News of the World*. Over 100 are injured in riots in Derry. Violent protests by students close the London School of Economics for three weeks.

1969

March Concorde makes its maiden flight.

April British troops arrive in Northern Ireland to reinforce the Royal Ulster Constabulary. Robin Knox-Johnston becomes the first person to sail around the world solo, without stopping. **May** The voting age is reduced to 18. **June** The UK and Rhodesia sever diplomatic ties. **July** Prince Charles is invested as Prince of Wales at Caernarfon. The halfpenny ceases to be legal tender. **August** British troops are deployed in Northern Ireland. **September** *Monty Python's Flying Circus* airs its first episode on the BBC. **October** The new seven-sided 50p coin is introduced.

Books & Literature: John Fowles *The French Lieutenant's Woman*.

Died: Richmal Crompton, writer; Osbert Sitwell, English writer; Brian Jones, musician (The Rolling Stones); Earl Alexander of Tunis, general; Dame Ivy Compton-Burnett, author.

1970 More working days are lost by strikes this year than any other since 1926. **January** The half crown ceases to be legal tender. **March** Ian Smith severs ties with Britain and declares Rhodesia a republic; Britain refuses to recognize the new state. **April** The Beatles split up. **May** A cricket tour by the South African cricket team is called off after African and Asian countries threaten to boycott the Commonwealth Games. **June** Edward Heath's Conservatives win the general election. Britain makes its third application to join the EEC. Riots break out in Londonderry, following the arrest of Mid-Ulster MP Bernadette Devlin. **July** The government declares a state of emergency to deal with a dockers' strike. The Commonwealth Games are held in Edinburgh. **November** The 10 shilling note ceases to be legal tender.

Books & Literature: *The New English Bible*.

Died: Bertrand Russell, logician and philosopher, recipient of the Nobel Prize in Literature; E M Forster, writer; Arkle, racehorse.

1971 Education Minister, Margaret Thatcher, abolishes free milk for schoolchildren. The Family Income Supplement is introduced. **January** A crush at the Rangers vs Celtic football match in Glasgow kills 66. BBC Open University broadcasts begin. Terrorist group, the Angry Brigade, explodes bombs in London. **February** The UK and Ireland both switch to decimal currency. 100,000 people march against the Industrial Relations Act. Rolls-Royce goes bankrupt and is nationalized. **March** A British postal workers' strike lasts for 47 days. **June** Workers at Upper Clyde Shipbuilders seize control of the shipyard when it goes into liquidation; the government refuses to help. **August** British security forces in Northern Ireland detain hundreds of suspected terrorists in Long Kesh prison; it marks the beginning of a policy of internment without trial; 20 die in ensuing riots; British troops patrol the Irish border to stop arms smuggling; the number of troops in Northern Ireland is raised to 12,500. **October** The House of Commons votes in favour of joining the EEC. The UK becomes the 6th nation to launch a satellite into orbit. The Rev Ian Paisley founds the Democratic Unionist Party. An IRA bomb explodes at the top of the Post Office Tower in London. **December** The UK gives up its military bases in Malta.

1972 The school leaving age is raised to 16. **January** Miners go on strike; there are power cuts and disruption to industry. Unemployment exceeds 1 million for the first time since the 1930s.

1972
January On 'Bloody Sunday', in Northern Ireland 13 Catholic civil rights protestors are killed when troops open fire on demonstrators.

February The miners' strike ends after seven weeks. A Provisional IRA bomb kills six at Aldershot Barracks. **March** Direct rule is imposed on Northern Ireland; the Stormont Parliament is suspended; William Whitelaw is appointed Secretary of State for Ireland. A CND demonstration is held against the nuclear base at Aldermaston. A report into the Bloody Sunday shootings exonerates British troops. **April** On the 13 April, there are 23 explosions in Ulster. The new state of Bangla Desh is admitted to the Commonwealth. **May** The Official IRA declare a ceasefire. The Duke of Windsor (Edward VIII) dies in Paris. **June** A Protestant demonstration in Londonderry turns into a battle. A British

European Airways plane crashes near Staines, killing 118. A strike by thousands of dockers leads the government to announce a state of emergency. **September** Thousands of Asian Ugandans arrive in Britain after being expelled by President Idi Amin. **November** The government introduces price and pay freezes to counter inflation. The Race Relations Act means that employers can no longer discriminate on grounds of colour.

Books & Literature: Richard Adams *Watership Down*.

Died: J Arthur Rank, industrialist and film producer; Cecil Day-Lewis, poet; King Edward VIII; Prince William of Gloucester (air crash); Sir Compton Mackenzie, author.

1973 **January** The UK joins the EEC. **March** IRA bombs explode in Whitehall and at the Old Bailey in London. In a referendum, Northern Ireland votes to remain within the UK; less than 1% of Catholics vote. **April** Value Added Tax (VAT) is introduced. **May** Frigates are sent to protect trawlers in disputed waters around Iceland. **July** Militant supporters of Ian Paisley disrupt the first sitting of the Northern Ireland Assembly. **August** The first in a series of IRA bombs goes off in London. **September** An IRA bomb explodes at Chelsea Barracks in London. The BBC introduces Ceefax, the world's first teletext system. **October** London Broadcasting Company (LBC) is Britain's first legal commercial Independent Local Radio station. **November** The Cod War between Britain and Iceland ends. A state of emergency is declared as miners and power workers strike. The 200th British soldier to die in Northern Ireland is killed. Princess Anne marries Captain Mark Phillips. **December** The Sunningdale Agreement is signed by Edward Heath, Irish premier Liam Cosgrave and representatives of the Ulster Unionist party, the Social Democratic Party, the Labour Party and the Alliance Party of Northern Ireland.

Died: JRR Tolkien, writer; WH Auden, poet; Noel Coward, actor, dramatist and songwriter.

1974 **January** Due to coal shortages caused by industrial action and an Arab oil embargo, Edward Heath introduces the Three-Day Week. **February** The general election almost results in a dead-heat; Harold Wilson becomes prime minister again. **March** The Three-Day Week comes to an end. OPEC nations end a five-month oil embargo. **April** The Local Government Act redraws the administrative map of England and Wales. **June** An explosion at a chemical plant in Flixborough kills 28 people. Members of the fascist National Front clash with leftist counter-protesters in Red Lion Square in London; one student is killed. Westminster Hall is damaged by an IRA bomb. **July** An IRA bomb explodes at the Tower of London, killing one person. **October** The second general election of the year results in a narrow victory for Labour. A bomb at two pubs in Guildford kills five people; there is rioting in the Maze Prison in Northern Ireland. **November** Lord Lucan disappears. An IRA bomb explodes at the Kings Arms, Woolwich; in Birmingham, two pubs are bombed, killing 21 people; Judith Ward is wrongly imprisoned for the blowing up of a coach on the M62, in which 12 soldiers die. The Prevention of Terrorism Act is passed.

Died: Sir James Chadwick, physicist.

1975 Allegations in the press about the sex life of Jeremy Thorpe, leader of the Liberal Party, embarrass the party. **February** Margaret Thatcher defeats Edward Heath in the Conservative leadership election. Five IRA bombs go off in London; an IRA terrorist shoots and kills an off-duty police officer. A tube train crash at Moorgate station kills 43. **June** 67 per cent of voters support continued membership of the EEC in a referendum. Parliament is televised for the first time. Lord Lucan is found guilty *in absentia* of murder. **September** Two die when the London Hilton hotel is bombed by the IRA. Dougal Haston and Doug Scott are the first Britons to climb Everest. **October** An IRA bomb outside Green Park tube station in London kills one. More than 16 million elm trees have been destroyed by Dutch Elm Disease. **November** The first petroleum pipeline in the UK, running from Cruden Bay to Grangemouth in Scotland, is opened by the Queen. Ross McWhirter, the co-founder of the *Guinness Book of Records*, is shot dead by the Provisional IRA for offering reward money to informers.

1975

December IRA members on the run from police break into a flat in Balcombe Street in London, taking the residents hostage; after six days, the gunmen give themselves up.

December British and Icelandic ships clash at the beginning of the Third Cod War. The Sex Discrimination aims to end inequalities in the workplace.

Books & Literature: Seamus Heaney *North*; Ian McEwan *First Love, Last Rites*.

Died: Julian Huxley, biologist; PG Wodehouse, writer; Barbara Hepworth, sculptor; Sir Arthur Bliss, composer.

1976 Two Northern Irish women, Betty Williams and Mairead Corrigan, win the Nobel Peace Prize. **January** 10 Protestant men are machine-gunned in South Armagh by the IRA; 12 IRA bombs explode in London's West End. HMS *Andromeda* is rammed by an Icelandic gunboat. Concorde makes its first commercial flight. **February** Iceland breaks off diplomatic relations with Britain. **March** The Maguire Seven are wrongfully imprisoned for possessing explosives; the Northern Ireland Constitutional Convention is dissolved, resulting in direct rule from London. Harold Wilson resigns as prime minister. Princess Margaret and Lord Snowdon separate. **April** James Callaghan becomes prime minister. Disgraced cabinet minister John Stonehouse resigns from the Labour Party, leaving the government with a majority of one.

Britain starts exporting North Sea oil. **June** The Cod War ends. **July** A heatwave brings record temperatures and drought. Christopher Ewart Biggs, UK ambassador to Ireland, is killed by a landmine. The UK severs diplomatic relations with Uganda. **August** 10,000 Protestant and Catholic women demonstrate for peace in Northern Ireland. **September** Rhodesian leader, Ian Smith, accepts the idea of majority rule within two years. **October** The Damned release *New Rose*, the first ever punk rock single. Intercity 125 trains are introduced on railways between London and Bristol. The Royal National Theatre opens. **December** Punk band the Sex Pistols achieve public notoriety as they unleash four-letter words live on Bill Grundy's TV show.

Died: Agatha Christie, writer; LS Lowry, artist; Bernard Montgomery, field marshal; Benjamin Britten, composer; Percy Shaw, inventor of the cat's eye; Sir Basil Spence, architect.

1977 **January** Seven IRA bombs explode in London. Ian Smith rejects British proposals for a transition to black majority rule in Rhodesia. **March** The government wins a vote of no confidence in the House of Commons.

1977
April Red Rum wins Grand National for the third time.

June Jubilee celebrations are held to celebrate 25 years of Elizabeth II's reign. **October** Former Liberal leader, Jeremy Thorpe, denies allegations of attempted murder of and having a relationship with male model Norman Scott. Police hunt a serial killer of young women known as the Yorkshire Ripper. **November** Firemen begin their first national strike. British Airways inaugurates a regular London to New York City Concorde service.

Books and Literature: Paul Scott *Staying On*; Bruce Chatwin *In Patagonia*.

Died: Anthony Eden, prime minister; Marc Bolan, musician; Clementine Churchill, Baroness Spencer Churchill, wife of Winston Churchill; Charlie Chaplin, comedian; Henry Williamson, writer.

1978 **January** The European Court of Human Rights finds the UK government guilty of mistreating prisoners in Northern Ireland, but not of torture. The Firemen's strike ends. **March** The Conservative Party recruit ad agency Saatchi & Saatchi to revamp their image. Ian Smith reaches an agreement with black leaders in Rhodesia. **May** The first May Day Bank Holiday is celebrated. **July** The Devolution Acts for Wales and Scotland receive Royal Assent. Louise Brown becomes the world's first human born from in vitro fertilization. **August** Jeremy Thorpe goes on trial for conspiracy to murder. **September** A series of strikes begins, lasting throughout the winter; bodies are unburied, people are turned away from hospitals and rubbish piles up on the streets. Bulgarian dissident Georgi Markov dies, after being stabbed with a poison-tipped umbrella in London. **November** Rioters sack the British Embassy in Tehran. **December** IRA bombs go off in many British cities.

Books & Literature: JRR Tolkien *The Silmarillion*.

The Winter of Discontent
1978–79

The Winter of Discontent is the name given to a period of widespread strike action which took place during the winter of 1978-79 in Britain. It marked the largest stoppage of labour in Britain since the 1926 general strike. It began with the Labour government's attempt to enforce a 5 per cent limit on wage increases in order to curb inflation. This was eventually achieved and inflation halved, but the government decided to stick to its policy of capping pay increases. In September 1978, workers at Ford Motors rejected the alloted 5 per cent pay increase. They wanted to be able to bargain for pay increases free of any government restriction. 15,000 workers at Ford walked off the job on 22 September, and by 26 September a further 57,000 people had joined them, leaving 23 Ford factories empty. The workers demanded a 25 per cent pay increase, and a 35 hour working week. By this time the TGWU had decided to support the strikers and helped to agree a 17 per cent pay rise. The government agreed to the pay rise on the condition that the Ford workers return to their jobs, but on 22 November the government changed its mind and attempted to impose sanctions on Ford Motors for acting against the government's policy. This was deemed unworkable in parliament and the proposed sanctions were rejected. This move rendered the government utterly powerless to stop further strike action, and as a consequence workers from many other industries, including lorry drivers and public sector workers like waste collection workers and even gravediggers, were able to hold the government to ransom and demand large pay increases. The nation ground to a halt, rubbish was not collected and was left in the streets to attract rats and other pests. Bodies went unburied, compromising public health and saftey. On 14 February 1979, the government finally struck a deal with the general council of the TUC, bringing the long Winter of Discontent finally to a close.

1979 **January** The Winter of Discontent; tens of thousands of public-workers strike. 49 die when an oil tanker explodes in Bantry Bay. **March** In referendums, Scotland votes narrowly for home rule, but the vote does not reach the required 40 per cent; Wales votes against it. Sir Richard Sykes, ambassador to the Netherlands, is shot dead by the IRA in The Hague. James Callaghan's government loses a vote of confidence by one vote, forcing a general election. Airey Neave, Conservative Northern Ireland spokesman, is killed by an Irish National Liberation Army bomb in the House of Commons car park. **May** The Conservatives win the general election; Margaret Thatcher becomes the first woman prime minister. Bishop Abel Muzorewa becomes Zimbabwe's (Rhodesia's) first black prime minister. **June** Jeremy Thorpe is acquitted of attempted murder. **August** Lord Mountbatten is assassinated by the Provisional IRA; 18 British soldiers are killed at Warrenpoint in Northern Ireland. **September** Police discover the Yorkshire Ripper's twelfth victim. **November** Anthony Blunt is named as the fourth man in the Cambridge Spy Ring. **December** The Housing Bill gives Council House tenants the right to buy their homes.

Died: Sid Vicious, musician (Sex Pistols); Airey Neave, politician (assassinated); Earl Mountbatten, last Viceroy of India (assassinated); Barnes Wallis, aeronautical engineer.

1980 **January** Workers at British Steel go on strike. **March** The British Olympic Association vote to defy the government by sending athletes to the Olympic Games in Moscow. 100 men die when a North Sea oil platform collapses in a storm. **April** Unemployment passes 1.5 million. The Iranian Embassy Siege begins; a six-man terrorist team captures the Iranian Embassy in Knightsbridge, London, taking 26 hostages. **May** The SAS storm the Iranian Embassy building, killing 5 terrorists and freeing the hostages. **June** There is a wave of bombings in Northern Ireland. **October** Margaret Thatcher makes her famous '*The lady's not for turning*' speech to the Conservative Party conference. **November** Michael Foot is elected leader of the Labour Party. **December** Unemployment passes 2 million, the highest since 1935. Former Beatle, John Lennon, is shot dead in New York. TVam is awarded the first ever breakfast TV contract by the Independent Broadcasting Authority.

Died: John Lennon, musician (The Beatles); Sir Cecil Beaton, photographer; Graham Sutherland, painter; Alfred Hitchcock, film director; Sir Oswald Mosley, fascist politician.

> " *To those waiting with bated breath for that favourite media catchphrase, the U turn, I have only one thing to say: You turn if you want to. The lady's not for turning.* "

Prime minister Margaret Thatcher, speaking at the Conservative Party Conference, 11 October 1980

1981 **January** 18 young black people are killed in an arson attack on a house in New Cross, London. Peter Sutcliffe, the Yorkshire Ripper, is arrested. **February** The National Coal Board plans to close 50 pits employing 30,000 men; miners consider a national strike. Rupert Murdoch buys *The Times*. **March** The Social Democratic Party is formed by former Labour MPs Shirley Williams, William Rodgers, Roy Jenkins and David Owen. The first London Marathon is held. **April** Bobby Sands, an IRA terrorist on hunger strike in the Maze prison, is elected MP for Fermanagh and South Tyrone in a by-election; he dies a few weeks later. Serious rioting breaks out in Brixton and Southall. **May** Peter Sutcliffe, the Yorkshire Ripper, is sentenced to life imprisonment. **July** 80 police are injured in two days of rioting in Toxteth in Liverpool; other riots occur in Manchester and Wood Green, in London; there is further trouble in Brixton. The Prince of Wales marries Lady Diana Spencer at St Paul's Cathedral. **October** The hunger strikes at the Maze prison end; 10 have died. An anti-nuclear march in London attracts over 250,000 people.

Architecture: The Barbican, London.

Books & Literature: Salman Rushdie *Midnight's Children*.

1982 **February** The European Court of Justice rules that schools cannot allow corporal punishment against the wishes of parents. **April** Argentina invades the Falkland Islands; the Falklands War begins; the British Falkland Islands government surrenders; a Royal Air Force Vulcan bomber bombs Port Stanley Airport. **May** The nuclear submarine HMS *Conqueror* sinks the Argentine cruiser *General Belgrano* killing 323; HMS *Sheffield* is destroyed by an Exocet missile; British troops land at San Carlos Bay and raise the Union Jack; HMS *Ardent* is sunk with the loss of 22 men; HMS *Antelope* is attacked and sunk; in the Battle of Goose Green, British paratroopers defeat a larger force of Argentine troops. **June** British forces reach the outskirts of Stanley; a formal surrender is agreed. **July** IRA bombs in Hyde Park and Regent's Park kill eight soldiers and injure 47 people. **October** The Thames Barrier is raised for the first time. The *Mary Rose*, Henry VIII's flagship that sank in 1545, is raised. Sinn Féin wins its first seats on the Northern Ireland Assembly. **November** Channel 4 is launched; the Welsh language station S4C launches.

Books & Literature: Thomas Kenneally *Schindler's Ark*.

Born: Prince William son of the Prince of Wales and heir to the throne.

1983 William Golding wins the Nobel Prize for Literature. The £1 coin comes into circulation. **January** Breakfast television begins. The wearing of seat belts in cars becomes compulsory. **February** Derby-winner Shergar is stolen in Ireland. **May** Wheel clamps are introduced. **June** Margaret Thatcher's Conservative Party wins a landslide victory in the general election. **September** 38 prisoners escape from the Maze Prison. **October** Over a million people demonstrate against nuclear weapons at a CND march in London. **November** The first US cruise missiles arrive at RAF Greenham Common amid huge protests. In London gold bars worth nearly £26 million are stolen from the Brinks Mat vault at Heathrow Airport; only a fraction is ever recovered. **December** A Provisional IRA car bomb kills six Christmas shoppers and injures 90 outside Harrods in London; another bomb explodes in Oxford Street.

Books & Literature: JM Coetzee *Life and Times of Michael K*.

Died: William Walton, composer; Arthur Koestler, writer.

1984 Chatham Dockyard in Medway closes after 400 years. **March** The National Coal Board announces it will close 21 pits and lay off 20,000 miners; a year-long long miners' strike begins; mass picketing leads to violence. Sinn Féin's Gerry Adams and three others are seriously injured in a gun attack by the Ulster Volunteer Force. The EEC summit breaks down over disagreement over Britain's budget rebate; Margaret Thatcher threatens to veto any expansion of spending plans. WPC Yvonne Fletcher is shot and killed by a gunman during a siege at the Libyan Embassy in London; Britain breaks off diplomatic relations with Libya. **April** Violence continues on the miners' picket lines. **July** Lightning sets fire to York Minster. **September** Britain and China sign the initial agreement to return Hong Kong to China in 1997. Prince Charles's second son, Prince Henry (Harry), is born. **October** The Provisional IRA attempts to assassinate the British Cabinet in the Grand Hotel, Brighton; four die. **November** 36 pop musicians record *Do They Know It's Christmas*, to raise money for Ethiopian famine relief. **December** British Telecom is privatized. Ted Hughes becomes poet laureate.

Books & Literature: JG Ballard *Empire of the Sun*; Anita Brookner *Hotel du Lac*.

Died: Sir John Betjeman, poet; JB Priestley, writer.

1985 British Antarctic Survey scientists discover the hole in the ozone layer. Spain reopens the border with Gibraltar after 16 years. **January** The first British mobile phone call is made by comedian Ernie Wise. British Telecom announces the end of red telephone boxes. **February** Nine die in a bomb attack at Newry police station. The first episode of the long-running soap, *EastEnders*, is broadcast. **March** The miners' strike ends. **April** Britain's first black bishop is appointed. **May** Fire kills 56 at a football match in Bradford.

1985
May 39 football fans die and hundreds are injured at the European Cup Final between Liverpool and Juventus at the Heysel Stadium in Brussels; English clubs are banned from playing in Europe.

June 13 are arrested in connection with the Brighton hotel bombing of 1984. Stansted is to become London's third airport. **July** Live Aid pop concerts, organized by Bob Geldof, raise over £50 million for famine relief in Ethiopia. The Church of England approves the ordination of women. **August** 55 die when a British Airtours Boeing 737 bursts into flames at Manchester Airport. **September** The wreck of the *Titanic* is located. There are riots in Brixton,

London and Handsworth, Birmingham. **October** There are riots in Toxteth, Liverpool and Peckham, London. **November** The Anglo-Irish Agreement is signed at Hillsborough Castle.

Books & Literature: Douglas Dunn *Elegies*; Keri Hulme *The Bone People*.

Died: Philip Larkin, poet; Robert Graves, writer; Lord George Brown, politician.

1986   Corporal punishment in schools is abolished. **January** Michael Heseltine and Leon Brittan resign from the Cabinet over the Westland affair. The UK and France announce plans to construct the Channel Tunnel. **March** Fire devastates Hampton Court Palace. The Greater London Council is abolished. **April** Journalist John McCarthy is kidnapped in Beirut. US planes bomb Libya, having taken off from British bases; there are widespread protests. Radiation from the explosion at the Chernobyl reactor in the Soviet Union reaches Britain. **May** There are violent clashes at Wapping between striking News International workers and police. **June** Ian Paisley's Ulster Unionist Party stages a protest at the dissolution of the Northern Ireland Assembly. **July** Prince Andrew, Duke of York, marries Sarah Ferguson at Westminster Abbey. The Commonwealth Games begin in Edinburgh. **October** The first edition of *The Independent* newspaper is published. Buses are deregulated. The M25 around London is completed.

1986

October Jeffrey Archer resigns as Deputy Leader of the Conservative Party over allegations concerning prostitutes.

November 47 oil-workers are killed when a Chinook helicopter carrying them from the Brent oilfield crashed. An AIDS advertising campaign is launched. **December** The government launches an inquiry into financial irregularities at Guinness. British gas is privatized.

Architecture: Richard Rodgers – Lloyd's, Leadenhall Street, London.

Books & Literature: Kingsley Amis *The Old Devils*.

Died: Harold Macmillan, Lord Stockton, prime minister.

1987 **January** Terry Waite, special envoy of the Archbishop of Canterbury, is kidnapped in Beirut while negotiating the release of hostages. 300 are injured in clashes at News International at Wapping. **February** British Airways is privatized. **March** British ferry *Herald of Free Enterprise* capsizes at Zeebrugge, Belgium, killing 193. 12 people die in violent storms. Nine IRA gunmen are killed by police and soldiers in County Armagh. **June** In the general election, Margaret Thatcher secures a third term in office. Princess Anne is created Princess Royal. Controversy increases over alleged child abuse in Cleveland. **July** The Queen opens the Docklands Light Railway, Britain's first driverless railway. The Social Democratic Party merges with the Liberal Party. **August** Michael Ryan shoots dead 16 people in Hungerford, Berkshire. Nazi Rudolf Hess kills himself in prison. **October** In the worst storm since 1703, hurricane-force winds kill 23 and cause extensive damage in south-east England. Black Monday; Wall Street crashes and £50 billion is wiped off the value of shares in London. **November** 11 people are killed by a Provisional IRA bomb at a Remembrance Day service at Enniskillen. The government announces plans to introduce the community charge. A fire at Kings Cross Underground station kills 31. **December** Work begins on the Channel Tunnel.
Books & Literature: Bruce Chatwin *The Songlines*.

> " *There is no such thing as society, there are individual men and women, and there are families.* "

Margaret Thatcher in Woman's Own, 31 October 1987

1988 **January** Margaret Thatcher becomes the 20th century's longest-serving prime minister. **February** Nurses go on strike. **March** The SAS shoot dead three unarmed Provisional IRA members in Gibraltar; at their funeral at Milltown Cemetery, Protestant terrorist Michael Stone kills six mourners; two British army corporals are killed by a mob after accidentally driving into a funeral cortege for the victims of the Milltown Cemetery attack. The Liberals and SDP form the Liberal Democratic Party. **July** The Piper Alpha oil rig in the North Sea explodes, killing 167. Paddy Ashdown is elected leader of the Liberal Democrats. **September** A Gibraltar jury decides that the three IRA members killed in March were killed lawfully. **December** Health minister Edwina Currie causes outrage by claiming that most of Britain's egg production is infected with salmonella; egg sales plummet; she resigns. 35 people die in a train crash at Clapham. A terrorist bomb explodes on Pan Am Flight 103 over Lockerbie, in Dumfries and Galloway, killing 270.
Books & Literature: Salman Rushdie *The Satanic Verses*; Stephen Hawking *A Brief History of Time*; Peter Carey *Oscar and Lucinda*.

1989 There is widespread protest in Scotland at the introduction of the Community Charge (Poll Tax) in place of rates. The remains of The Rose and Globe theatres are discovered in London. **January**

A British Midland Boeing 737 crashes onto the M1 at Kegworth, killing 44. **February** In Iran, Ayatollah Khomeini orders the execution of *The Satanic Verses* author, Salman Rushdie. **March** Iran severs diplomatic ties with Britain over *The Satanic Verses*. **April** 95 fans are killed in a crush at the Hillsborough Stadium in Sheffield during the FA Cup semi-final between Nottingham Forest and Liverpool. **July** Lady Porter, Tory Leader of Westminster City Council, is accused of gerrymandering. **August** *The Marchioness* pleasure cruiser collides with a barge in the River Thames, killing 30 people. **September** 11 soldiers are killed by an IRA bomb at Deal barracks in Kent. **October** The Guildford Four are released from prison after the high court quashes their convictions for a 1975 terrorist atrocity. Britain and Argentina formally end hostilities.

Books & Literature: Kazuo Ishiguro *The Remains of the Day*.

Died: Daphne du Maurier, writer; Stella Gibbons, writer.

1990   **January** Violent storms kill 39 people in England and Wales. **March** Iraq hangs British journalist Farzad Bazoft, for spying.

1990
March 200,000 protesters take part in Poll Tax Riots in London.

April A riot at Strangeways Prison in Manchester, lasts for over four weeks. An earthquake in Wrexham measures 5.2 on the Richter Scale. **May** Agriculture Minister John Gummer feeds a hamburger to his five year-old daughter to counter rumours about the spread of mad cow disease. **July** An IRA bomb explodes at the London Stock Exchange; an IRA car bomb kills British MP Ian Gow. **August** Iraq invades Kuwait; British Airways Flight 149 is seized by the Iraqi army at Kuwait International Airport; British hostages are paraded on TV. **October** Sterling joins the Exchange Rate Mechanism. **November** British Sky Broadcasting is founded following a merger between Sky Television and British Satellite Broadcasting. Geoffrey Howe, deputy prime minister resigns over European policy, attacking the prime minister in his resignation speech. Margaret Thatcher resigns as prime minister; John Major succeeds her. **December** British troops assemble in the Gulf in preparation for the Gulf War. Channel Tunnel workers from Britain and France meet beneath the English Channel seabed; it is the first ground connection between the UK and the mainland of Europe since the last ice age. The first British hostages held in Iraq are released.

Died: Lawrence Durrell, writer; Roald Dahl, writer; Ian Gow, politician (assassinated); AJP Taylor, historian.

1991 **January** The UK expels Iraqi diplomats. 'Operation Desert Storm', the Gulf War begins; the Royal Air Force mounts bombing raids on Iraq. Gales kill 27. **February** The IRA launch a mortar attack against 10 Downing Street; the IRA explodes bombs at Paddington and Victoria stations in London. In the Gulf War, Kuwait City is liberated; the Iraqi army is defeated. **March** The Poll Tax is to be replaced by a property-based tax. VAT is increased to 17.5 per cent. The Birmingham Six are freed after the court of appeal quashes their convictions over the 1974 Birmingham pub bombings. **May** Helen Sharman becomes the first Briton in space. A series of attacks by pit bull terriers leads to a ban on the importation of the breed. **June** The British army kills three IRA terrorists in Northern Ireland. **August** John McCarthy, held hostage in Beirut for more than five years, is freed. **October** The 1991 Rugby World Cup is staged in England; Australia win. **November** Robert Maxwell, owner of the *Daily Mirror*, is found dead off the coast of Tenerife. Terry Waite is freed in Lebanon. **December** The Robert Maxwell business empire goes into receivership; Maxwell had removed £350 million from its pension fund shortly before he died.

Died: Graham Greene, writer; David Lean, film director; Angus Wilson, writer.

1992 **February** The Maastricht Treaty creates the European Union. **March** The Duke and Duchess of York separate. **April** The Conservative Party, under John Major, is re-elected for a fourth term. Neil Kinnock resigns as leader of the Labour Party. Betty Boothroyd is the first woman to be elected Speaker of the House of Commons. **August** The first Premier League football matches are played. **September** On Black Wednesday, the government suspends Britain's membership of the European Exchange Rate Mechanism, following a wave of speculation against the Pound. **October** The government announces the closure of a third of Britain's deep coal mines, with the loss of 31,000 jobs. **November** The Church of England votes to allow women to become priests. Fire causes serious damage in Windsor Castle. The Queen describes this year as an '*Annus Horribilis*' (horrible year). **December** The Prince and Princess of Wales separate.

1993 **January** British Airways apologises for an alleged 'dirty tricks' campaign against Virgin Atlantic. **February** On Merseyside, toddler James Bulger is murdered by two ten year-old boys. **March** An IRA bomb on Warrington, Cheshire, kills three-year-old Jonathan Ball and 12-year-old Timothy Parry. **April** A false start forces the Grand National to be cancelled. A massive bomb explodes at Bishopsgate, in the City of London. **June** Andrew Wiles announces a proof to Fermat's Last Theorem at the Isaac Newton Institute. **September** The British National Party wins its first council seat in Tower Hamlets. **October** A bomb in Belfast's Shankill Road kills 10; Protestant Ulster Freedom Fighters kill eight in a bar in Greysteel in revenge. **December** The Downing Street Declaration is signed between the UK and Irish governments on the future of Northern Ireland.

Died: Bobby Moore, footballer; William Golding, writer and Nobel Prize laureate.

The Channel Tunnel

It was technically possible to build a channel tunnel for over a hundred years before the project was actually put into action. The idea was first discussed during the Napoleonic wars during a brief period of peace between England and France in 1802. But war soon broke out again and the idea was abandoned. It was not until the Victorian era, when engineers' experience of major tunneling works had sufficiently increased, that a channel tunnel became a real possibility. Confident English and French engineers began planning and designing the 40.23-kilometre (25-mile) -long undersea rail tunnel in earnest, but they faced a whole host of difficulties. Firstly, engineers had limited knowledge of the geology underneath the channel, secondly, they needed to devise a system for allowing smoke to escape from the steam trains so that passengers would not be choked to death during their journey. Finally, they were concerned about providing an easy route for invaders across the channel. The British were correct to be concerned, if a channel tunnel had been open and operational during World War I, Britain's borders could have been seriously compromised. As it happened, England and France agreed to work together towards building a tunnel in 1870, but the construction of a viable tunnel did not actually begin until 1987, and the tunnel did not officially open until 1994, two years late and hugely over budget.

1994 **January** The Duchess of Kent is the first member of the Royal Family to convert to Catholicism for more than 300 years. **March** The IRA launch three mortar attacks on Heathrow Airport. The Church of England ordains its first female priests. **May** The Channel Tunnel is opened. John Smith, Leader of the Opposition, dies of a heart attack. The Camelot Group wins the contract to run the UK's first National Lottery. Tony Blair and Gordon Brown have dinner at the Granita restaurant in Islington and allegedly make a deal on who will become the leader of the Labour Party. **June** An RAF Chinook helicopter crashes on the Mull of Kintyre, killing all passengers and crew, including 20 intelligence experts. **July** Tony Blair wins the Labour Party leadership election. **August** Sunday trading becomes legal in England and Wales. The Provisional IRA declares a ceasefire. **October** The cash-for-questions affair; *The Guardian* claims that two Conservative MPs Neil Hamilton and Tim Smith, took bribes from Harrods chief Mohamed Al-Fayed to ask questions in the Commons. **December** 52-year-old builder, Fred

West is charged with the murders of 12 people; his wife Rose is charged with 10 of them.

Died: Matt Busby, football manager; Derek Jarman, film director; John Smith, politician; Dennis Potter, writer; Dorothy Crowfoot Hodgkin, chemist and Nobel Prize laureate.

1995 **January** Fred West is found hanged in his cell at Winson Green Prison in Birmingham. **February** Barings Bank collapses following $1.4 billion of losses by rogue trader, Nick Leeson. **November** The Princess of Wales gives a television interview in which she candidly discusses her adultery, depression, bulimia and her children. **December** Rioting breaks out in Brixton. The Queen writes to the Prince and Princess of Wales, urging them to divorce as soon as possible.

Died: Alec Douglas-Home, prime minister.

1996 **February** The first genetically modified food products go on sale. A large IRA bomb explodes in the London Docklands area, killing two people; it signals the end of a 17-month ceasefire; a bomb explodes on a bus in Central London, killing the IRA bomber transporting it. **March** At a primary school in Dunblane, 43-year-old Thomas Hamilton kills 16 children, their teacher and himself. **May** The Duke and Duchess of York are divorced. **June** England hosts the 1996 European Football Championship; it is won by Germany. A bomb devastates Manchester city centre. **July** Dolly the sheep is the first mammal to be successfully cloned from an adult cell. **August** The Prince and Princess of Wales divorce. **October** There is a fire in the Channel Tunnel.

1997 **January** In North Wales, more than 80 people are named as child abusers in care homes. **May** In the general election, the Labour Party under Tony Blair wins a landslide victory. The new chancellor of the exchequer, Gordon Brown, announces that the Bank of England, is to assume independent responsibility for UK monetary policy. **June** McDonalds wins the 'McLibel' libel case, the longest trial in English legal history, against two environmental campaigners. The UK transfers sovereignty of Hong Kong to the People's Republic of China as the 99-year lease on the territory ends. The first *Harry Potter* novel, *Harry Potter and the Philosopher's Stone* is published. **July** The IRA declares a ceasefire. **August** Diana, Princess of Wales, and Dodi Al-Fayed are killed in a car crash in Paris; the country enters a period of national mourning. **September** French investigators reveal that Princess Diana's driver, Henri Paul, was over the drink-driving limit; he had been travelling at over 100mph (160kph); lawyers for Mohamed Al-Fayed, father of Dodi Al-Fayed, blame the paparazzi who were pursuing the Princess's car; widespread criticism of the Royal response to Diana's death forces the Queen to pay tribute to Diana in a nationwide broadcast; Diana's funeral takes place at Westminster Abbey, followed by a private burial at the estate of the Earl Spencer in Althorp, Nottinghamshire; the Earl Spencer, brother of Diana, attacks the Royal Family's treatment of his sister in his funeral eulogy. In referendums in Scotland and Wales, voters back plans for national parliaments with devolved powers. British scientists claim a link between Creutzfeldt-Jakob disease and the consumption of BSE-infected meat. **December** The bill to establish the Scottish parliament is unveiled by Donald Dewar, secretary of state for Scotland. The government announces an independent inquiry into the BSE crisis.

Died: Diana, Princess of Wales; WV Awdry, writer; AL Rowse, historian.

1998 Ulster politicians John Hume and David Trimble win the Nobel Peace Prize. **April** The Good Friday Agreement, an agreement between the UK and Irish governments and the main political parties in Northern Ireland is signed. **May** The Good Friday Agreement is given support by referendums in the Republic of Ireland and Northern Ireland. **August** A car bomb in the Northern Irish market town of Omagh kills 29 people; it is the worst terrorist atrocity in the history of the troubles. **October** At the request of Spain, General Augusto Pinochet, former dictator of Chile, is placed under house arrest during medical treatment in Britain. **November** The Human Rights Act receives Royal Assent. The Queen's Speech is interrupted by MPs and peers, when the Queen announces the Government's plan to abolish the rights of 700 hereditary peers to sit and vote in the House of Lords.

Died: Ted Hughes, poet; Enoch Powell, politician.

> " *Now is not the time for sound-bites. I can feel the hand of history on my shoulder.* "
>
> Tony Blair on the signing of the Good Friday Agreement, 10 April 1998

1999 **April** A minimum wage is introduced. Edgar Pearce, the so-called 'Mardi Gra bomber', is sentenced to 21 years for a series of bombings. David Copeland, the 'London nailbomber', attacks the black, Asian and gay communities in London with three bombs; he is given six life sentences. **May** The first elections to the Scottish parliament and Welsh Assembly are held; Labour and the Liberal Democrats form a coalition government in Scotland; Donald Dewar becomes first minister of Scotland; Labour wins in Wales. **June** Former cabinet minister Jonathan Aitken is sentenced to 18 months for perjury. Prince Edward marries Sophie Rhys-Jones and is created Earl of Wessex. **August** Charles Kennedy becomes leader of the Liberal Democrats. **October** The Rugby World Cup takes place in Wales; Australia win. 31 people are killed in a train crash at Ladbroke Grove in London.

2000 **January** Millennium celebrations are held; the Queen opens the Millennium Dome. Dr Harold Shipman in sentenced to life imprisonment after being found guilty of murdering 15 patients in Greater Manchester; he has actually killed 250. **February** The Royal Bank of Scotland takes over NatWest Bank. The Northern Ireland Assembly is suspended. **March** Britain sends Augusto Pinochet back to Chile to face trial. **May** Anti-capitalist protestors riot on May Day in central London. Ken Livingstone is elected Mayor of London. Tate Modern is opened by the Queen. **July** As part of the Northern Ireland peace process, the last prisoners leave the Maze Prison in Northern Ireland. **August** The Queen Mother celebrates her 100th birthday. Oil refineries are blocked by protests against high fuel prices; panic-buying leads to petrol shortages. **September** Steve Redgrave rows to his fifth Olympic gold medal. **October** Wembley Stadium closes after 77 years; it will not reopen until

2007. Henry McLeish becomes first minister of Scotland. **December** The Millennium Dome closes after one year.

Died: Donald Dewar, first minister of Scotland.

2001 VS Naipaul wins the Nobel Prize for Literature. **January** Peter Mandelson resigns from Cabinet for the second time. A Scottish Court in the Netherlands convicts a Libyan for the 1988 Lockerbie bombing. **February** A serious foot and mouth epidemic breaks out. A train crash at Selby kills 10 people. Britain and the US bomb Iraq's air defence network. **April** The population of the United Kingdom is 58,789,194, according to the 2001 census. **June** Tony Blair's Labour Party secure a second term in the general election. There is a race riot in Burnley. Two people are stabbed in race riots in Bradford. Politician and novelist Jeffrey Archer is sentenced to four years for perjury and perverting the course of justice. **September** One Canada Square, the UK's tallest building, and the London Stock Exchange are evacuated following the 9/11 attacks in the US; Tony Blair pledges to 'stand shoulder to shoulder' with the United States. Iain Duncan Smith becomes leader of the Conservative Party. The Bank of Scotland and the Halifax merge to form HBOS plc. **October** The US invades Afghanistan. The Provisional IRA announces that it has begun to decommission its weapons. **December** Using explosives hidden in his shoes, British-born terrorist, Richard Reid, attempts to blow up American Airlines Flight 63 en route from Paris to Miami.

Died: Fred Hoyle, astronomer; George Harrison, musician (former Beatle); David Astor, newspaper publisher.

2002 **February** Princess Margaret, sister of the Queen, dies aged 71. **March** The Queen Mother dies, aged 101. **May** A train crash at Potters Bar in Hertfordshire kills seven people. **June** The Queen celebrates her Golden Jubilee. **July** Iraq rejects weapons inspector proposals. The Commonwealth Games are held in Manchester. **August** 10-year-olds Holly Wells and Jessica Chapman are killed in Soham, Cambridgeshire by Ian Huntley; he is sentenced to life imprisonment. **November** Firemen go on strike. Politicians in England and Wales lose the power to set minimum terms on life-sentence prisoners.

Died: Princess Margaret, sister of the Queen; Queen Elizabeth, the Queen Mother, consort of King George VI.

2003 **January** Britain and other nations show support for the US against Iraq's violation of UN resolutions. **February** The government issues a dossier purporting to show that Iraq has weapons of mass destruction; a million people demonstrate against the imminent war. **March** The Second Gulf War begins; troops from the UK, the US, Australia and Poland invade Iraq; a massive air strike is centred on military targets in Baghdad. **April** British forces take Basra; Baghdad falls. The Labour and Liberal Democrat coalition, led by Jack McConnell, wins the Scottish parliamentary election; in the Welsh Assembly election, Labour remains in power. **May** The end of major combat operations in Iraq; former UN weapons inspector Dr David Kelly, meets BBC journalist Andrew Gilligan; a political scandal ensues. **July** Dr David Kelly appears before the Commons Foreign Affairs Select Committee; he commits suicide in Oxfordshire. **November** Bombs explode in Istanbul at several British targets; the British consulate-general, Roger Short, is killed. England wins the Rugby World Cup.

Died: Roy Jenkins, politician; Dolly the Sheep (cloned sheep).

THE 20TH CENTURY – PRESENT DAY

Anti Iraq War Demonstrations
2003

On 15 February 2003, over one million British citizens descended on London in order to protest against their government's plan to invade Iraq and overthrow its dictator: Saddam Hussein. The Labour government's argument for the invasion depended heavily on intelligence indicating that Saddam Hussein was developing weapons of mass destruction and was intent on using such weapons against his enemies in the Middle East and in the West, as well as on his own people. This intelligence was thought by many to be dangerously flawed. The London protest was coordinated to coincide with a huge number of other protests in major cities all over the world. Globally the number of protesters has been estimated at as many as 30 million people, but for an enormous number of British citizens this was the first time they had played such a direct role in their own political system. Ordinary people who had never been motivated to do so before, took to the streets to show their anger at a government they felt were unwilling to listen to the views of the electorate. The anti-war protests of 2003 have come to represent a subtle shift in contemporary British politics. The previously popular Labour government (and the prime minister, Tony Blair) came in for a barrage of criticism following the international protests and the subsequent invasion of Iraq, and the repercussions are still being felt in Westminster today.

2004 **January** The inquest into the death of Diana, Princess of Wales and Dodi Al-Fayed is opened. Serial killer Dr Harold Shipman hangs himself in prison. The Hutton Inquiry into the death of Dr David Kelly is published; director-general, Greg Dyke, Chairman of the Board of Governors, Gavyn Davies and journalist, Andrew Gilligan, resign from the BBC. **February** 23 Chinese cockle pickers drown in Morecambe Bay. **June** Labour loses seats in the European, local and regional elections. Ken Livingstone wins a second term as Mayor of London. In Iraq, sovereignty is passed to the Iraqi provisional government. **July** 100,000 civil service jobs are cut. The Butler Inquiry criticizes the government in their use of intelligence relating to weapons of mass destruction in Iraq. The Queen opens the Scottish parliament building. November Voters reject elected regional assemblies in a referendum in north-east England. **December** £26.5 million in used bank notes is stolen from the Northern Bank in Belfast.

2005 Harold Pinter wins the Nobel Prize for Literature. **January** Storms cause disruption. Four Britons are released from Guantanamo Bay. **February** The Provisional IRA withdraws from its commitment to the decommissioning of weapons. Englishwoman Ellen MacArthur sets a record for the quickest solo voyage round the world. The Hunting Act, banning hunting with dogs, becomes law. Three British soldiers are found guilty of abusing Iraqi prisoners. **April** The Prince of Wales marries Camilla Parker-Bowles at Windsor

Guildhall. **May** Tony Blair's Labour Party wins the general election with a reduced majority. **June** Ugandan-born John Sentamu is appointed Archbishop of York, the first black person to become an archbishop in the Church of England. **July** Tony Blair assumes the Presidency of the Council of the European Union. Protesters riot in Edinburgh before the G8 conference at Gleneagles in Perthshire. London is chosen as the host city for the 2012 Olympic Games. The IRA orders an end to its armed campaign.

2005
On 7 July a series of coordinated suicide bombings by Muslim extremists strikes London's public transport system during the morning rush hour; three bombs explode within 50 seconds of each other on three London Underground trains; a fourth explodes on a bus in Tavistock Square; 52 die. On 21 July, there are four more attempted, but smaller, bombings on London Transport; Metropolitan Police shoot and kill Brazilian Jean Charles de Menezes, mistakenly believing him to be a suicide bomber; police arrest suspects of the 21 July bombings in London and Rome.

September The IRA's arsenal has been 'put beyond use'. **November** Pubs in England and Wales are permitted to open 24-hours a day. **December** David Cameron is elected leader of the Conservative Party. The Civil Partnerships Act becomes law, granting same-sex couples similar legal rights to heterosexual couples.

2006 **January** Charles Kennedy, leader of the Liberal Democrats, resigns because of his drinking problem. **February** Around £53 million is stolen from the Securitas depot in London; the largest cash robbery in British history. **March** The Queen opens the Welsh Assembly Building. Sir Menzies Campbell becomes leader of the Liberal Democrats. **April** Queen Elizabeth II celebrates her eightieth birthday. **August** Police arrest conspirators in a plot to detonate liquid explosives on transatlantic flights. **September** 14 military personnel are killed when a Nimrod aircraft crashes in Afghanistan. **November** Former lieutenant-colonel in the Russian Federation's Federal Security Service, Alexander Litvinenko, dies in London having been poisoned by Polonium 210.

Died: John Profumo, politician; Muriel Spark, novelist.

The Murder of Alexander Litvinenko

On 1 November 2006, former Lieutenant Colonel in the Russian Federation's Security Service (the FSB) Alexander Litvinenko, suddenly fell ill and was hospitalised in Barnet, London. He was a well-known and outspoken critic of Russia's government, and in particular of its President, Vladimir Putin – the former head of the FSB. In his previous job, Litvinenko had headed-up one of the internal investigation branches charged with looking into cases of corruption and coercion within the FSB itself. As a result he made a number of enemies within its ranks – many of whom could have wanted him permanantly out of the way. Doctors were initially mystified by the symptoms shown by Litvinenko, but it eventually emerged that he had been poisoned with a radioactive substance called polonium 210, adminstered in a cup of tea at the Pine Bar at the Millenium Hotel in central London. An enormous investigation was launched to discover the source of the polonium 210. The trail seemed to lead back to Moscow; a Finnish aeroplane used on a journey from Moscow to London in the days preceeding the poisoning was found to carry traces of the radioactive poison. Various theories concerning the murder continue to emerge. Some powerful Russians have claimed that the British Secret Service were responsible for poisoning Litvinenko in order to cast suspicion on Vladimir Putin's administration. The case is still officially open for investigation, the British have requested the extradition of Russian businessman (and former colleague of Alexander Litvinenko) Andrei Lugovoi, but the Russian administration has so far forbidden it.

2007 **January** New rules outlawing businesses from discriminating against homosexuals are upheld in the House of Lords. Home Secretary John Reid faces mounting problems with escapes from open prisons, the absconding of people under Control Orders and missing sex offenders. Tony Blair is interviewed by police regarding the Cash-for-honours allegations. The Bank of England raises interest rates for the third time in five months. Britain is hit by torrential rain and gale-force winds, resulting in the deaths of at least nine people. **February** Passenger duty for flights from the UK doubles. **March** MPs vote for a fully elected House of Lords. In the Northern Ireland Assembly elections the DUP and Sinn Féin make gains; for direct rule to end, both parties must cooperate in a power-sharing Executive. In spite of a revolt in its ranks, the government wins Commons support for the updating of the Trident missile system. 15 Royal Navy servicemen operating in Iraqi waters are seized by Iranian authorities. Members of the Democratic Unionist Party and Sinn Féin, led by Ian Paisley and Gerry Adams, meet face to face for the first time; they agree a timetable for the implementation of the St Andrews Agreement. **April** Smoking is banned in public places in Wales. The 15 British soldiers held captive in Iran are freed. In Iraq, four British soldiers are killed in an explosion near the Iraqi city of Basra. There is an earthquake measuring 4.3 on the Richter scale in Kent. **May** Elections are held for the Scottish parliament and National Assembly for Wales; Scottish Nationalist Alex Salmond is elected First Minister of Scotland; in Wales, labour retain power. The power-sharing executive in the Northern Ireland Assembly is formed. The Ministry of Justice is created. The Ministry of Defence announces that HRH Prince Harry will not be sent to Iraq. Tony Blair is succeeded by Gordon Brown as prime minister; Blair becomes an envoy to the Middle East. Two car bombs are found and defused in central London. Terrorists attack Glasgow Airport; they are found to be doctors employed by the NHS. **July** The smoking ban begins in England. **August** Heavy rain causes flooding in many parts of northern England, the midlands, Gloucestershire, Oxfordshire and surrounding areas **September** A global credit-crunch triggers mortgage lenders, Northern Rock, to accept a loan from the Bank of England; thousands of Northern Rock customers begin closing their accounts, causing share prices to plummet sharpely. **October** Figures published show that record numbers of people will enrol in University for the autumn term **November** Two computer disks, containing all the government's data pertaining to recipients of child benefit, go missing in transit. Niether disk has been properly encrypted, meaning that the names, addresses and bank details of all child benefit recipients living in the UK have been made available to whoever finds the disks; prime minister, Gordon Brown, apologizes to the House of Commons and to the British public.

2008 **January** The queen supports a strict dress-code, outlawing the wearing of miniskirts and bare midriffs at this year's Ascot, in an attempt to 'keep the chav-factor down'; Intelligence services investigate an on-line Al-Qa'eda threat to kill prime minister Gordon Brown.

Died: Sir Edmund Hillary, the first conqueror of Everest.